VANCOUVER & BEYOND

Pictures and Stories
from the Postcard Era
1900 – 1914

Fred Thirkell and Bob Scullion

Heritage House

CANADIAN CATALOGUING IN PUBLICATION DATA

Thirkell, Fred, 1930-
    Vancouver & beyond

    Includes bibliographical references and index.

    ISBN 1-894384-15-6

    1. Vancouver Metropolitan Area (B.C.)—History—Pictorial works.
2. Vancouver Metropolitan Area (B.C.)—History.
3. Postcards—British Columbia—History.
I. Scullion, Bob, 1937-
II. Title.
FC3847.37.T56 2000   971.1'3303'0222   C00-911193-X
F1089.5.V22T56 2000

First edition 2000

    Heritage House acknowledges the financial support of the Government of Canada through the Book Publishing Industry Development Program (BPIDP) for our publishing activities, the British Columbia Arts Council, and the support of the BC Archives.

Front cover
    Line car at Edmonds and Kingsway, 1912.

Back cover
    Top photo: Prince Fushimi and party at the Big Tree in Stanley Park, 1907.
    Centre photo: The Melanope under tow near the mouth of the Columbia River, 1906.
    Bottom photo: Jack Johnson and Victor McLaglen exhibition bout at the Vancouver Athletic Club, 1909.

Design and layout by Bob Scullion
Edited by Terri Elderton

HERITAGE HOUSE PUBLISHING COMPANY LTD.
#108 - 17665 66 A Avenue, Surrey, BC V3S 2A7

Printed in Canada

Canadä

ACKNOWLEDGEMENTS

We owe a particular debt of gratitude to the many people who staff the various archives we used. It would not be an exaggeration to say that without their assistance it would have been impossible for us to have produced a book like *Vancouver and Beyond*. While the researcher may know that much-needed information is buried somewhere in a collection, it is so often only with the expert assistance of professional archivists that the material can be unearthed. Computer listings and card catalogues can only do so much; it is the "cross-referencing" minds and memories of the individuals who work day in and day out with a collection that makes all the difference.

For their very special help we are grateful to Kelly Nowlin of the British Columbia Archives and Records Service and to Elaine Miller of the Washington State Historical Society. As always, Leonard McCann and Rachel Grant of the Vancouver Maritime Museum and Sue Baptie and her staff at the City of Vancouver Archives deserve special mention. We have also received much help from community archives in Richmond, North Vancouver, West Vancouver, Delta, and Bowen Island. To Frank Kamiya and the Japanese Canadian National Museum and Archives Society as well as to Linda Tzang, Curator of the Local History Archives of the Chinese Cultural Centre, we express appreciation. As well, much assistance has been provided by Doreen Stevenson of the Anglican Provincial Synod of B.C. Archives, Patricia M. Ryan of the Salvation Army Archives and Museum (Toronto), Bob Stewart of the B.C. Conference Archives of the United Church of Canada, Ralph Hughs of the Archives of the Oblates of Mary Immaculate, and Lila Pritchard who provided access to the Archives of the Anglican Parish of St. James, Vancouver. We also want to say "thank you" to staff working in Special Collections at the University of British Columbia.

And where would researchers be without the help of reference librarians! Particular thanks go to Rosemary Keelan, Sheila Roberton, and Wendy Turnbull of New Westminster Public Library, and to Pat McCalib and Miriam Moses of the Burnaby Public Library. We also appreciated the help of the many Vancouver Public Library staff members who nearly always found answers to seemingly impossible questions! They so often came to the rescue when our own research seemed to be going nowhere.

We sought advice from a number of individuals, each an expert in his or her field. We particularly appreciated information provided by Lorraine Irving, Don Luxton, Peggy Imredy, Daphne Sleigh and Jim Wolfe. Special thanks are extended to John Davies, Alan Dawe, Ron Greene and Trish McGeer, not only for information provided, but also for permission to use photographs and other material from their files.

Photo Credits are as follows: Vancouver Maritime Museum: pages 20, 31, 39, 46, 48, 50, 177; Washington State Historical Society: page 21 (photo by Curtis), Neg. No. 58885-B; BC Archives: pages 28 (G-00405), 88 (A-02521), 184-185 (I-51848); City of Vancouver Archives: pages 37, 60, 61, 65, 76, 112, 113, 147, 154-155.

While we may have seemed a tad defensive on occasion, we really did appreciate the helpful suggestions and comments made by our spouses as we laboured to produce *Vancouver and Beyond*; to Beth Fish and Lil Thirkell goes our very special "Thank you."

THE PHOTOGRAPHS

The production of picture postcards was a flourishing business during Vancouver's late adolescent and early adult years, the years that were also those of the "golden age" of postcards. While almost all printed postcards sold locally (both coloured and black and white cards) were printed in Europe, the so-called "real photograph" cards were almost all produced locally. Practically every commercial photographer in Vancouver, North Vancouver and New Westminster cashed in on the postcard craze that was at its zenith between 1900 and 1914.

It is difficult today to imagine just how popular postcard collecting was in the years before the First World War. Although we have no sure way of knowing how many postcards were bought by individuals for their own postcard albums, the recorded number of postcards that passed through the mail certainly indicates with accuracy just how widespread the postcard craze was in the early years of the 20th century. The postcard—an open correspondence card that could pass through the mail at a rate significantly lower than letter rate—first appeared on October 1, 1869 in Austro-Hungary, but it was the Germans who were first to run with the idea in a big way. By 1903 they were already sending over 1.1 billion postcards a year to each other! Postal statistics for other countries show the postcard collecting mania spreading like wildfire. By 1908, for example, over 677 million postcards were mailed in the United States, a country with a population of only 88 million.

Here in Canada postcard collecting was as popular as it was in the United States and abroad. While our country only had a population of 5.4 million in 1901, an estimated 25 million postcards passed through the mail. By 1910, when the country had a population of just over 7 million, Canadians sent off 45 million postcards. The statistics for British Columbia tell much the same story. In 1901 when the province had a population of only178,657, residents and visitors mailed 760,000 postcards. In 1910 by which time B.C.'s population had reached 350,000, over 1.8 million cards passed through the mail. Two years later, when the provincial population had grown to 525,000, federal postal statistics tell us that over 2.7 million postcards were mailed in B.C.

To focus on one specific year, it would probably be safe to assume that at least 95 percent of the cards sold in Vancouver in 1912 would have been printed coloured cards; they were not only bright and attractive but cheap as well, selling at a penny each. Photographic cards would have cost at least five cents apiece, and therefore appealed to a much more limited market. Nevertheless, if only five percent of the postcards sold in B.C. in 1912 were "real photo" cards, the number would still have been a significant 135,000. It has to be remembered that in many of the province's smaller communities the only postcards available would have been "real photograph" ones since the small town market would have been far too small to interest the large commercial firms that produced printed cards.

Assuming half the photo cards produced in 1912 in B.C. were the work of Greater Vancouver's professional photographers, their combined output would have been 65,000 cards. Of that number, at least half the postcards would have been picturing Stanley Park, English Bay, Burrard Inlet, Capilano Canyon and the mountains. The remaining 37,500 cards would have covered a vast array of subjects. Some runs doubtless numbered as few as 50 or 100 cards. After all, just how many pictures of the corner of Edmonds and Kingsway, or the abandoned Cariboo Road could a photographer expect to sell in a year?

Of the 160 illustrations used in *Vancouver and Beyond*, 124 are taken from "real photograph" postcards. One of the things that give many of the pictures their special appeal is their rarity factor; their subject matter is such that they would have been printed only in very limited numbers. Still thinking of rarity, a few of the postcards used were undoubtedly the work of anonymous amateurs armed with what were popularly known as postcard cameras. These cameras produced pictures in a 3½- by 5½-inch format which were printed on paper that came supplied with the familiar postcard back. For the most part, however, the photographic postcards used in *Vancouver and Beyond* were the creations of professionals who deserve to be much better known than they are today. Their number includes F.J. Baglow, Chris Bannister, G.A. Barrowclough, Richard Broadbridge, William Brown, H.E. Bullen, W.T. Cooksley, A.T. Ellkiott, Frank Gowen, F.L. Hacking, and C.F. Smith, to name but a few among the many early B.C. photographers whose stories are still waiting to be told.

The remaining 36 illustrations to be found on the pages that follow were taken from non-postcard photographs, paintings, drawings, and sketches.

To Beth and Lil

for their patience and understanding

TABLE OF CONTENTS

PREFACE

Welcome to *Vancouver and Beyond*. We hope you enjoy this book of pictures and stories relating to Vancouver, the Fraser Valley, and the Coast, as much as we have enjoyed producing it. For the most part its focus is Vancouver during the years when the city came of age, that is, between 1900 and 1914. In a few stories we do, however, go beyond our self-imposed time parameters and geographic limits.

While most writers begin with ideas, we start out with some old photographic postcards and a hunch that they have stories to tell. "Old postcards, you say?" Yes, and while they do sound prosaic, it is amazing how many of them have become rarities, even though they may well have originally been produced in the hundreds, if not in the thousands. If not unique, many of the images are at the very least uncommon survivors.

There is often a serendipitous quality to stories waiting to be told; one never knows when a story will take off in an unexpected direction. Who would have thought, for example, that a story about Canada's first West Coast naval vessel would end up including an episode involving the *Komagata Maru?* Or that an account describing the visit to Vancouver of the first Black world heavyweight champion would, of necessity, have something to say about another boxer who later in life was to win an Oscar for best actor?

Each story in *Vancouver and Beyond* has been produced without reference to any other story in the collection. Nevertheless, taken as a whole, the pictures and text in this photo anthology reflect recurring themes. It is, of course, only in hindsight—always an exact science—that these themes become apparent.

By way of example, one theme that quickly becomes obvious is just how British *British* Columbia was in the years between 1900 and 1914. In each of the years between the census of 1901 and that of 1911 something like 75 percent of Vancouver's population was either British-born, or of British ancestry. Given the ethnic origin of nearly three-quarters of the city's population, it is not too surprising that local belief in the British Empire as God's preordained plan for the social, economic, spiritual and political salvation of the world was popular. Before the First World War there would have been few in Vancouver who did not believe that patriotism meant, almost by definition, loyalty to the Crown—the imperial ideal—and to Great Britain.

In the early years of the 20th century those Vancouverites who were not British by birth or heritage were definitely below the salt. And no one was farther from the salt than Asians, particularly Orientals. Sadly, it is the deep-seated—albeit irrational—fear and distrust of Japanese, Chinese and East Indians that presents itself as a second theme in *Vancouver and Beyond*. In Vancouver before the First World War Asians were at best patronized and at worst despised.

While the "Britishness" of British Columbia and the anti-Asian hostility of the White population clearly come through as facts of Vancouver life in times gone by, there are other themes that thread their way through the stories. For instance, there are all the postcards picturing both Vancouver's harbour and the ships that carried passengers and cargo in and out of it. And ruling over all else on the waterfront were the CPR's majestic empresses. There were always crowds of people on hand to watch their arrivals and departures. For many, these magnificent ships were the stuff of which impossible dreams are made.

To identify any more themes would be to spoil the fun. Everyone sees and feels things differently, and no doubt other themes will suggest themselves to each reader of *Vancouver and Beyond* as its images and stories are perused. Discovering connectedness has been but one of the pleasures we have enjoyed as we brought together the series of pictures and stories in this book. Hopefully it will also be among the many hidden pleasures waiting to be discovered by all who read the pages that follow.

Fred Thirkell

Bob Scullion

Burrard Inlet

THE "ST. GEORGE"

With the mountains in the background, and passengers waiting to disembark, it can be assumed that the St. George *is approaching the ferry slip on the Vancouver side of Burrard Inlet. Beyond the ferry can be seen a sailing ship riding at anchor, waiting to load lumber at Hastings Mill.*

Although passengers had been transported back and forth across Burrard Inlet on something resembling a scheduled service since 1893, it was not until 1900 that the Municipality of North Vancouver came to operate a ferry service of its own. In fact, the municipal council was forced into the ferry business because the Union Steamships had given notice that it was about to discontinue the unprofitable service.

In 1899 the district municipality had a vessel, appropriately named the *North Vancouver*, built at a cost of $16,458. It was loaded from the side, but could only accommodate small wagons. Needless to say, the loading and unloading of horse-drawn wagons was an awkward and time-consuming business. While the service provided was better than it had been in the past, the municipality councillors soon came to appreciate the fact that operating a ferry service was not only a money-losing proposition but also a sure way to lose friends!

If not exactly a knight in shining armour, Lt. Colonel A. St. George Hamersley, K.C. arrived on the scene with a plan to rescue the unprofitable ferry service. The British-born Hamersley had come to Vancouver in 1888 from New Zealand, where he had fought in the Maori wars of the 1870s and 80s. He was a legal advisor to the CPR and was also the City Solicitor. Doubtless the idea of conflict of interest would never have crossed his mind, since he would have seen whatever he was doing as being very much in his own best interest! His contemporaries might have referred to him as a gentleman adventurer, but today he would probably be regarded as just another self-serving real estate or stock promoter.

Hamersley had bought North Vancouver's District Lot 274, a tract of land east of Lonsdale that had been part of the Moodyville timber holdings. He had it subdivided, and set out to attract buyers. Since good reliable transportation to and from Vancouver was essential if purchasers were to be found, Hamersley had the North Vancouver Ferry and Power Company incorporated in Ontario in early 1903. On March 3 of the same year he approached North Vancouver Council with an offer to buy the municipal ferry system, promising to add a second and more efficient vessel as soon as his company took over. On May 9 the ratepayers authorized the sale, and on July 15 the ferry system, such as it was, passed into Hamersley's hands.

Plans for the new ferry were presented to council and approved on November 16. It was to be a double-ended vessel that would allow horses and wagons to board the ship at one end and get off at the other end. Comprising 544 tons, with a length of 131 feet and a breadth of 28.5 feet, it was to be capable of making the trip each way in less than twenty minutes.

Most of the ship's principal components were prefabricated in Collingwood, Ontario and shipped by train to Wallace's Ship Yard on False Creek for assembly. Launched in August 1904, and not surprisingly named the *St. George*, the new double-ended ferry with its twin pilot houses and ability to load and unload from either end was a unique sight for local residents. Dividing the vehicle deck were stairs that led up to the passenger deck. In addition to an open deck, there were separate enclosed cabins on either side of the stairwell: one was for women and the other for men. And luxury of luxuries—both had toilets!

While ferries are thought of today as strictly utilitarian vessels, back in 1905 they were viewed differently, and owners encouraged people to use them for sheer pleasure. Hamersley's company tried a variety of schemes to attract passengers. For a time a Black husband and wife team of entertainers sang, danced and told stories on the passenger deck. Before the ferry ended its crossing the woman passed the hat for donations.

Alfred St. George Hamersley *was born into a prominent Oxfordshire family in 1850. After living in New Zealand he moved on to Vancouver in 1888. Very much in the social, political and financial swim, he was soon recognized as a rather large frog in what was still a relatively small pond.*

Some of the patrons found the jokes offensive, and the act was discontinued before too long. Shipboard refreshment stands were opened. While the coffee was doubtless appreciated by those who were a bit late setting off for work, the refreshment stands didn't do anything more to increase patronage than had the minstrels.

In 1905 Hamersley hit upon a more ambitious scheme for attracting passengers. He opened Lonsdale Gardens at the foot of St. Patrick's, complete with a wharf and floats, bathhouse, refreshment booths, picnic sites and a baseball diamond. Special evening events were staged to attract Vancouverites, but neither band concerts nor dancing on the beach drew the hoped-for crowds. The season ended, and so did Lonsdale Gardens as a scheme for attracting patrons to the ferry service.

As 1907 drew to a close, the North Vancouver Ferry and Power Company announced that it was discontinuing the money-losing ferry service. The municipality had no choice but to run the system itself. The North Vancouver ferries continued to be operated as a public utility until the last vessel completed its final trip on August 30, 1958.

Hamersley had left Vancouver in 1906. Evidently he had had enough of colonial life, returning to Britain where, in 1910, he became a Conservative member of parliament. His namesake, the *St. George* (which had along the way become the much more prosaic *North Vancouver Ferry No. 2*), provided a longer and more worthwhile service for the people of North Vancouver than he did. The ship continued in service until 1936, when newer ships made old *No. 2* superfluous to the needs of the ferry system. Sold to Gibson Brothers, the vessel was moved to Tahsis Inlet off Nootka Sound, where it became a floating store and bunkhouse for loggers. Not long after being moved to the west coast of Vancouver Island it caught fire and burned to the waterline. Thus, after its 31 years of service during which it carried over 30 million passengers and two million vehicles between downtown Vancouver and the North Shore, the old *St. George* rather appropriately had a kind of belated Viking burial, going out in a blaze of glory.

"Vancouver's Own"
PAULINE JOHNSON

Pauline Johnson had a strong sense of theatre, dressing as occasion demanded in the costume of a Mohawk princess or in the high fashion of the wealthy Edwardian lady.

There may be any number of unmarked aboriginal graves in Stanley Park, but there is only one burial site identified by a monument of any sort. It is near Siwash Rock, at the place where the earthly remains of Pauline Johnson lie buried. How did her ashes come to be buried in a public park? The exceptional place of interment relates directly to the exceptional life of this unique personality. Although she lived in Vancouver for only five short years, her popularity, prestige (and connections!) were such that her request to be buried in Stanley Park, a federal military reserve leased to the city, seems never to have been questioned. The city fathers, the provincial attorney general, and the federal minister of militia all approved the burial without hesitation. Who was this woman?

Emily Pauline Johnson was born March 10, 1861 on the Six Nations Reserve near Brantford, Ontario. She was the youngest of four children born to George Henry Martin Johnson, Chief of the Mohawks, and his English wife Emily Howells, a cousin of William Dean Howells, the American novelist, critic and editor. Pauline, as she was called, was educated for the most part at home, and while still quite young became familiar

with both English and American poetry. At the same time she grew to appreciate the legends and stories of her father's people. Even though she was of mixed parentage, Pauline Johnson always regarded herself as Indian.

Although two of her poems had appeared in an anthology of Canadian verse in 1889, Johnson's career didn't really take off until 1892 when she read before the Young Liberal Club of Toronto. The enthusiastic reception launched a stage career that kept her travelling for the next seventeen years.

It was the age of the Chautauqua, a movement that took its name from a Methodist camp meeting ground in upstate New York. A Chautauqua circuit quickly developed, booking family programs that provided a blend of education, inspiration, and entertainment into towns and hamlets in both the United States and Canada. Everyone loved these programs that brought both culture and colour into small town life. Pauline Johnson was very much the right person, at the right time, in the right place. Her warm and winning personality easily reached beyond the footlights, and she was a huge success wherever she appeared, whether on the Chautauqua circuit or under local sponsorship.

Throughout her career, dressed in native costume, she always included readings of her own works in her recitals. Her ability to reach an audience did much to popularize her poems and stories. It has to be said that while Johnson used her aboriginal heritage to advantage in her stage performances, she did not abuse it. Although she wore the costume of a Mohawk princess on stage when she presented her own material, for those parts of her program that had no connection with Indian legend or culture she always wore the evening dress appropriate to any Edwardian lady of fashion and status. And she was very much the elegant Edwardian celebrity. Not only was she admired by thousands of ordinary people who had read her poems and stories, or who had seen her in person, but she was admired by the rich and famous as well.

During her career Pauline Johnson crossed Canada nineteen times, appearing in small towns and cities alike. She also performed regularly in the United

States. As well, she travelled to Britain in 1894 and in 1906. The primary reason for going to the United Kingdom in 1894 was to arrange for the publication of her first book, *The White Wampum*. While she was in London she appeared on stage under the patronage of the Earl of Aberdeen, who introduced her to many well-placed people. Among those she met, and with whom she established life-long friendships, were two of Queen Victoria's daughters, Princess Louise (whose husband, the Marquis of Lorne had earlier been Canada's Governor General) and Princess Helena. Her 1906 trip was sponsored by Lord and Lady Strathcona. Again, by all accounts, the poetess had a remarkable ability to make and *keep* friends. In 1909 Johnson decided to give up her stage career with the endless travel it involved. It had been a strenuous life, and she simply didn't have either the energy or will to continue a life on the road. As well, her boys' stories—later to appear as *The Shagganappi*—had sold well.

Johnson decided to spend her retirement freelance writing in Vancouver, a city that had come to mean much to her over the years. During her many visits she had established warm and genuine friendships with a vast circle that included Chief Joe Capilano and other local aboriginal leaders. She learned much of local Indian myths and stories during the many hours she spent with the people of the Squamish Nation.

As it turned out, her idyll was not long-lived. Her lack of stamina and drive had less to do with what today would be called burn-out than it did with the fact that she had unknowingly been enduring the debilitating effects of breast cancer, which had advanced beyond the point where surgery could be of use. And bad enough that Johnson was already dying when she came to Vancouver, but she had precious little money with which to meet on-going expenses. Although her stage career and her books

had been successful, travel costs and a comfortable lifestyle had left her with little savings.

When in 1910 her financial situation began to look desperate she went to see her old acquaintance W.C. Nichol, owner of the *Vancouver Province*. She told him of the stories she had written about The Lions (the "Two Sisters" of Indian legend) of Siwash Rock and of other local tales that had been shared with her by the chiefs and elders of local tribes. Nichol introduced her to L.W. Makovski, editor of the paper's Saturday magazine section. He liked the stories and asked Johnson to provide a series of tales based on local native myths and stories that could appear weekly. The "Legends" were immensely popular, and their author was paid seven dollars for each story! The last of the series appeared on January 7, 1911, by which time she was no longer well enough to write.

In September, 1911 a group of her friends met at the home of Mayor Douglas to set up the Pauline Johnson Trust Fund. Sir Charles Hibbert Tupper was chairman and L.W. Makovski was secretary. The group helped Johnson by financing the publication of her series of stories that had appeared weekly in *The Province*. The first and second printings of 1,000 copies each sold out quickly, and the third printing of 10,000 copies of *Legends of Vancouver* moved equally well. Over and above printing costs, all proceeds were credited to Johnson's bank account. The venture was so successful that the committee went on to publish *Flint and Feather* in 1912. Through the effort of those involved in what came to be known as "the Friendship Plot," Pauline Johnson had more than enough money to meet her needs over the remaining months of her life.

In May 1912, Walter McRaye arranged for Johnson to be moved to the Bute Street Private Hospital. McRaye had long had a special place in her life. They

The overly sentimental Spirit of Siwash Rock, *Charles Marega's proposed memorial to Pauline Johnson, never got off the drawing board: it was too expensive for the burghers of Vancouver.*

Pauline Johnson's grave near Siwash Rock was initially enclosed by a rustic fence, and marked only by a boulder bearing the name, Pauline.

had first met in Winnipeg in 1897 where they were both performing. McRaye called himself an "Entertainer and Monologist," and his speciality was the recitation of the narrative verse of W.H. Drummond, whose poems were in the broken English of the French-Canadian *habitant.* The fashion for what would today be regarded as ethnic parody has long past, but it was immensely popular in McRaye's day. He and Johnson began giving joint recitals in 1899, and continued to do so until 1909. He travelled to London with her in 1906, and acted as her manager throughout their years together.

At the Bute Street hospital Johnson was given a room on the second floor which she could furnish to her own taste. As well, she was free to come and go as long as she was able to do so. When she could no longer leave the hospital, her many friends came to visit her. One particular visit that did much to lift her spirits took place in September 1912 when the Governor-General, the Duke of Connaught, took time from his official visit to Vancouver to call on her privately. Johnson had first met the duke many years before when her father had made him an honorary chief of the Mohawks. When she was told that the duke was coming to see her she had his chair draped with one of her prized possessions—the red broadcloth blanket upon which he stood when he had been made a chief of the Six Nations. She was well-dressed for the royal visit, wearing a new blue and gold kimono, which was a gift from her friends in the Vancouver Press Club. As always, Pauline Johnson never lacked for friends!

One special friend was Mrs. Jonathan Rogers, president of the Women's Canadian Club of Vancouver. If not *the* leader of local society, she was at the very least a power to be contended with in local women's social, volunteer and philanthropic circles. Johnson had often told Mrs. Rogers how happy she would be to be buried in Stanley Park. Mrs. Rogers recognized the impracticality of the request, suggesting to the poetess

that cremation might make it possible for her wish to be fulfilled. Johnson enthusiastically accepted Mrs. Rogers' advice, and in her will directed that her body be cremated. She also instructed that she be cremated wearing her mother's wedding ring, and a gold locket which was not to be opened by anyone. Years later Mrs. Rogers recalled that Pauline Johnson had shown her, "what [the locket] contained. It was a photograph of a man." Mrs Rogers also said, "I refrained from asking who it was, and she did not inform me."

Death came to Pauline Johnson on March 7, 1913. Although she had requested that no one see her body after death, and that there be no flowers at her funeral, her wishes were ignored. Her body lay within an open grey coffin in the hospital's reception room until her funeral, which took place on March 10, 1913, at Christ Church. At the service the bier was surrounded by a sea of floral tributes. The wreath upon the coffin was put in place by the mayor on behalf of all the citizens of Vancouver. Special invitations to attend went to Chief Matthias of the Squamish Nation, and to other local Native leaders. On the day of the funeral the flags on all city schools were at half-mast, and civic offices were closed for the afternoon.

Three days after the funeral Mrs. Rogers and Makovski were called to the crematorium to "view the ashes" before they were sealed in what Mrs. Rogers described as "the roughest stone box of concrete." Besides the tin containing the ashes, "the small concrete sarcophagus" allowed room for two white satin cushions between which the tin and copies of *Legends of Vancouver* and *Flint and Feather* were placed. At Mrs. Rogers' suggestion, Makovski wrote an inscription in one of the books. Mrs Rogers took the concrete box to the spot near Siwash Rock where it was interred.

Initially the burial site was temporarily marked by a large boulder upon which the name *Pauline* had been carved by a park workman. The Vancouver branch of the Women's Canadian Club, which had taken responsibility for all the funeral arrangements, fully intended to mark the spot with a more elaborate and permanent monument.

The design of choice was that of Charles Marega, the city's premier sculptor. Called *The Spirit of Siwash Rock,* it was a grandiose affair that posed a seated life-size figure of the poetess across an open space from a native couple and child—the family featured in the legend of Siwash Rock. The piece was to cost $30,000, an amount equivalent to over $400,000 in today's dollars. The First World War put fund raising on hold, and by the time peace returned there was little enthusiasm for Marega's expensive and overly sentimental sculpture.

In 1922 the women's club recruited the services of James A. Benzie, a local architect, and Major Harry Patterson, president of Patterson, Chandler & Stephen, Ltd., a local art monument works. The two men were willing to design a monument "as a labour of love."

Dedicated on May 26, 1922, the memorial could be described as a rusticated fountain. Trickles of water run down the sides of a pile of large rocks taken from the nearby beach. The water flows into an ornamental pool, beneath which lies the concrete casket buried in 1913. Patterson's foreman, James McLeod Hurry, carved the cameo portrait of the poetess, the canoe, and the flint-tipped feathered arrow that decorate the cairn.

The grave marker cum monument was never viewed with much enthusiasm by either the Women's Canadian Club, which had rather reluctantly accepted the design, or by the general public. The cairn looks like what it is—a pile of rocks decorated with a Grecian profile that bears little resemblance to the woman whose features were so well-known to the public of her day. Over the years it has often been asked why Johnson's portrait does not face toward the sea and Siwash Rock, which she loved so much. The answer to the many criticisms of the memorial may lie in the fact that it only cost $1,200, and one gets what one pays for.

Today's literary establishment considers Johnson, like Robert Service, to be somewhat below the salt, and her work to be derivative and shallow. Nevertheless, her popular appeal is such that her books, like those of Service, remain in print while the works of other Canadian writers of her day, judged by the professionals to be much more significant, have long been forgotten in all but academic circles. As was said at the dedication of her grave marker in 1922, in her life and work Pauline Johnson "linked together the race that first occupied this land with those who came after." Perhaps there is a certain poetic justice in the fact that the only monument marking a burial site in Stanley Park identifies the final resting place of this daughter of a First Nations chieftain and his English wife.

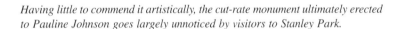

Having little to commend it artistically, the cut-rate monument ultimately erected to Pauline Johnson goes largely unnoticed by visitors to Stanley Park.

PUBLIC ENEMY NUMBER ONE

At the beginning of the twentieth century British Columbia's cities, towns, and villages all shared one common fear: fire! A number of factors conspired to make fire Public Enemy Number One.

The fact that most buildings were of frame construction meant that once fire took hold the structures would soon be nothing more than charred ruins. Then, too, building codes were almost non-existent before the Great War. Stoves and heaters could be placed near unprotected walls, and stove pipes that could literally become red-hot, passed through nothing more than lightweight sheet metal thimbles as they snaked from one room to the next or from one floor to another on their way to the brick chimney. And many a fire was caused by a carelessly handled candle or oil lamp. In the early years of electric lighting poorly insulated wires in attics and walls caused many fires that ended tragically.

Although they provided the best they could afford, most towns had meagre fire protection. Generally there was an enthusiastic but poorly-equipped volunteer hose company of a dozen or so men, one of whom was "fire chief." Equipment was almost invariably limited to one hose reel, a contraption consisting of a pair of spoked wheels six feet in diameter, between which the length of hose was wound around a spool, through the centre of which passed the axle. These hose reels were pulled not by horses but by the men of the volunteer hose company! Not surprisingly the firemen were noted for their physical fitness and places on the team were much sought after.

Competition between teams from neighbouring towns were popular on July first, or Dominion Day as it was then called. Even the larger communities were proud of their hose companies. And rightly so. In 1889 Vancouver's Hose Company was good enough to win the North American championship, even beating New York City's team.

Larger communities like Vancouver, Victoria, and New Westminster acquired horse-drawn steam pumps, hose wagons, and ladder trucks as soon as civic budgets allowed. Still later, as motorized fire engines

In earlier days, before it was moved to its present location, St. Thomas' Anglican Church *marked Five Corners at the heart of Chilliwack. The building on fire in the picture on the following page is the white structure across the street from the church.*

Not a woman in sight! Watching fires must have been a male-only pastime in Chilliwack's earlier years. The ornate structure in the right background is the town's courthouse.

came on the scene, the older horse-drawn apparatus was sold to smaller communities that couldn't afford the sophisticated new equipment. (Vancouver's first motorized hose wagon, purchased in 1907, cost an astronomical $4,950.) Towns in the Fraser Valley and in the Interior were happy to get the used equipment. After all, a second-hand horse-drawn ladder truck was better than no ladder truck at all. Chilliwack's horse-drawn ladder truck, doubtless just such a hand-me-down, is pictured being put to good use.

It is difficult to date the photo exactly, but it is most likely of the period 1917 to 1920. The fire took place at Five Corners, the commercial and geographic centre of Chilliwack. It appears to have started in a second storey photographic studio, above William G. Lillies' grocery store. Since the town is not numbered among those that burned to the ground in the early part of the century, it can be assumed that the fire brigade successfully contained the blaze. Generally speaking, protecting neighbouring buildings from flying sparks was the measure of success for small town volunteer firefighters, who had little to work with other than primitive equipment, and a commitment to doing their very best.

COALING-UP THE EMPRESSES

Sailing ships continued to carry most of the world's grain, lumber and other raw materials across the seven seas until the beginning of the twentieth century, but their days were numbered. By the 1850s, the world's major steamship companies—firms like Cunard, White Star, and Hamburg Amerika—had come into being, and by the 1870s virtually all passengers and manufactured goods were crossing the Atlantic in steamships. And why not! After all, a steamer could travel between Liverpool and New York in two weeks, while a sailing ship was lucky to make the same crossing in six weeks.

Even after the advent of steam, sailing ships did, however, continue to travel the world's less profitable routes. In fact, rigged as either barques or schooners, the last of the sailing ships were those in the Australian grain trade with Britain and those in the North and South American Pacific Coast trade. These sailing ships didn't disappear until the 1920s, by which time steam-powered vessels ruled the seas.

Steamboats, modelled after the American Robert Fulton's successful paddlewheeler of 1807 soon became popular on both the inland and coastal waters of Great Britain, the United States and British North America. British Columbia was to become one of the places that proved the worth of steam power at sea. Built in 1835, the Hudson's Bay Company's *Beaver*—rigged as a sailing ship—travelled halfway around the world to the Columbia River in 1836. Almost immediately upon its arrival on the Pacific Coast the *Beaver's* sidewheels, which were carried as cargo for the voyage, were fitted. Soon, with its two engines fired up, it began its 52 years of service. Each of its 35-horsepower non-condensing engines was fuelled by wood, and under normal conditions it took 26 cords of wood to keep the ship moving for two or three days. If it was towing a boom of logs it burned 40 cords every 24 hours. Even when it was fed coal, it gobbled up 700 pounds an hour.

The *Beaver's* non-condensing engines, which were typical of the day, consumed huge amounts of fuel to produce very limited motive power. It was for this reason that steamboats did not enter transoceanic service until the mid 1850s, that is, until after the double-expansion engine had been invented. The double-expansion engine reused the steam exhausted from an engine's pressure cylinder to power another lower pressure cylinder, thereby increasing the overall efficiency of the engine. In practical terms this meant that a ship equipped with double-expansion engines could go farther on the same amount of fuel as that used by a single-expansion engine. Going one step further and operating on the same principle the triple-expansion engine, which first appeared in 1873, meant even more fuel economy. With double- and triple-expansion engines, the day of steamships had finally arrived; they could at last carry enough coal to get themselves across the oceans of the world. Having overcome the need to carry impractically large amounts of coal, the last obstacle in the way of those who yearned to build larger and larger vessels was defeated.

However, the amount of coal a ship required to get itself across the Atlantic, let alone the Pacific Ocean, was still huge. One problem that remained was the great uncertainty as to just how much coal would be used in a crossing. Weather, currents, weight of both the ship and its cargo, and speed were factors that affected the number of tons of coal consumed on a voyage. There was so much uncertainty, in fact, that early ocean going steamships were rigged to carry sails that could be used to cut fuel consumption or as an emergency power source should there be an engine failure or should a propeller be lost.

The first steamships used by the CPR on the Pacific were the *Parthia, Abyssinia,* and *Batavia,* which had originally sailed as Cunard liners. All three had been built in 1870 for the North Atlantic service and carried sails. While steam plus sails reflected a kind of "belt and suspenders" mentality, at the time it was considered much better to be safe than sorry. In the early 1880s Cunard no longer needed the vessels and they were sold to owners who made them available for lease. Not being sure just how well-received a trans-Pacific service would be, and whether a long-term Royal Mail subsidy could be secured, the CPR thought it more prudent at the time to lease vessels rather than buy them. Before they were put into service the three ships were refitted and modernized. These are relative terms, however, since none of the three ships had either heat or electric lighting in its staterooms. The first of the chartered vessels to reach Vancouver was the *Abyssinia,* which tied up at the CPR's new landing stage on June 14, 1887.

Having unloaded passengers and cargo, the *Abyssinia* crossed the Strait of Georgia to coal-up. After

The Robert Kerr *was the CPR's coaling barge from 1888 until 1911 when it sank off Thetis Island. Often such barges had a live-aboard barge master, and it was not unusual for his family to live aboard with him. This picture, taken alongside the CPR's wharf, dates from the period 1903 – 1907.*

bunkering, it returned to Vancouver from whence it sailed for the Orient on June 20, 1887. From its inception the CPR was noted for and successful in large measure because of its ever-frugal management. Since sailing to Vancouver Island to coal-up wasted time and therefore money, a derelict barque was bought in 1888. The old wooden-hulled sailing ship was refitted as a coal barge, and for 20 years it was to be towed back and forth between Ladysmith, Comox or Nanaimo and Vancouver with coal for the CPR's ships.

Before its conversion, the vessel had been the *Robert Kerr,* a ship that already had a special place in Vancouver's history. After a dreadful voyage to the West Coast, which had begun in September 1884, the ship finally reached Vancouver in September 1885, almost a year to the day after leaving Liverpool. Enroute the ship's officers had to sail through damaging storms, deal with a near-mutinous crew, contend with winds off Staten Island that battered both rigging and hull, deal with the death of their captain a few weeks out of Panama, and last but not least, refloat the vessel after it grounded in the shallows off San Juan Island.

In Vancouver, after a marine survey had been undertaken, it was decided that the crew should be paid off and the ship sold. As it happened, Seraphim "Joe" Fortes, who was to become English Bay's legendary lifeguard, was one of the crewmen paid off. William Soule, the loading superintendent at Hastings Mill, bought the vessel. After Soule had made necessary repairs the ship was riding at anchor in Burrard Inlet not only on April 6, 1886, the day of Vancouver's incorporation as a city, but also on June 13, 1886, the day of Vancouver's "Great Fire." Upward of 200 people found refuge aboard the *Robert Kerr,* where Soule and his family were living while their new home at Dunlevy and Powell Streets was being built.

On October 3, 1888, Soule sold the ship to the CPR for $7,000. After being stripped of most of its superstructure, losing its rigging, and having its holds made larger, the coal barge went to work servicing the company's liners. From 1888 until 1891 it was the *Parthia, Abyssinia,* and *Batavia* that were coaled, and from 1891 onward the principal ships to be coaled were the new *Empress of India, Empress of China,* and *Empress of Japan.* And these *Empresses* knew how to

17

In that the Empresses of Japan, China, *and* India *were virtually identical, their figureheads being their only obvious distinguishing features, it is impossible to tell from this Lyall photograph of either 1911 or 1912, which of the three is being bunkered.*

Pictured in this undated photograph is either the Empress of Asia *or the* Empress of Russia. *The ship is being coaled-up by the* Melanope, *which had lost its mainmast by the time this picture was taken. The coal was being loaded onto the ship by a steam crane.*

burn coal! While there were sails aboard, they were safely tucked away in a locker "just in case." They were not intended, as had been the case with older ships, to serve in a fuel-saving capacity as an auxiliary power source.

Given that the three ships were for all practical purposes reliant solely on their engines for power, knowing just how much coal was need for a trip was crucially important. The *Empress of India* ended its maiden voyage in Vancouver with only 32 tons of coal in its bunkers. On its next crossing from Yokohama the *India* sailed with extra coal on deck. On average the first three *Empresses* burned between 1,350 and 1,500

Bunkering was a hateful job. It was dirty and time-consuming. Interestingly, while the ships were in Vancouver their officers and White crew were allowed shore leave, but the Chinese crew members—which included all the stokers—were not allowed ashore because of immigration regulations.

Until 1911 all the thousands of tons of coal that fuelled the CPR's Pacific fleet which included *Empresses*, coastal *Princesses*, and a variety of other ships, was brought from Vancouver Island to ship side by the *Robert Kerr*. The *Robert Kerr's* career ended unexpectedly on March 4, 1911. The barge was being towed from Ladysmith to Vancouver by the tug, *Coulti*,

By 1906 trade was such that an additional freighter that also had good passenger accommodation was needed for the trans-Pacific service. The 6,163-ton Monteagle which had been launched in 1889 was transferred from the CPR's Atlantic service. This undated picture of the Monteagle with the Melanope at its side is probably circa 1910 – 1912.

tons of coal on the crossing from Vancouver to Yokohama. On the longer voyage between Vancouver and Hong Kong 2,750 tons of coal were burned. The early *Empresses* each had twin 16.5 foot propellers driven by a pair of triple-expansion reciprocating engines, which in turn were powered by four double-ended Scotch cylindrical boilers. Each boiler had eight *hand-fired* furnaces! The fact that there was a pair of engines and twin screws meant that there was relative safety; should one engine fail the other was still capable of moving the ship, and if a propeller was lost or damaged the other could still be counted on to function.

when during the night the tug went off course and towed the *Robert Kerr* onto a reef at the north end of Thetis Island. The old hulk quickly filled with water and sank to the bottom carrying 1,800 tons of coal intended for the waiting *Empress of India*.

It was determined that the *Robert Kerr* was a total loss and would have to be replaced as quickly as possible. The company bought another tall ship shorn of rigging and spars, with hatchways enlarged, and part of the main deck removed. It was purchased from James Griffiths of Seattle, a man who had made a fortune in large part by purchasing old retired windjammers to turn into barges.

This idealized "ship's portrait" of the Melanope *was probably painted for either its captain or its owners, W.H. Porter and Company of Liverpool, soon after it put to sea in 1876.* Melanope, *after whom the vessel was named, was a daughter of Aeolus, Greek god of the winds. She had two children by Poseidon, god of the sea. Their eyes were put out by Aeolus, but their sight was restored by Poseidon.*

The vessel sold to the CPR by the Griffiths Coastwise Steamship and Barge Company was the *Melanope*.

Built in Liverpool in 1876 the *Melanope* was an iron-hulled three-masted clipper ship that first saw service as an emigrant ship sailing between Great Britain and Australia. Later the ship carried lumber from Puget Sound to Cape Town. One such voyage was made in an unequalled record of 72 days. On December 10, 1906 the *Melanope's* years as a sailing ship came to an end when the ballast shifted in a gale off the mouth of the Columbia River. The vessel lay over on its beam ends and held fast in what was fortunately shallow water. The crew abandoned ship and made it safely to shore. The *Melanope* was later found by the steamer *Northland*, which towed the distressed vessel across the Columbia River sand bar, upon which it had foundered, into Astoria. The 30 year old vessel was considered beyond repair and sold to Griffiths who four years later sold it to the CPR.

The *Melanope* coaled the original three *Empresses*, the older coal-burning *Princesses*, and sundry other vessels belonging to the CPR. Aside from

the *Princess Beatrice*, which was built in Esquimalt in 1903 and not withdrawn from service until 1928, all the other coast boats at some time in their careers were eventually converted to oil.

To meet increasing competition from newer and faster liners sailing on the trans-Pacific routes between both Seattle and San Francisco and the Orient, the CPR ordered two new liners from Fairfield's Shipbuilding in Govan (Glasgow) in mid-1911. At just under 17,000 tons, they were over three times the size of the original *Empresses*. They were coal-burning and designed to operate with only two coaling ports, one on either side of the Pacific. A large pair of holds were required for coal storage. It may be wondered why coal was still the fuel of choice in 1913 while a ship like the new Union Steamships of New Zealand's liner *Niagara* normally burned oil, though it was equipped to burn coal if necessary or expedient. As well, the newer Nippon Yusen Kaisha (NYK) liners with which the *Empresses* were in competition were all oil-burning.

The answer to the question has a number of parts. First of all, good coal was both cheap and available, while oil in Chinese ports at that point in time may or may not have been easily obtainable. Then, too, the major British and German steamship companies were still fitting out their new ships as coal-burners. Cunard's *Lusitania* (1907), *Mauritania* (1907), and *Aquitania* (1914) as well as White Star's *Olympic* (1911) and *Titanic* (1912) were all coal-fired; it was not until after the First World War that the three surviving vessels were converted to oil. And it was only after the CPR purchased Hamburg Amerika's *Tirpitz* (1913) from the British war reparations commission in 1921 that the vessel was converted to oil.

The last two coal-burning Empresses—never converted to oil—continued to sail the Pacific even after the Second World War had begun. In November 28, 1940 the *Empress of Russia*, while in Hong Kong, was requisitioned as a troop transport. The *Empress of Asia* followed its sister ship into war service on January 11, 1941. Both Empresses left Vancouver for the last time in February 1941. Neither ship ever made it back to Vancouver; the *Asia* was bombed and sunk by the Japanese off Singapore in February 1942, and the *Russia* was destroyed by fire in Barrow-in-Furness during a refit in September 1945. Throughout the war and on into 1946 the 70 year old *Melanope* continued, though with much less frequency, to move coal from Vancouver Island to the CPR's wharves at the foot of Burrard Street. Coal was still needed by the company's tugs and in the galleys of the Coast Service's *Princesses*. But it was really all over for the *Melanope* in April 1946. At that time it was announced that the old windjammer-cum-coaling barge was to be sunk in shallow water off the Comox Logging and Railway Company's wharf at Royston on Vancouver Island, to become part of a breakwater. Such was the end of the *Melanope* and of coaling-up in Vancouver.

Looking less than the noble clipper ship that it had been, the Melanope *was towed off the sandbar at Cape Blanco near the mouth of the Columbia River, where it had run aground in a storm on December 10, 1906. The steamer* Northland *towed the derelict into Astoria. Considered beyond repair the* Melanope *was sold to a Seattle firm that specialized in converting old sailing ships into barges.*

Port Moody

"NUMBER PLEASE"

Alexander Graham Bell patented the telephone in March 1876, and it was first seen by the general public at the Centennial Exhibition in Philadelphia in June of the same year. Its popularity spread quickly, and as early as 1878 single line phones—sort of "distance intercoms"—were in use by a few businesses in British Columbia's capital city. One line ran a quarter of a mile from W. J. Jeffree's clothing store to Pendray's soap factory. The Victoria *Daily British Colonist* reported that "the mode of communication is very simple. In the office at each end of the wire [there is] a small black walnut box. At the side of the box is a small crank, which a person desirous of communicating with another turns. The movement of the crank rings an alarm bell and the attention of the person sought being directed to the instrument, he...takes the speaking-tube in his hand,...places it near his mouth and asks what is wanted. The sound of the voice strikes against a diaphragm within the tube and is conveyed by the wire to the other end, and so on. A conversation thus commenced may be carried on as long as desired." On May 8, 1880 an act of the British Columbia legislature established the Victoria and Esquimalt Telephone Company. The legislation set the rate at five dollars per month per subscriber, with certain "additional charges" permitted.

On the Lower Mainland telephone service had its beginning in Port Moody in 1883, when two of the many local real estate speculators received permission from the city of New Westminster to erect telephone poles from the Royal City to Port Moody. In February 1884 they received a provincial charter for the already operating New Westminster and Port Moody Telephone Company. The company quickly found itself in debt, and when the CPR announced that it was moving its terminus to Vancouver, the telephone company had to declare bankruptcy. The Bank of British Columbia and Joseph C. Armstrong, who were the principal creditors, were forced to foreclose.

The manager of the bank and Armstrong quickly realized that the only way they were going to be able to protect their investment was by up-grading and expanding the telephone system they now owned. In 1886 they extended the company's phone lines to the newly-named city of Vancouver. Changing the firm's name, it became the New Westminster and Burrard Inlet Telephone Company.

Vancouver's first telephone exchange was a switchboard located in S.T. Tilley's Bookstore at 11 Cordova Street. The operators were Tilley's son, Charlie and J.W. King. By 1888 they were each paid $20 a month for providing a 24-hour service for approximately one hundred subscribers. It wasn't long, however, before telephone companies everywhere were employing women as switchboard operators. It seems that women were less likely to be rude to subscribers, play practical jokes on customers, and needed less supervision.

Like other North American telephone companies, the local phone company grew by leaps and bounds. As one writer rather patronizingly put it, "The people of the [North] American continent are noted for the readiness with which they adopt any contrivance that tends to lessen labour or increase convenience, and the telephone [has] won its way into favour." Much credit for the rapid growth of the Lower Mainland's telephone company must go to Dr. James M. Lefevre who purchased an interest in the company in 1886. Over the years until his death in 1906 he, more than anyone else, provided leadership and direction.

Lefevre had come to Vancouver as the surgeon for the CPR's Pacific division. He quickly involved himself in both the political and business life of the city. He was elected to City Council in 1886, served as president of the Board of Trade, and ran unsuccessfully as a Conservative candidate. He built a downtown business block, owned a significant number of shares in the BC Electric Railway, and speculated successfully in local real estate.

In 1898 Lefevre supported the sale of the telephone company to the Yorkshire Guarantee and Security Company which already had a number of business interests in British Columbia. These investments were watched over by the firm's Vancouver manager, William Farrell. The reason for the sale of the company was to gain access to the kind of capital that was necessary for immediate further expansion.

It was at this time that the New Westminster and Burrard Inlet Telephone Company became the British Columbia Telephones Limited. By 1901 it had a controlling interest in telephone companies in Vancouver and New Westminster, Victoria and Nanaimo, and in Kamloops, the Okanagan, the Boundary country, and the West Kootenay area.

In 1902 Dr. Lefevre and one other director bought the controlling shares in the company, and the

The crew putting up a telephone pole in Port Moody didn't appear to lack for sidewalk superintendents. As is made obvious by the picture, the men erecting the pole had to do their job with little equipment. To help with the heavier work they probably had the use of a team of horses.

business once again became locally owned. In 1904 there was again a name change, and the British Columbia Telephone Company Ltd., came into existence. By 1906 Lefevre and William Farrell were the company's principal shareholders. Farrell remained in control until the mid-twenties when the firm was again sold in order to raise capital for continued expansion. It was bought by an American utilities company headed by Theodore Gary. In 1955 Gary's holdings were merged into General Telephone Company, thereby giving the latter firm control of BC Tel. In 1959 Sylvania merged with General Telephone to form General Telephone and Electronics (GTE) a company with world-wide interests. It became the owner of BC Tel, and at least 25 other North American telephone companies.

While the telephone company has been foreign-owned since the mid-twenties, BC Tel continued to foster its image as a locally-owned family business right through to the mid-fifties. The image did reflect reality at least to a limited extent in that the Farrells held a significant block of shares in the American company, and first William Farrell, and then his son, Gordon Farrell, were given what amounted to a free hand in the management of BC Tel. The degree of local autonomy allowed to the Farrells helped the company avoid the fate of that other large local public utility, the BC Electric, which of course, was taken over by the government in the days of Premier W.A.C. Bennett to became BC Hydro. Again, the reality is that the company that British Columbians loved to hate had been American-owned for three-quarters of a century.

Burrard Inlet

BRIDGE OVER TROUBLED WATERS

While some sort of Burrard Inlet crossing had been suggested as early as 1895, it was another fifteen years before any concrete action was taken. On May 4, 1910 the federal government granted a charter to the newly-formed Burrard Inlet Tunnel and Bridge Company, allowing it to run a tunnel under the First Narrows, and build a bridge across the Second Narrows. The firm decided that the bridge would be built first, and in 1913, after government subsidies had been secured, the company solicited tenders. Unfortunately, the tenders submitted all called for more money than the company had on hand.

It was not until after World War One that a contract was finally signed. On July 23, 1923 Northern Construction Company and W. Stewart & Company jointly contracted to build a Second Narrows bridge designed by William Smaill, their chief engineer, for 1.25 million dollars. It wasn't long before costs escalated, however, and a number of players got into the act, causing the design to be altered several times. None of the changes corrected the bridge's principal design fault, which was that its moveable span was in the wrong place given the currents created by the rush of water coming down both the Seymour River and Lynn Creek, and by the severe riptides created daily within the narrows. And, of course, all the changes cost money.

The original design called for a 300-foot swing span but the federal government insisted that a bascule be used instead. The argument put forth was that a bascule, which was a counter-weighted draw bridge operating on the principle of the see-saw, was "much more up-to-date,

easier on manipulation and much more speedy." Ottawa agreed to meet the $100,000 cost of this design change.

In response to the request of towboat owners, who were concerned about the currents swirling through the much-narrowed Second Narrows, the number of supporting piers was increased from six to eight to allow for two additional 150-foot spans at the north end of the bridge. This change meant that over 1,000 feet of trestle that had already been built had to be demolished. Shipping interests also pointed out that the clearance was not enough to allow the majority of small boats that would be passing through the narrows to sail under the fixed spans; they would have to wait for the bascule to be opened each time they wanted to pass through the narrows. Unfortunately, this concern only came to the attention of the builders after the piers had been finished, meaning that a concrete cap had to be placed atop each pier in order to raise the height of the bridge five feet throughout its length. Not to be left out, the provincial government demanded that there be another design change.

While the original specifications called for a bridge that could carry motor vehicles with a gross tonnage of not more than ten tons, Victoria said that the maximum allowable vehicle weight had to be raised to fifteen tons. The cost of this change, $200,000, was paid by the province. By the time all the design changes had been made the cost of the bridge had gone from 1.25 million to 2.1 million dollars. Through the purchase of shares in the company, and by guaranteeing its bonds, the City of Vancouver, the City and the District of North Vancouver, West Vancouver, the federal and provincial governments, and the Vancouver

Burrard Inlet's first rail and road crossing was at the Second Narrows, slightly to the east of the present bridge. It first opened to traffic on November 7, 1925.

Harbour Board underwrote the cost of the bridge. The tolls to be charged were intended to pay off the bond issues, meet operating costs, and provide a reasonable profit for the bridge's owners. Such optimism!

The crossing very quickly turned out to be a bridge to disaster. Not only did none of the investors ever make any money, but in the five years following its opening there were over twenty accidents, causing half a million dollars damage. While most were relatively minor, a few of the accidents were of major proportions. On March 10, 1927, for example, the steamer *Eurana* struck the main span, causing $30,000 worth of damage. On April 24, 1928 the *Norwich City* being caught in the current sailed under the main span and lost its forward derrick booms, bridge, funnel, and much of its superstructure. While damage to the bridge was relatively slight, repairs to the 5,627 ton ship cost over $50,000.

By sheer coincidence it was exactly two years later (April 24, 1930) that the riptide swept another freighter, the 10,000 ton *Losmar* into the bridge. Caught in the cross current, the pilot ordered both anchors dropped, but they failed to hold. Since the vessel could not be steered clear, it crashed into the southern span, dropping it into the inlet, and severing the electric cable supplying power to the bascule. The bascule was open when the accident happened, so shipping was able to continue moving through the narrows; however, rail and road traffic to the North Shore was cut off for weeks.

Having little room to manoeuvre after hitting the Second Narrows Bridge, the Losmar *with engines reversed ran hard aground on the Knuckle, a shoal off the south (Vancouver) shore of Burrard Inlet. This picture looks eastward through the bridge toward Barnet and Port Moody.*

Serious though it was, the accident involving the *Losmar* seemed like little more than a dress rehearsal for what was to come in just a matter of months. On September 19, 1930 the empty hulk, *Pacific Gatherer*, a cumbersome 300-ton log carrier, was under tow when it was caught by the riptide and driven under the centre span where it became firmly wedged. Because the hulk had no seacocks it couldn't be scuttled, and since Vancouver's fireboat was in False Creek it wouldn't have been able to get to the scene in time to sink the log carrier. There was nothing to do but wait and watch as the tide rose. On the rising tide the *Pacific Gatherer* simply lifted the span and dumped it into Burrard Inlet! Bridge traffic was not restored until June 18, 1934.

The account of how the bridge was rebuilt, and just why it took so long to be repaired is another story to be told at some other time. One does wonder, though, how the North Shore would have developed had the Burrard Inlet Tunnel and Bridge Company chosen in the 1920s to run a tunnel under the First Narrows rather than build its Second Narrows Bridge over both troubled, and very troubling waters.

Vancouver
ONLY IN BRITISH COLUMBIA

British Columbia's politics have long confused Canadians in other provinces. And, indeed, there are even times when they mystify British Columbians themselves. One unhappy aspect of local political life relates to what was once the prevailing attitude to Asians. Fear, hostility, suspicion, and distrust of "Orientals," as these people invariable would have been called when they weren't being called "Chinks" or "Japs," coloured race relations in Vancouver and the Fraser Valley until the Second World War and beyond.

In 1907 long-standing anti-Asian feeling was particularly high. Labour saw the Orientals as competing unfairly for jobs, churchmen saw them as opium-smoking heathen who would all be White slavers given half a chance, and politicians saw them as a threat to political stability and to White (i.e. European and Christian) values. In 1907 the provincial government had even gone so far as to pass legislation curtailing the immigration of Orientals into the province. Even though the measure was vetoed by the federal government as being beyond the legislative power of the provincial government, it had overwhelming popular support.

Generally speaking, White Vancouverites had little difficulty assigning the Chinese and East Indians in their midst to a "below stairs" position of social, cultural, economic and racial inferiority. In 1907, however, the White population was not so easily able to look down its nose at the Japanese with total assurance of its own manifest superiority. And why not? Because the Japanese had not only proved their military expertise

Prince Fushimi's carriage can be seen passing beneath the evergreen welcome arch that was erected in front of the CPR's train station. Amazing though it may seem, over 120 such ceremonial welcoming arches are reported to have been built in British Columbia between 1869 and 1946. Although they were made of a variety of materials, these temporary arches were most often made of logs or poles and covered in evergreen branches as was the arch erected in 1907 for the visit of Prince Fushimi.

and might by defeating the Chinese in the Sino-Japanese War of 1894-95, but much more significantly, had decisively defeated the czar's forces in the Russo-Japanese War of 1904-05.

As well, by the beginning of the twentieth century both Japan and Great Britain were beginning to see Russia as militarily threatening. Russian troops were already in Manchuria and were known to have designs on both Chinese and Korean territory. On January 30, 1902, an Anglo-Japanese Alliance was signed. While the treaty was in itself important, it was most significant because it was the first treaty between a Western power and an oriental nation in which the Asian country was treated as an equal. Not only did the treaty create strong pro-British feeling in Japan, but enhanced Japanese prestige everywhere—even in Vancouver with its large and unpopular Japanese population. The treaty was renewed in 1905 for a further ten years.

For the West, the Russian defeat was a kind of wake-up call; Japan in less than half a century had moved from being a feudal society ruled by local shoguns or warlords to become a powerful national state united under the Emperor Mutsuhito, whose rule name was Meiji. This Meiji period saw the country become a modern industrial state. The 1889 constitution made the emperor the paramount symbol for a united Japan, and created a diet with an upper house selected from the nobility and an elected lower house. Together they were to advise the cabinet, which was regarded as above politics and was accountable only to the emperor. The Meiji reforms—administrative, economic, social, legal, educational and military—were carried out under the slogan: "enrich the country and strengthen the military."

While Vancouver's anti-Asian feelings were running particularly high in the summer of 1907, the city had a Japanese visitor it could not ignore. After all, the man had been received by King Edward who made him a Knight Commander of the Order of the Bath, had travelled across Canada in a special train provided by the CPR, and was accompanied by Joseph Pope, the federal Deputy Minister of State; Miles Lampson, M.V.O. of the British Foreign Office; Captain D.O.C. Newton, aide-de-camp to the Governor General Earl Grey; and W.R. Baker, representing the CPR. Given that he was a prince, albeit an Oriental prince, undoubtedly in the minds of civic politicians and the self-anointed socially elite, his rank would have separated him from "the little brown men" they were working so hard to have excluded from local residency and Canadian citizenship. At this point it is tempting to say that political pragmatism overriding principle is nothing new.

The distinguished visitor was His Imperial Highness Prince Sadanaru Fushimi, first cousin of the Emperor Meiji, and after the Crown Prince first in line to the throne of Japan. The 49-year-old prince was on his way home from London, where he was returning the 1906 official visit of Prince Arthur of Connaught to Japan. Prince Arthur, who was the son of the Duke of Connaught, had gone to Japan representing his uncle King Edward VII. On the King's behalf he presented Emperor Meiji with the Order of the Garter. As it happened, Prince Arthur passed through Vancouver on March 30, 1906 on his way to Japan.

On February 12, 1907 Prince Fushimi, who had been appointed to head a mission to London, left Japan for Great Britain. He was sent by the Emperor to thank King Edward for the Garter. Rather surprisingly he went to London empty-handed; there was no reciprocal order for the British monarch. Nevertheless, the visit was considered to have been a huge diplomatic success. Precautions had been taken, of course. One "precaution" was generally seen as misguided, to say the least; the Lord Chamberlain's office had withdrawn the license for the performing of Gilbert and Sullivan's *Mikado* for the duration of the prince's visit.

Prince Fushimi's visit to London was something more than a social call. Together with Admiral Yamamoto he was involved in secret negotiations with Sir Edward Grey of the Foreign Office regarding an extension of the scope of the Anglo-Japanese agreement that was already in effect, so that Japan would be bound to assist Great Britain, should India come under attack by a foreign power. The assistance would be naval and the country perceived as the potential aggressor was, of course, Russia. In return for Japan's promise of naval support, Britain proposed to help Japan maintain financial stability and gain enhanced international standing. Returning home by way of Canada Prince Fushimi and his party crossed the Atlantic to Quebec City where they disembarked from the CPR's *Empress of Ireland*. Not only was Prince Fushimi a senior member of the Japanese Imperial Family, he was also both a distinguished general and respected diplomat. On earlier occasions he had represented the emperor as Ambassador Extraordinary at the coronation of Czar Nicholas II in 1896 and had attended the St. Louis World's Fair in 1904 as the official representative of his country.

Prince Fushimi's military career was equally impressive. By the time of his visit to Vancouver he was a full general and a member of Japan's Supreme Council of War. As a major-general in the Sino-Japanese War he had successfully led campaigns in the Kei-hai-wei region and in Formosa (Taiwan). During the Russo-Japanese War, by which time Prince Fushimi had reached the rank of lieutenant-general, he led a division in the attack on

Prince Fushimi and members of his entourage were photographed in front of Stanley Park's Hollow Tree. The Prince and some of the others in the party can be seen to be wearing the "Prince Fushimi Medal" they had received earlier in the day. The Daily Province *described Prince Fushimi as having "the typical face of the Japanese patrician, sharp but whimsical, almond shaped eyes, [and] a well-set and determined mouth …." One wonders just how many "typical" Japanese patricians the writer had met.*

Nansan, which later made the capture of Ryojun (Port Arthur) possible.

As the city fathers planned their welcome for Prince Fushimi, Ottawa let them know exactly what was expected of them. They were told "that while it is not expected that a civic address should be delivered, both the Imperial [British] and Canadian Governments desired that the visitor be accorded a full state reception and treatment." The federal government also decreed that the local regiment would provide a guard of honour during the visit, and that there would be royal salutes marking the prince's arrival and departure. As well, it was suggested that the streets be decorated "with intertwined Japanese and English [sic] flags." Ottawa offered to lend the city Japanese flags should they be needed.

The prince and his party arrived aboard a "Royal Train … a marvel of luxury in the manner of [its] appointments" at Vancouver's CPR station on the morning of Saturday, June 22, 1907. Local dignitaries, headed by Mayor Bethune, were waiting on the platform to greet the royal visitor and his retinue. Prince Fushimi inspected a guard of honour, and the band of the Duke of Connaught's Own Rifles played the Japanese national anthem.

The Vancouver Daily Province reported: "Following the inspection His Imperial Highness quickly stepped into a waiting carriage which was driven rapidly up the hill leading from the depot to Granville Street. In front of the station a 75-foot high evergreen ceremonial arch of welcome had been erected by the Japanese community. Following the instructions of Vancouver's

Japanese Consul it was designed by local architect W.A. Arthur, and erected by Coulson & Laidlow." The *Province* report went on to say that "several thousand Japanese who were lined up in military order upon the embankment overlooking the depot broke out in an enthusiastic, swelling roar of 'Banzais'—the national cheer of Japan—as their Prince was driven up the hill. Daylight fireworks from barges anchored in the stream were sent up in profusion ….'Banzai!' greeted the prince wherever and whenever the carriage passed the little brown men. Even the Hindu, loyal British subject that he is, cheered for the Prince and incidentally for the British-Japanese alliance."

An interesting personal recollection of the day has come down to us from one of the men in the D.C.O.R. Honour Guard. He was none other than J.S. Matthews, later to become Vancouver's first City Archivist. Written years after the visit of Prince Fushimi, Major Matthews recalled the "odd [Japanese] custom of putting all the men in one place, the women in another, and the children in another. The men were nearest Granville, the women nearest Cordova, and the children down the slope to the station. When we saw the number of them we got a bit of a fright; we had never dreamed that our … fisheries, etc., had so passed out of our control. Even at that long ago date we foresaw that … it would lead to trouble."

A luncheon for fifteen guests was held at the Hotel Vancouver, where Prince Fushimi and his party were staying overnight as guests of the CPR. In the afternoon there was a drive along decorated streets to Pacific Coast Mills where the prince had an opportunity to tour the plant. As it happened, most of the city's other sawmills were shut down during the Fushimi visit; their many Japanese employees had simply taken time off to be among those welcoming the prince. Following the visit, the procession of seven carriages then made its way around Stanley Park, stopping of course at the Hollow Tree for the obligatory photograph. With two exceptions, the same guests who had been present at luncheon were at dinner with the prince in the evening. Both the luncheon and dinner were served in the hotel's Green Room at an oval table that could accommodate twenty diners. The table had been built specially for the visit of Prince Arthur the year before.

It has to be wondered why there was neither a large civic luncheon or dinner to honour the visitor. While it may have been because the prince spoke no English, it is much more likely that both the British and Canadian governments wanted to avoid creating any situation which might be cause for embarrassment for their Japanese guest and his government.

We can be sure that the prince and his party would have been well aware of the high level of anti-Japanese feeling that existed in Vancouver, not only among the ignorant and uniformed but also among the community's political, social and business leaders as well. It is not surprising, therefore, that one of his very few expressions of appreciation while in Vancouver related to the quality of service provided by the CPR's

The "Prince Fushimi Medal" was made in Seattle by Jos. Mayer & Bros. At its centre is the Japanese rising sun, on either side of which appear to be Canadian maple and British oak leaves. The pin from which the medal is suspended features Japanese and Canadian flags with an Imperial emblem, the chrysanthemum blossom.

Hotel Vancouver. He said that the service was the best he had experienced since leaving London. No small endorsement! To mark his appreciation Prince Fushimi presented Frank Cummings, the hotel's manager, with a gold cigarette case bearing the Japanese imperial crest. One of the two gifts the prince received during his visit to Vancouver was presented to him by the Japanese community. It was a giant mounted moose head. Following dinner, the prince appeared on the hotel's verandah to acknowledge the "Banzai's" of the hundreds of Japanese who had gathered in front of the hotel with their swinging coloured lanterns. Before he left Vancouver he expressed his appreciation for the affection shown to a member of the Japanese Imperial Family by making a donation of 1,000 yen to the city's Japanese School in support of its work.

The prince, together with others in his party, did receive one other gift. It was what is now known as the "Prince Fushimi Medal." Made of silver-plated copper, it was manufactured by Mayer Bros. of Seattle. The Japanese inscription on the obverse translates as, "To His Imperial Highness Prince Fushimi / A Respectful Welcome to a Member of the Royal House." The English inscription on the reverse reads, "H.I.H. Prince Fushimi / Royal Ambassador / and / Envoy Extraordinary / to the / Court of St. James [sic] / Vancouver, B.C. / June 22, 1907." The names of those who commissioned the medal's creation and were responsible for its distribution remain a mystery. The best guess is that the donors were members of Vancouver's Japanese community. To date the whereabouts of fifteen "Prince Fushimi Medals" is known. Just how many medals were cast and to whom they were presented is not known.

On the second and last day of his visit the prince insisted that the trip around Stanley Park be repeated. After this second visit to the park, the procession of seven carriages moved on to the Davie Street residence of the Japanese Consul for a reception and luncheon. Leaving the Consul's house the procession made its way down to the CPR docks, passing again beneath the evergreen welcome arch, to where the company's *Princess Victoria* was waiting to transport the royal party and the British and Canadian officials accompanying him to Victoria.

Before departing, Prince Fushimi (through his interpreter) expressed his appreciation of the cordiality of Canada's people for their hearty demonstrations of goodwill. He also expressed thanks to the federal government, and to the CPR for the great consideration shown to him and Japan. His aide-de-camp added that "the many manifestations of cordiality and friendly feeling through the Envoy's tour to and from London would undoubtedly strengthen the very basis of the British-Japanese alliance." As the prince and his party prepared to embark, Mayor Bethune said that "the Mayor and Aldermen, and the whole of Vancouver are deeply grateful for the honor [sic] of the prince's visit." Again, through his English-speaking aide Major Higashi, the prince politely returned the compliment. Following the party on board was the giant moose head and half a carload of baggage. To the strains of the Japanese and British national anthems the *Princess Victoria*, decked out in flags and bunting, set sail and passed through a decorated flotilla of local yachts and Japanese fishing boats from Steveston and Delta.

After a day in Victoria Prince Fushimi and his suite sailed for Japan aboard H.M.S. Monmouth, a China-based battle cruiser made available for the trip by the British Admiralty. Once again, the level of hospitality provided by both the British and federal governments would suggest that His Imperial Highness Prince Fushimi was a Very Important Person indeed.

To end the story, having seen their royal guest safely off to Japan, one can imagine Messrs Pope, Lampson, Newton, and Baker back in Vancouver boarding their private train for the trip to Ottawa and Montreal. Once they were on their way and as they congratulated themselves on a job well done, one of them might have said something like, "Time for a whiskey … cheers … and thank God the Vancouverites didn't ruin everything." After all, there had been no anti-Japanese protests, no negative comments in the newspapers, and no remarks made that might have offended anyone in the prince's party. And the four men might well have been amused to read in *The Daily Province*: "to the reception committee and Chief of Police Chamberlin, assisted by the Dominion officers and the local detective force, is due the credit for perhaps the best arranged and best carried out reception it has been Vancouver's privilege to accord a distinguished visitor." The newspaper quoted was dated Monday, June 24, 1907. It was to be less than seven weeks after the visit of Prince Fushimi—on Saturday, September 7, 1907 to be exact—that Vancouver's anti-Oriental riot took place, fomented by the words and actions of the city's Asiatic Exclusion League.

Having read the newspaper article, the four who were jointly responsible for insuring that all proceeded without incident may have looked at each other and smiled knowingly. Perhaps one of them might even have said that it was indeed unfortunate that British Columbians and their political, business, social, and religious leaders weren't nearly as adept at building bridges between peoples as they were at building ceremonial arches.

PAT BURNS' LITTLE BROTHER

There are some men who seem destined never to have an identity of their own. One such chap was a Vancouver businessman and entrepreneur who was almost invariably identified in print as the brother of his much more famous sibling. The man was Dominic Burns, and his much better known brother was Senator Pat Burns. Even his obituary in the *Vancouver Province* was headlined, "D. Burns Dead–Brother of Senator; Funeral Thursday."

P. Burns & Company was the biggest name in Canadian meat packing for several decades. Burns' pails of *Shamrock Lard* were a staple in nearly every home in Western Canada. In B.C. alone, before the First World War, P. Burns & Company meat markets could be found in 25 cities and towns; and in Vancouver itself Burns had outlets in eleven locations. In 1912 Pat Burns became one of the four founders of the Calgary Stampede, each of whom donated $100,000 to get the show up and running. Burns sold his meat packing business in 1928 for $15 million, while keeping his vast cattle ranches. In 1931 he was appointed to the Senate by Conservative prime minister, R. B. Bennett. With a brother like the senator, its easy to see how difficult it must have been for Dominic Burns to be known in any other way than as a younger brother of Pat Burns.

Dominic Burns, like his two brothers and his sister, was born in Ontario. He eventually joined his brother Pat in his cattle business and in 1898 accompanied P. Burns & Company's second cattle drive to Dawson City. While getting the beef to the Yukon by

Today's Workers' Compensation Board would love the Vancouver Block's ground floor scaffolding; it looks like a Laurel and Hardy movie set. The firm of Mason & Risch, a leading Canadian piano manufacturer, was the original occupant of the building's ground floor and mezzanine.

The unfinished Vancouver Block is still without its magnificent clock. Once a landmark that could be seen for miles around, the Vancouver Block's clock tower is now largely hidden from view by its much newer and taller neighbours.

way of Vancouver, Skagway, and over the Dalton Trail was both difficult work and a risky way to try to make money, these trips, and later ones like them, were a huge success financially. Dominic stayed on in the Yukon managing his brother's booming northern business until 1903 when he moved to Vancouver to manage the B.C. end of P. Burns & Company, "Wholesale and Retail Meat Merchants–Beef and Pork Packers," with its "Special Attention given to the Shipping Trade." At the same time he took a hands-on interest in the local real estate market. In 1909 Pat Burns gave company shares to a number of individuals who had a legitimate claim on them. Dominic received 1,500 shares. With a par value of $100 per share, his stock had a market value of 1.5 million dollars.

In spite of the fact that Dominic Burns lived much of his life in the shadow of his brother Pat, who was quite literally a household name, he did manage to leave his very own mark on Vancouver. Whether his new-found and sudden wealth was an influencing factor we do not know; however, in 1910 he decided to build a 15-storey skyscraper, the top two floors of which would be his own private penthouse. The building's Granville Street site is 75 feet by 120 feet, and the 70,000-square foot structure is steel-framed with reinforced concrete on the ground floor and brick "Spandel" interior walls above. The building's street side facade is faced with white glazed terracotta, and the light wells on either side of the structure are of reinforced concrete. The building permit for the $400,000 skyscraper was issued on January 23, 1911, and construction began in March of the same year. The contractor was the Norton Griffiths Steel Construction Company. While under construction the building was popularly known as the Burns Block, and it was not until it was opened on August 21, 1912 that it became the Vancouver Block.

For over sixty years the Vancouver Block suffered by comparison with the now demolished Birks Building, architecturally Vancouver's most sophisticated pre-World War One office building. Compared to its elegant neighbour, the Vancouver Block was decidedly "plain Jane." In that Burns selected Par and Fee as his architects, the structure's lack of finesse is not surprising. J.E. Parr and T.A. Fee were the principals in a firm that was highly successful because it gave clients the biggest economic bang for their buck. The partners advertised their firm as "built upon a strictly commercial basis," and stated that "while they welcome any incident that gives expression or beauty to their work, their chief endeavour is the production of buildings that will pay." They also advertised "Utilitas" [Utility] as "their motto and revenue their aim." Since the Birks Building cost $1.25 million to build, and the Vancouver Block only

$.4 million, its easy to see why Parr and Fee were so successful in attracting a large clientele.

Even though Parr and Fee were the architects of record, it seems that the actual design was the work of Parr, MacKenzie and Day. In all probability MacKenzie and Day were staff architects employed by Parr and Fee. It would be interesting to know which of the three men came up with the idea for the building's crowning glory, Canada's largest clock! It stands atop Burn's two-storey penthouse. The design not only provided the building owner with his unique residence, but gave the clock an elevation that would greatly enhance its visibility. The clock was installed by its makers, the Standard Electric Time Company of San Francisco at a cost of over $10,000. Each of its four faces is 22-feet in diameter with a minute hand 11-feet long, and a second hand 8-feet long. The glass protecting each face is seven-eighths of an inch thick, and weighs four tons.

Dominic Burns lived in his Vancouver Block penthouse until his death on December 19, 1933. His estate sold the building to Samuel Zacks of Toronto for one million dollars. Three years later Zacks sold it to a consortium of local investors for $1.355 million.

Though few would know that the Vancouver Block began its life as the Burns Block, today Dominic Burns' name is known far and wide in connection with another local landmark. It relates to his on-going interest in farming. He owned a 2,425 hectare farm in Delta, which was something of a show place. It was when additional land was needed for cattle range that he bought the last parcel of undeveloped land in the municipality, the 4,000 hectare property that had been purchased by John Douglas Sutherland Campbell, Marquis of Lorne, who had become Canada's Governor General at age thirty-three in 1878. Lord Lorne, later ninth Duke of Argyle, was married to Princess Louise, Queen Victoria's second daughter. The Lorne's made a vice-regal visit to British Columbia even though the transcontinental railroad (the CPR) was not yet finished. Lorne in fact did much during his term of office to reconcile B.C. to Confederation. While buying a piece of land that covered a quarter of Delta municipality may have been a wise political move, it did the Campbell family no good economically. The land still remained vacant when Dominic Burns bought it.

As it turned out, Burns' newly acquired ranch lands were too marshy to be used successfully for grazing cattle. While his Vancouver Block was a consistent money-maker, his ranch lands were considered worthless by most people until the 1990s. That was when conservationists and ecologists ranked them as being of inestimable value. Dominic Burns' 4,000-hectare folly we now know today as Burns Bog.

THE ONE-ROOM SCHOOLHOUSE

Very few among us can claim the pioneer status that comes to those who were born in a log cabin. At the same time, however, there are still many in our midst who can lay claim to that other mark of the pioneer, namely, learning their "three Rs" in a one-room schoolhouse.

British Columbia's first school was opened in Victoria in 1855 by the Hudson's Bay Company for the children of its employees. By 1895 the provincial school system had grown to the point where there were not only a great many schools, but four classifications of schools within the system. There were high schools and graded schools which, of course, were only found in the cities and larger towns. Then there were rural municipal schools, and in unorganized territory, rural assisted schools. Almost without exception, the schools in the latter two categories were of the one-room variety.

A typical rural school opened at Harrison River in the early spring of 1901. Seventy-five miles east of Vancouver, Harrison River (known as Harrison Mills after May 1, 1910) is not surprisingly on the Harrison River. The settlement is about half a mile above the point where the Harrison River joins the Fraser. The area's first European settlers arrived in 1869. Since much of the land was heavily forested, one of their number, Henry Cooper, built a small water-powered sawmill on the west bank of the Harrison River in 1870 to produce rough lumber from local fir and cedar. However, it really wasn't until the Canadian Pacific's main line came through the settlement in 1885 that there was any significant growth. In 1892 Joseph Martin and his sons built a sawmill on the east side of the Harrison River, just to the south of the rail line. The Martins had earlier bought the mill first operated by Cooper and ran it for a few years. In 1901 John Fulbrook and Joseph Innis of Chilliwack built a seven-machine shingle mill on the Harrison's west bank, across the river from Martin's mill. At the beginning of the twentieth century the future looked bright at Harrison Mills. There was not only a lumber mill, a shingle mill, and a growing number of nearby logging operations, but also a railroad that could carry the local output both east and west to markets hungry for lumber and shingles.

Naturally where there were mill workers and loggers there were families, and by 1900 these families wanted a school built in their community. In October of the same year the provincial Department of Education acquired a half acre of land, and hired J.W. Machan of Chilliwack to build a schoolhouse over the winter of 1900-1901. Those children who had already been attending makeshift classes in the home of Emma Menton, plus one five-year-old (enrolled in order to meet the minimum number of pupils required for a school to be built) were all in their places when the school inspector paid his first visit in April 1901.

Known as the Harrison River School, the building was simple enough. The entrance was through a large cloakroom. In the centre of the classroom stood a large woodstove, with a protecting steel guard on three sides. There were the usual classroom furnishings, including an eight-day clock that hung high on the wall, well above the reach of pupils. In common with all the other buildings at Harrison Mills, the school was a frame structure raised six feet above ground to protect it against flooding. A web of catwalks and ramps connected virtually all the buildings in the settlement so life could go on without serious interruption during the spring floods, which were a fact of life at Harrison Mills.

The teacher never had to wonder what was to be done in a day—the provincial Department of Education saw to that. It expected all pupils to be in "constant employment in their studies … " with the teacher "to render the exercises pleasant as well as profitable, … to supervise the playground," and to practise discipline "such as may be exercised by a judicious parent in his (sic) family." Commenting on the Public Schools Act of 1895, one writer pointed out that it "admirably [illustrated] the Imperial Spirit animating those who control the cause of public education."

Among other things, the act dictated that certain days, including Empire Day, Dominion Day, and the King's birthday, be observed as school holidays. Regarding Empire Day, the act stated that its object was "the development of the Empire idea." Consequently, "the lessons, recitations, and other exercises of the last teaching day preceding Empire Day [were to] bear directly upon the history and resources of Canada and the British Empire [and] to promote a spirit of true patriotism and loyalty." For all patriotic holidays the teacher was to raise "the school flag (British or Canadian)."

And what was the teacher paid for doing these and many other things? In 1910, according to the

Harrison River School, built in 1901, was typical of the more than 200 one-room schools existing in rural and semi-rural communities throughout British Columbia in 1910.

Provincial Year Book, salaries for teachers in rural municipal schools like the one at Harrison River ranged from fifty to one hundred dollars a month. The higher figure was "an extreme allowance" with the average "between fifty and sixty dollars per month." It would be safe to assume that the salaries approaching the "extreme allowance" of one hundred dollars would only have gone to married male teachers. And undoubtedly the all-male school boards of the time would have thought that right and proper.

The schoolhouse built for the Harrison River School in 1901 continued in use until 1922, by which time Harrison Mills had seen many changes. The mill built by the Martins in 1892, and owned since 1898 by James and Arthur Tretheway, had burned to the ground in July 1903. The Tretheways had sold the site to Sir Douglas Cameron's Manitoba-based Rat Portage Lumber Company in 1904. The mill built at Harrison Mills became the company's seventh when it was completed in 1908. It employed over 200 men and kept 400 more at work in the surrounding logging camps. While optimism for the future was naturally high, it didn't last long. An

"inadequate log supply " and other "insurmountable problems" led to the mill's temporary closure in 1910. "Temporary" has a way of becoming "permanent," and when the sawmill equipment was removed to Vancouver in 1923, the community's hope that it would become a major lumbering centre faded forever.

As fate would have it, Harrison Mills future lay in quite a different direction: it was to become a prosperous agricultural community. Farming got a boost when the portion of the Scowlitz Indian reserve north of the CPR line was released by the band and put up for sale. Chief Joe Hall signed the necessary documents on October 20, 1920, and the land was divided into 25-acre lots which were put on the market in 1922.

The reshaping of the community led the School Board to relocate the Harrison River School to a site more central to the expanded farming community. A new and larger school, standing on a two-acre site, opened in 1922. The old one-room schoolhouse was sold by tender in 1927. The successful bidder dismantled the building and used the lumber to build his barn. The days of the one-room school at Harrison Mills were over.

Coming ashore in Vancouver from the USS Henderson, *Mrs. Harding precedes the president down the gang plank as they leave the American naval transport to begin their heavily programmed day of formal and semi-formal functions.*

Vancouver

A NEIGHBOUR CALLS

Americans visiting Stanley Park for the first time must be more than a little surprised when they come upon the memorial to President Warren G. Harding. Until relatively recent times when serious competition has been provided by Richard Nixon and Bill Clinton, it was a toss-up as to whether the administration of Harding or that of U.S. Grant was the most corrupt in the history of the United States.

The 29th president of the United States was a man of limited intellect who was blessed with a large measure of charm, good looks, and a mastery of the high-sounding (if empty) phrase. He was also a man who was far too loyal to his friends and cronies, many of whom used his trust to line their own pockets and those of their friends. How did such a man become president of the United States and end up with a rather imposing memorial in Vancouver, B.C.?

Warren Gamaliel Harding was born in Ohio. When he was nineteen, he and two friends whom he later bought out, paid $300 for the *Marion Daily Star*. Harding's affable nature and his willingness to work hard made the newspaper a success. Through its pages he supported the Republican party, and thereby came to the attention of the Ohio GOP political machine.

Elected to the Ohio State Senate in 1899, he served until 1902 when he was elected lieutenant-governor for one term. In 1915 he was elected to the U.S. Senate where he served until 1921. Throughout his years in both state and federal senates, Harding's name was never attached to any legislation of consequence. What, then, was his secret of success? Basically it was his unswerving party loyalty, coupled with a conviviality and a gift for public speaking.

Mediocrity was unquestionably Harding's long suit, and it served him well. With his many friends and few enemies, he emerged as the ideal compromise candidate for president. At the 1920 Republican convention there were two strong contenders, but neither could command a majority. In what later was to become known as the "smoke-filled room" of American politics, a gathering of powerful conservative senators agreed to support Harding and secured his nomination. He conducted a "front porch" campaign calling—in his own words—for a "return to normalcy." Being a candidate who asked for neither domestic reform nor international involvement, he won the presidency by the widest margin to date.

Although Harding's term of office began well enough, it wasn't long before there were rumours of political, as opposed to personal, impropriety. Not that Harding's life was without a darker side. His marriage to a domineering woman, whom he called "the Duchess," brought him little happiness. He was involved in a number of affairs, one lasting fifteen years, and another producing his only child. Illicit White House sex is not exclusively a post war phenomenon: the mother of his daughter visited him regularly at the White House. In Harding's day, of course, the goings-on in the bedrooms of the Executive Mansion were considered off-limits by the press.

By the spring of 1923 rumours of corruption within the administration were circulating widely. Three members of Harding's cabinet and a number of his patronage appointees were not only unsuited for public office but downright dishonest. Particularly venal was his secretary of the interior, who secretly leased naval oil reserves near Tea Pot Dome, Wyoming to his friends. After seeing his party do badly in the 1922 congressional elections, Harding set out on a transcontinental "Voyage of Understanding" that was to take him as far as Alaska.

It was on July 26, 1923, while he was en route from Alaska to California, that Harding disembarked from the *USS Henderson* in Vancouver to become the first president to set foot on Canadian soil. *The Vancouver Sun* reported that as the visitors came ashore they received "a 21-gun Royal (sic) salute." The presidential motorcade travelled first to Stanley Park where at noon Harding delivered an address to over 40,000 people. He was at his most eloquent, describing his visit "as just a neighbourly call" made "in much the same spirit as one runs next door to borrow a couple of eggs." The day also included a luncheon jointly hosted by the province

Travelling south on Granville Street, the presidential motorcade approaches the Dunsmuir Street intersection. In the lead car with the Hardings are W.C. Nicol, Lieutenant-Governor of British Columbia, and the Hon. J.H. King, Minister of Public Works representing the federal government.

and city, a round of golf at Shaughnessy Golf Club, a state dinner tendered by the federal government, and a reception hosted by the Hardings. The president also found time to drop in on the Police Chiefs' convention, and on the dinner being sponsored by the B.C. Institute of Journalists for those members of the press travelling with him. Harding told the reporters that "the newspaper game had always succeeded because it [had] always played on the square." He also said that a good reporter "never knocks but always boosts." With impromptu visits like these, and his gift for the appropriate off-the-cuff remark, it is not surprising that he enjoyed great personal popularity. The presidential party returned to the *Henderson* by ten o'clock and the highly successful "neighbourly call" ended.

Doubtless Vancouverites were still talking about the affable American president when just a week after his visit (on August 2) he died in San Francisco. Already suffering from a heart condition, his strenuous schedule and the knowledge of the scandals that were threatening his administration were probably responsible for bringing on the thrombosis, from which he did not recover.

Although Harding may have been a politician of mediocre talent with little more than a gift for the well-turned phrase, he was not a party to the political corruption that marked his administration. Respecting him for his personal commitment to international goodwill, his fellow Kiwanians collected fifty cents from each of their 95,000 members to meet the cost of a suitable memorial to their most illustrious brother. At its 1924 convention the Kiwanis Club International selected Vancouver's Stanley Park as the site for their memorial to him.

An international design competition was held, and Charles Marega of Vancouver was awarded the commission. Well sited against a forested background, the memorial succeeds in suggesting peace and tranquillity. Officially known as "The Harding International Goodwill Memorial," the monument was intended to do three things. First, memorialize "the high character, broad statesmanship, and lofty purposes of President Harding." Second, mark the "respect and generous goodwill of the people of Canada and of the United States each for the other." And, third, witness to "the immense power of the Kiwanis Club of Canada and the United States in promoting [the] close friendship which has characterized the relations of these two mighty peoples." The Harding Memorial was dedicated on September 16, 1925 in the presence of a large crowd which included over 1,500 Kiwanians from both sides of the border.

Warren Harding's life says something about leadership: being well-intentioned and well-liked isn't enough; vision and resolve must also be present in one who would lead. Harding's political legacy is a lot less solid than his memorial in Stanley Park.

Charles Marega won the design competition for the Harding International Goodwill Memorial. With its unadorned surfaces, simplicity of form, and minimal ornamentation, his Art Moderne monument would have been considered avante-guarde when it was first seen in 1925.

With its deck stacked ten feet high with lumber, the Mabel Brown *is pictured leaving Vancouver on its maiden voyage across the Pacific. Each of the schooners built for the Canada West Coast Navigation Company was named after the wife of a director. The fleet included the* Laurel Whalen, Jessie Norcross, Janet Carruthers, *and the* Margaret Haney.

Vancouver

WOODEN SHIPS:
NECESSITY'S STEP-CHILDREN

Being a seaport, facilities for ship repairs have always had a place on Vancouver's waterfront, which is more than can be said for shipbuilding. Although it is true that from time to time larger vessels had been built in either Burrard Inlet or False Creek, and scores of fishing boats and other small craft have been built in Vancouver's harbour, the reality is that shipbuilding first became a significant local industry only when wartime conditions made it a necessity, and when it was supported financially—either directly or indirectly—by government. Vancouver's development as a shipbuilding centre during the First World War was not motivated primarily by patriotism, but rather by economic opportunism.

The need for huge numbers of trans-Atlantic troop and supply ships, many of which were to replace

those lost through enemy submarine attack, meant that there was a severe shortage of ships available to serve the needs of West Coast lumbermen and sawmill owners. By the spring of 1915 piles of logs and stacks of lumber were everywhere, waiting shipment to what are now called Pacific Rim markets. These lumbermen and mill owners found an ally in the Canadian Manufacturers' Association that took up their cause and with whom they lobbied governments in Ottawa and Victoria for ships. Although Ottawa wasn't moved by this united appeal, in the spring of 1915 the provincial premier, Sir Richard McBride, set up a cabinet committee to determine whether or not a "made in British Columbia" ship-building program was feasible. Given that both loggers and mill workers were being laid off because forest products could not be moved overseas, it was very much in the provincial government's interest to find a positive answer to the question. Not surprisingly, there was wide

support within the business community for the idea of building wooden ships locally, on the understanding of course that provincial financial incentives would be forthcoming. Among those supporting the idea was H.R. MacMillan who wrote from London in August 1915 saying that "ships of steel" and also "wooden vessels … which can be built cheaply now and operated cheaply now" should be built on the West Coast. Finally, in the spring of 1916 the legislature passed the B.C. Shipping Act to encourage the building of ships "for the carriage of freight on ocean routes," but specifically excluding "coastwise or inland water trade."

The bill had the desired effect; suddenly there was an abundance of venture capital, much of it in central Canada, ready and waiting to be used for the construction of West Coast shipyards. While a half dozen firms were quick to respond, none was faster than Wallace Shipyards, Limited in North Vancouver. In June 1916 at

The War Atlin, War Cariboo, War Cayuse, War Nicola, War Puget, *and* War Suquash
were the six wooden merchant ships built at the Lyall shipyard in North Vancouver.
The War Puget, *pictured left of centre, was the first of the six completed.*

a cost of $165,000 the company bought 21 acres of reclaimed waterfront property at the foot of Fell Avenue as a site for wooden shipbuilding berths. Wallace's first contract was with a consortium operating as the Canada West Coast Navigation Company. The new shipyard built three auxiliary five-masted gaff-rigged lumber schooners at a price per ship of $121,200. The first of these 2,500-ton deadweight schooners, built with assistance under the B.C. Shipping Act of 1916, to go into service was the *Mabel Brown,* launched in January 1917. These 243-foot lumber schooners, each equipped with a pair of Swedish 160 horsepower auxiliary internal combustion engines, were among the most elegant vessels ever to sail the seven seas. While they were designed by J.H. Price, an American

who had built the world's largest wooden schooner—the *City of Portland*—and was the acknowledged expert in schooner design, they were out of date before they were built. After building only three more of these schooners, Wallace had decided to concentrate on building steel ships, and in August 1916 the North Vancouver yard laid the keel for a 3,200-ton steel freighter. It was to become the first steel ocean-going merchant ship launched in B.C. The successful and profitable completion of this steel freighter convinced Wallace that the firm's future success lay in building steel not wooden ships. The Fell Avenue yard was sold to W. Lyall S.B. Company, which was a wholly owned subsidiary of W. Lyall Construction Company of Montreal.

Lyall built six more of the Price-designed 2,500-ton auxiliary schooners for their own account. The ships were intended for sale to Belgian interests, but delivery was refused. It was only with great difficulty that Lyall was able to sell them to French and Italian companies. In all, fifteen of these schooners were built in Vancouver and Victoria, but none was ever commercially successful. Their capacity was too limited, their underpowered engines were unreliable, they were too susceptible to the vagaries of the weather and sadly, they were too poorly built to stand up to either rough seas or rough usage. Ironically the huge amount of timber required to build both these wooden schooners, and the wooden freighters that were to follow, meant that B.C. mills were so busy meeting the needs of local shipyards that they had only a very limited amount of timber available for export!

By 1917 Allied shipping losses to German U-boats were seriously hindering the war effort. The situation had in fact reached the point where the Imperial Munitions Board in London had taken over the contracting for all shipbuilding. While steel ships were being ordered in large numbers from Canadian shipyards, 46 wooden freighters were ordered from yards on both the East and West Coasts. These single deck sister ships of 2,325 gross registered tons (3,300-tons deadweight) and powered by triple-expansion engines were 250 feet in length with a superstructure well aft. They had three hatches, two in the long forward deck, and one near the stern.

Under the direction of R.P. Butchart, director of shipbuilding for B.C., and his assistant Captain J.W. Troup, B.C. yards received orders for 27 of these wooden steamers. Built of Douglas fir, they were powered by triple-expansion engines which were expected to move the vessels along at ten knots. Butchart of course is much better known today for his famous gardens in Victoria

The War Nootka *was built by Western Canada Shipyard. This False Creek yard was created during the First World War specifically to produce wooden freighters. Western Canada built six ships, as did the Lyall Shipbuuilding Company in North Vancouver, before closing at the end of the war.*

The wooden freighters built by Lyall had their engines installed either at the Wallace Shipyards at the foot of Lonsdale in North Vancouver, or at B.C. Marine, at the north end of Victoria Drive in Vancouver. Here the War Puget *is pictured leaving B.C. Marine on August 21, 1918 for the fitting-out dock at Victoria's Ogden Point.*

and Troup for his highly successful years as manager of the Canadian Pacific's coastal steamship service.

Butchart and Troup awarded contracts for five ships to Foundation Company and four ships to Cameron-Genoa, both of Victoria. On the mainland, six ships were to be built by Lyall of North Vancouver, six by Western Canada Shipyards in False Creek, four by Westminster Construction in the Royal City, and two by Pacific Construction in Coquitlam. In February 1918 contracts were awarded to two other firms for 40 more ships. They were never built, however, since the war ended before the companies—British American Shipbuilding of Vancouver and Victoria Shipbuilding on the Island—could get their yards up and running. These were the last wooden freighters ordered by the Imperial

Munitions Board. All 27 of the "made in B.C." wooden freighters that were built set off across the Atlantic with cargoes of timber, flour, and other such badly needed supplies. None ever returned to the West Coast.

Although the ships could be built quickly, albeit of unseasoned softwood, their cargo capacity was too limited and they were too slow to compete successfully for post-war trade. Of those that survived the war, all but one were either laid up or scrapped by 1925.

The wooden schooners and freighters built on the West Coast during the First World War had short lives, but those responsible for building them had long memories. During the Second World War no one suggested that West Coast shipyards could or should again be building wooden ships.

Thirteen (count 'em) of Vancouver's fire engines—8 Seagraves, 3 American-LaFrance, 1 Webb and 1 Amoskeag—appear to be decked out for a parade or celebration of some sort. They were posed in the summer of 1913 for this "photo op" in the CPR's freight yards, which were on the south side of Pender Street in the block between Carrall and Abbott Streets.

Vancouver

A FIRED-UP FIRE CHIEF

In his role as Vancouver's first fire chief, John Howe Carlisle must have had his fair share of problems. However, getting City Council to vote money for fire-fighting equipment and fire halls wasn't one of them. The fire of Sunday, June 13, 1886 that virtually destroyed the two month old city and left 2,000 homeless predisposed the city fathers to support Carlisle as he laboured to make the city's fire department Canada's finest. His success was clearly evident when in 1909 a special commission in Britain ranked Vancouver's fire department with those of London and Leipzig as the "world's best in efficiency and equipment."

Always up-to-date, if not actually ahead of his time, Carlisle began his program to develop a fully motorized department in 1907, buying three fire engines from the Seagrave Company of Columbus, Ohio. The firm was so new, in fact, that the two hose wagons and one chemical wagon Vancouver purchased were the first three fire engines produced by the firm. The vehicles were each equipped with a 53 horsepower, four-cylinder air-cooled engine. Together they cost $16,870, which was a lot of money in 1907. Not to be outdistanced by his fire engines, the fire chief also bought in the same year a two-cylinder McLaughlan-Buick for his own use.

One of the motorized hosewagons and the chemical wagon were assigned to the West End's new No. 6 Fire Hall at Nicola and Nelson. This hall, opened on March 1, 1908, was the first in Canada built expressly

Pictured in the CPR's freight yard are Vancouver's first two motorized aerial ladder trucks. On the left is the 1909 4-cylinder, 90 horsepower air-cooled Seagrave *75-foot tractor and aerial trailer. It was the first motorized aerial ladder truck manufactured by* Seagrave. *On the right is the 1912 85-foot* Webb *front-wheel drive gas electric.*

for motorized equipment. As it happened, 1908 was also the year in which the last piece of horse-drawn equipment was bought for the city. From then on it was motorized equipment all the way. Even the city's fire wardens, who regularly patrolled the business and factory districts, were provided with motorcycles.

Just as all automobiles weren't powered by internal combustion engines, some being steamers and others being electric, so it was with fire engines. In 1908 Carlisle bought the city's first (and last) steam propelled pumper. The eight-ton behemoth cost $12,480 and was build by the Amoskeag Manufactory and Manchester Locomotive Works of Manchester, New Hampshire. It was the only Amoskeag sold in Canada, and the last one built by the company. In spite of its ungainly appearance and top speed of 12 m.p.h., it remained in service until the early 1940s when it was sold to Fernie.

In 1912 Chief Carlisle bought an 85-foot aerial ladder truck which, like the Amoskeag pumper, was unique. Manufactured by the Webb Motor Company of St. Louis, Missouri, it was a front-wheel drive couple-gear electric. A gas motor drove a generator, which in turn supplied power to the two electric motors that powered each of the front wheels. Even though the vehicle was so slow that a kid on a bicycle could easily

out-distance it, the gas-electric remained in service for twenty years.

It was in 1914 that delivery was taken on the last Seagrave fire engine to be bought until 1943 when Seagraves were once again purchased. In 1912 the city had bought its first equipment from the American-LaFrance Fire Engine Company, and it was LaFrance that was to supply most of Vancouver's fire engines over the next half century.

In the fall of 1917 Vancouver became the first city in Canada to have a completely motorized fire department. Chief Carlisle's leadership and drive were recognized in 1922 when he was presented with Vancouver's first Good Citizen Award. He retired in 1928, and died at age 84 in 1941. Interestingly, the combined years of service of the seven men who in turn succeeded him as chief didn't equal the 42 years John Howe Carlisle served as Vancouver's fire chief.

There was a time when the comings and goings of the little West Vancouver ferries were a familiar sight in Burrard Inlet. In this quintessential view, West Vancouver No. 6 is pictured on its way to downtown Vancouver from Dunderave in West Vancouver. The crossing generally took from 20 minutes to half an hour, depending on tides, currents, and weather.

The Harbour

"A FERRY STORY"

For older long-time Vancouverites, it will seem like only yesterday that the little ferries were crossing back and forth between Ambleside in West Vancouver and the foot of Columbia Street in Vancouver. "Only yesterday" was in fact actually more than half a century ago.

The West Vancouver municipal ferry system was originally the creation of four West Vancouver real estate developers. Although there were a few settlers living in what is now West Vancouver by the mid-1880s, development didn't really amount to much until 1906 when the provincial government offered large parcels of land for sale at auction. John Lawson bought 160 acres and in the following year settled on the North

Shore. Lawson sold William C. Thompson, his brother-in-law who had also acquired acreage, on the idea of promoting land development. By 1909 the two men had subdivided their properties and were ready to market building lots. There was one problem, however, and it was that there was no way in which prospective buyers could get back and forth to West Vancouver unless they owned their own boats. Lawson and Thompson solved the problem by having a boat built, not only for their own use, but to transport the community's new residents to and from the city.

The boat, built in Vancouver by John J. Harford, was designed to carry 35 passengers. Teaming up with two other real estate developers, Robert

Macpherson and John Sinclair, Lawson and Thompson formed the West Vancouver Transportation Company, Limited, on February 22, 1910. On July 10 in the same year the *West Vancouver*, as the ferry was called, went into service, operating between Hollyburn (now 17th Street) in West Vancouver to a landing on English Bay, near the foot of Denman Street. Crossings were made every two hours from 7:00 a.m. until 7:00 p.m. The ferry did the trick, and it was not long before there was a growing population spreading out from the ferry's Hollyburn landing.

The new residents were not long in petitioning the provincial government for the creation of the District Municipality of West Vancouver to include that part of the North Shore stretching westward from the Capilano River to a point on Howe Sound beyond Horseshoe Bay. The new municipality came into being on April 6, 1912. Almost immediately its first municipal council passed a resolution authorizing the organization of a limited company to own and operate a ferry service between West Vancouver and Vancouver. This West Vancouver Ferry Company, as it was called, bought out the

privately-owned ferry company's assets for something like $6,500. The developers' ferry service had operated at a loss throughout its short existence and its owners were no doubt happy to be free of it. At the time of the takeover they were operating two vessels: the *West Vancouver* and the *Sea Foam*. The *Sea Foam*, which had been built by William Simpson in Vancouver in 1906 and re-engined in 1911, could carry 55 passengers.

It was not long before the new municipal ferry company went in search of a large ferry that would provide a better service for the increasing number of passengers travelling to and from Vancouver each day. The 80-passenger *Doncella*, which had been built in 1908 in Tacoma, Washington and was sailing out of Redondo Beach California, was bought and brought north. After the vessel had been upgraded to meet Canadian safety standards, it went into service on July 14, 1912. At the same time a new schedule was introduced that provided for sailings every half hour.

The municipal ferry company not only bought a new ship, but also relocated its Vancouver landing site. English Bay's exposure to westerly winds often made

It was not always smooth sailing through the First Narrows. The Sonrisa, which measured 72.9 feet by 16 feet with a 6.2-foot draft, had "seating accommodation for 150 with ample cabin room for wet weather." Like all the other West Van ferries, it could weather a crossing that was challenging for skipper, crew, and passengers alike.

The ill-fated West Vancouver No. 5, built in 1914, was an attractive vessel. The ferry is pictured leaving the Columbia Street wharf for West Vancouver. The ship sank with the loss of one life on February 4, 1935 after a collision with the CPR's Princess Alice.

docking difficult. Space was leased in the harbour, first of all from the North American Steamship Company, and then in 1913 from the city of North Vancouver, which had space available on the west side of its Vancouver ferry slip at the foot of Columbia Street. The West Vancouver Ferry Company build a ticket office and waiting room at the approach to its new wharf.

On the North Shore the ferries continued to use the Hollyburn (17th Street) wharf. In 1912 a morning and an evening trip to Skunk Cove, known today as Caulfeild, was added to the schedule. While a small community had grown up around the marine pilotage station, the settlement had no road connection with the rest of the district municipality. The service to Skunk Cove only lasted until the Pacific Great Eastern Railway opened its North Vancouver to Whytecliff line on August 1, 1914.

The growing number of residents made it necessary for the municipal ferry company to yet again order larger vessels. In 1914 the 120-passenger *Sonrisa* was built by G. Wessell of Vancouver, and the 200-passenger *West Vancouver No. 5* was built by Vancouver Shipyards. Other developments prior to the First World War included the building of a new $40,000 concrete pier at Dunderave and a new wharf, freight shed, and administration building at the foot of Fourteenth Street. When this new "Ambleside" facility was completed the company severely reduced the frequency of service to Dunderave and eliminated stops at Hollyburn (17th Street) altogether. Considering the amount of money spent on the new Hollyburn wharf, it can only be concluded that municipal planning wasn't all that sophisticated.

The cut in service to Dunderave led to loud complaints reaching the ears of municipal councillors.

Council, recognizing that the complaints were justified, agreed to do something about the situation. The "something" that it did was to introduce a jitney or bus service between Dunderave and Ambleside, a distance of two miles. Operating the bus service was the responsibility of the manager of the ferry system. The ferry manager's car was stretched and—*voila!*—West Vancouver's first blue bus was born. Service began on December 6, 1915. In 1916 a Pierce-Arrow sedan was purchased and ferry staff converted it into the municipality's second bus.

Also in 1916 the Municipal Council transferred the West Vancouver Ferry Company's assets and liabilities to the municipality. Since the municipality was the company's sole shareholder the move was uncomplicated. Its purpose was to make the ferry service directly responsible to the elected council, rather than to an appointed board that could make decisions without reference to the wishes of the Municipal Council. The ferry system had alway operated at a loss, and the council did at one point write to the provincial government, urging it to take over and operate the ferry service. Victoria declined the invitation!

It is interesting to note that the West Vancouver Municipal Ferries had a 242-passenger ferry built by Wallace's in North Vancouver in 1925, the same year in which the Second Narrows Bridge was opened. As things turned out, while there was a drop in the number of passengers using the North Vancouver ferries, the West Vancouver ferries experienced no similar loss of passengers. In fact, by 1927 the number of passengers had risen to 780,000. For West Vancouver residents it was as fast, if not faster, to travel to town by ferry than it was to make the trip by car or bus by way of the Second Narrows Bridge. And it was a lot cheaper, too.

While there were times when the relatively short trip between downtown Vancouver and West Vancouver could be a rough crossing, and occasions when heavy seas meant cancelled sailings, the ferries had an enviable safety record. There was only one occasion in the history of the ferry service when a passenger was lost. That was on February 4, 1935 when *West Vancouver No. 5* was rammed in dense fog off Brockton Point by the CPR's *Princess Alice.* Having sliced the ferry amidship on the port side, cutting in on an angle for about six feet, the captain of the *Alice* realized he had to keep his ship's bow firmly in the side of the ferry to keep the smaller vessel afloat and allow time for those aboard to be rescued. While five of the six passengers and all four crew men were saved, one woman was trapped in the after (rear) cabin. Both the ferry's captain and the mate tried valiantly to rescue her, but they could not reach her because of the wreckage. The ferry stayed afloat for nine minutes before sinking. The official inquiry, having found neither captain to blame, went on to commend the captain of *West Vancouver No. 5* for being "gallant

The West Vancouver looks more like a family pleasure boat that has seen better days than a seaworthy ferry boat. West Vancouver's first ferry, launched in 1909, was in service until 1915 when it was sold. It sank in Thunder Bay, B.C. in 1928.

… in endeavouring at great personal risk, to save life," and praised the captain of the CPR steamer for displaying "skill in the incident following the collision in the handling of his vessel, and his crew in rendering assistance to the ferry."

Raised two days after the sinking, the *West Vancouver No. 5* was found to be damaged beyond repair. The vessel was dismantled and burned. A replacement was immediately ordered from North Vancouver Ship Repairs Limited. This new 237-passenger ferry, powered by the engine salvaged from the sunken ferry, was put into service in June, 1935. In 1936 the municipal ferries had to order another new ship, the 23 year old *Sonrisa* having failed to meet the safety standards for passenger ferries. The new replacement ferry, the last to be built for West Vancouver Municipal Ferries, was the *Hollyburn*. Like the *Bonabelle*, the *Hollyburn* was built by North Vancouver Ship Repairs Limited.

That year, 1936, was also the year in which construction began on the Lions Gate Bridge that spans the First Narrows. The new bridge opened to traffic in November, 1938. Although the number of people using the ferries went down, the Second World War extended the life of the West Vancouver ferries for a few more years. Gas rationing and a reduced bus service to and from West Vancouver encouraged people to use the ferries. But the war only postponed the inevitable. While there had been 95,442 ferry passengers in the year ending in April 1944, just twelve months later the number was down to 48,265. The handwriting was on the wall. To keep costs down, the newest ferry—the *Hollyburn*—was sold in June 1945 to Harbour Navigation Company Limited. A referendum, held in 1945 and at the same time as the West Vancouver municipal election, asked taxpayers to decide whether or not to end the ferry service. Eighty percent of those who voted favoured discontinuing the ferry service. The ferries were only to continue operating until adequate bus service to and from Vancouver could be assured. That day came on February 8, 1947. It was just three weeks short of 37 years from the day the *West Vancouver* inaugurated ferry service between Hollyburn and English Bay that *West Vancouver No. 6* tied up for the last time. The ferry story was over.

West Vancouver No. 6 is shown approaching the Dunderave (14th Street) wharf in West Vancouver at sunset. Launched in 1925, West Vancouver No. 6 was the last ferry to tie up on February 8, 1947, the final day on which the West Vancouver Municipal Ferries operated.

Vancouver

KING EDWARD'S FOUNTAIN

King Edward VII died at Buckingham Palace on May 6, 1910. He was born on November 9, 1841 and had become king upon the death of his mother, Queen Victoria, on January 22, 1901. Being 59 years old when he came to the throne, he had briefly considered abdicating until he discovered that he quite enjoyed being king!

Edward was a pleasure-loving man whose style appealed to all segments of society. He loved parties, yachting, cards, and racing; one of his horses, *Minoru*, won the Derby in 1909. While he was easily bored, and was neither an intellectual nor widely read, Edward as both Prince of Wales and as king liked to be surrounded by clever and interesting men and beautiful women.

After the 63-year reign of "Victoria the Good", people quite enjoyed the nine years when "Good Old Teddy" was king. While he could be a stickler when it came to matters of protocol, his genial good humour and warmth generally won him friends wherever he went. King Edward was as popular in Vancouver as he was throughout the rest of his empire and when he died people everywhere felt a genuine sense of loss.

His funeral in London on May 20, 1910 could be called the high point of empire. His nephew, the Emperor of Germany; his sister-in-law, the dowager Czarina of Russia; eight kings; and a mob of crown princes, grand dukes, and other exalted beings were present. In the King's funeral procession they walked behind his fox terrier Caesar, who followed immediately after his master's coffin.

Special parades and services were held throughout the empire to honour King Edward's memory. In Vancouver the service was held at Recreation Park, and according to the newspapers, a crowd of over 20,000 people turned out to pay its last respects to the man who gave his name to an era of optimism, invention, and seemingly inevitable progress. In those Edwardian days few would have doubted that on every day, in every way, things were getting better and better.

King Edward VII, who reigned from 1901 to 1910, gave his name to a flamboyant period in British history. The Edwardian days were the halcyon days of the "empire upon which the sun never sets." Pictured with the King is his grandson, Prince Edward, who later was to become King Edward VIII.

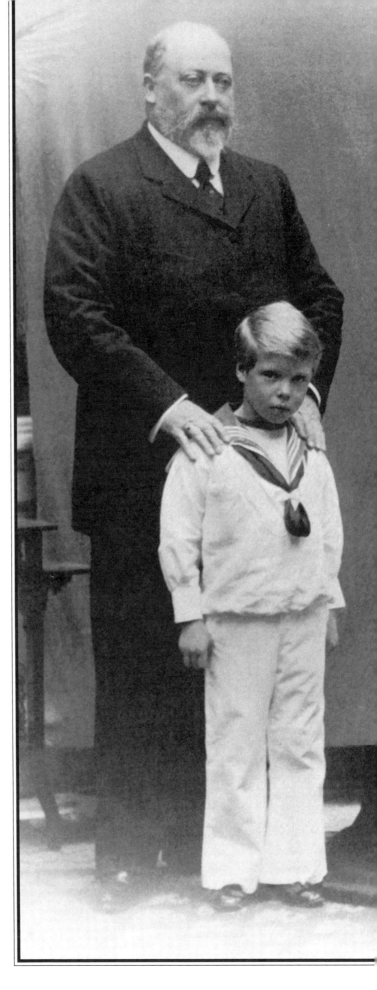

On May 20, 1910 crowds line the streets as the military units marched in the procession to Vancouver's Recreation Park for King Edward's memorial service.

In addition to the civic parade and memorial service, King Edward's passing was marked in other suitable ways. On May 24, 1910, what had been Vancouver High School officially became King Edward High School. As well, in 1912 the municipality of Point Grey decided to name its new east/west boulevard that ran from Camoson to Macdonald, King Edward Avenue.

Perhaps King Edward's most impressive local memorial is the drinking fountain that was erected by the Imperial Order, Daughters of the Empire in 1912. It seems that earlier on the Dufferin Chapter of the I.O.D.E. had decided to erect a relatively modest memorial to the dead monarch. As so often happens, the small and uncomplicated became large and involved. The scheme grew until it was decided that all eleven local chapters of the Order would contribute to the project. The design was to have a drinking fountain as its focus, and the memorial was to located on the lawn in front of the new Provincial Court House on Georgia Street.

Funds were raised without difficulty; someone was found to design the fountain and oversee its construction, and on May 6, 1912 in the presence of about 3,000 people, the memorial was unveiled by Mayor James Findlay. Lady Hibbert Tupper, as regent of the local Municipal Chapter of the I.O.D.E., presided over the ceremony. As would be expected, the usual complement of Seaforth Highlanders, men and officers of the Duke of Connaught's Own Rifles, Boy Scouts and high school cadets were on hand. In his remarks the mayor said that "the members [of the I.O.D.E. had] shown for all times that they are worthy of their forbears (sic). It is women who make strong the hearts and arms of men. It is they who encourage men to noble deeds. It is they who today are helping us to serve the cause of Imperialism." The newspapers also reported that Findlay "quaffed the first draught of water from the fountain, and his example was quickly followed by a number of those present."

The papers went on to say that a reception for invited guests followed the dedication of the memorial. It was held at Glencoe Lodge, which in 1912 was *the* place to stay for those who wanted something better than the Hotel Vancouver. Glencoe Lodge stood on the

northwest corner of Georgia and Burrard. While both *The Province* and *The Sun* listed the principal guests who gathered for tea, nowhere in either paper was the name of the man who created the monument mentioned!

The designer and sculptor was Charles Marega, an artist who has still to this day not received the recognition he deserves. Marega designed the Harding Memorial in Stanley Park, the bust of Mayor Oppenheimer at the Beach Avenue entrance to the park, the Joe Fortes memorial fountain at English Bay, the figures of Captains Vancouver and Burrard that are mounted on Burrard Bridge, the bronze casting of Captain Vancouver in front of City Hall, and the pair of lions that guard the Lions Gate Bridge, as well as the King Edward VII fountain.

Marega's Beaux Arts fountain harmonized perfectly with the courthouse. Centred on its granite facade is a bronze plaque bearing a cameo profile of King Edward. The water spout, above a large stone bowl, is in the shape of a lion's head. Ionic columns frame the fountain, and the whole structure is tied together by a neo-Classical pediment.

The King Edward fountain stood in front of the courthouse until 1966 when it was removed to make

The King Edward VII memorial fountain stood in front of the courthouse until 1966. Water poured from the lion's mouth and chained to the fountain were two bronze drinking cups. As might have been expected, the cups were stolen in next to no time.

space for the provincial government's sculpture erected to commemorate the union of the crown colonies of Vancouver Island and British Columbia a century earlier. The old fountain was stored away in the courthouse basement until public opinion forced the powers that-be to refurbish and reassemble the memorial on a new downtown site. Its present rather out of the way location is on the west (Hornby Street) side of the courthouse.

It should be mentioned that lines from Shakespeare appear on the back of the fountain. They read:

"Not monumental stone preserves our fame,
Nor sky-aspiring pyramids our name;
The memory of him for whom this stands
Shall outlive marble and defacers' hands."

In this day of spray paint cans and thick felt markers, so beloved of local graffiti artists, these words have taken on new meaning.

Harrison Lake

THE WORLD'S LARGEST FISH HATCHERY

The words, "What has happened before will happen again: there is nothing new under the sun" were written 2,300 years ago. They could, however, have been describing the seemingly endless federal/provincial arguing over West Coast fisheries. Nearly one hundred years ago the author of the *Provincial Year Book* reflected local frustration when he wrote that among questions not understood in Ottawa were those relating to the economic necessity of hatcheries, methods of incubation, disposing of fry, and the necessity for fishing limits and a clearly defined fishing season.

While it is true that Ottawa had opened a fish hatchery in 1884 at Bon Accord, five miles east of New Westminster on the south side of the Fraser River, and put in place some basic regulations governing salmon fishing, federal concern and action was seen locally as hopelessly inadequate. The federal government was spurred into action after 1901, by which time the provincial government had created its own department of fisheries and hired John Pease Babcock as its first deputy. Babcock was an internationally recognized authority who had saved California's salmon industry and was employed to fulfill a similar role in British Columbia.

Not long after taking up his new post, Babcock established a provincial salmon hatchery at Seaton Lake. He also got W.J. Bowser, who was commissioner of fisheries in Richard McBrides's government, to establish stricter regulations governing salmon fisheries. Included in the new guidelines was a shorter fishing season. It was at this point that provincial jurisdiction was challenged by the federal government in the courts. Being largely successful in court, Ottawa had no choice but to take its responsibility for maintaining a healthy West Coast fishery more seriously. Not only did the federal government promulgate regulations remarkably similar to those put in place by B.C., but it set about building seven salmon hatcheries.

The third of these new hatcheries was built in 1904 at Green Point on Harrison Lake. The site was on the east side of the lake, three miles from present-day Harrison Hot Springs. Although there was a primitive trail providing access to the site, the main route was by water. Construction got underway in September 1904, with W.W. Forrester of New Westminster as contractor. The unknown architect was probably someone in the federal department of public works.

As the largest fish hatchery not only in Canada but in the world, it was an imposing structure. Decorated with more restraint than was usual for Edwardian buildings, the exterior was painted canary yellow with white trim. The whole of the interior was painted white. There were two principal ancillary buildings. One was a seven-room superintendent's cottage, and the other was a boarding house for the men employed at the hatchery. The buildings were lighted by electricity, and "the water which [supplied] the power afterward was used in hatching the eggs." A dam on Trout Creek connected to the hatchery by a 500-foot flume carried the water to the building.

The eggs came from the spawning ground at nearby Morris Creek. Over the winter of 1904-05 some 6.5 million salmon fry hatched. A year later, by which time the hatchery was in full operation, nearly 29 million fry were released from the Harrison Lake hatchery. In its report for 1908 the federal Department of Marine and Fisheries described the hatchery at Harrison Lake as the "banner fish-breeding establishment in the Dominion." By 1909 it had distributed over 84 million fry.

The fish-breeding program came to a sudden end in 1936 when on March 19 the Chief Supervisor of Fisheries for B.C., J.A. Motherwell, announced that all the salmon hatcheries in the province would be closed within three months. The official explanation for the decision was that natural spawning grounds and propagation was able to maintain the salmon population satisfactorily, and therefore the benefits of the hatchery program didn't warrant the expenditure. Given that the year was 1936, and the Depression was at its worst, the decision was probably more political and economic than anything else.

Soon after the Harrison Lake hatchery closed, the rather magnificent structure was demolished. Its site is now beachfront in Sasquatch Provincial Park.

The salmon hatchery on Harrison Lake bore a strong family resemblance to so many other Edwardian frame structures in Canada, whether they be exhibition halls, sport or seaside pavilions, or even monkey houses in the zoo! In spite of their size these buildings all had a lightness and whimsy that gave them strong visual appeal.

THE CHAMP COMES TO TOWN

While there must be any number of easier ways to make a living, there are men who choose the boxing ring as their route to what they hope will be fame and fortune. Among others who travelled along this rough road to riches was John Arthur "Jack" Johnson.

An Afro-American, Johnson was born in Galveston, Texas in 1878. His father was a school janitor, and when still a teenager Jack went to work on the Galveston docks. He was big and strong for his age and while working as a longshoreman, he also had a part-time job as a gym attendant. He liked boxing and quickly picked up the rudiments of the fight game. From Galveston he made his way to Chicago, New York and Boston, where he hung around fight gyms, sparring whenever he could with seasoned veterans.

Johnson had a long hard road to the top. It wasn't until he had been boxing for nine years and had 91 recorded fights behind him that he got his chance at the world heavyweight title. That was in 1908. He had already won the Coloured Heavyweight World Championship in 1903, but that wasn't enough; he wanted to be world heavyweight champion, period!

The man he had to beat for the title was Tommy Burns, the reigning champion. Burns was from Hanover, Ontario and had played both hockey and lacrosse professionally earlier in his career. After winning the heavyweight title in 1906 Burns set off on a money-making world tour. Along the way be fought eight title bouts and flattened the English, Irish and Australian champions of the day. Johnson was ready for Burns, and Burns knew it. In a way Burns and Johnson deserved each other; both men were arrogant and boastful blow-hards. While Burns tried to avoid meeting Johnson, he finally had to fight him.

The bout took place on December 26, 1908 in Sydney, Australia. It was to be a 41-round fight to the finish. Burns called Johnson every foul name he could think of to get the Black man angered to the point where he would lose his cool, make mistakes, and lose the fight. Burns was hopelessly outclassed, however, and Johnson could have finished him off at anytime. By the 14th round it was obvious that Burns was through, and the police stepped in and put a stop to the fight. The world now had its first Black heavyweight champion. Burns got his guaranteed $30,000 for the fight, and Johnson got $5,000.

After the fight Johnson sailed for Vancouver aboard the New Zealand Shipping Company's new turbine steamship, the 8,075-ton *Makura*. Johnson liked to travel in style but he didn't like to travel alone; he was accompanied by a beautiful White woman whom he passed off as his wife when they arrived in Vancouver on March 9, 1909. The couple did not receive a particularly warm welcome in Vancouver. Even though he was wise enough not to try getting into the city's top hostelries like the Hotel Vancouver or Glencoe Lodge, Johnson couldn't even get a room in the St. Francis, Rainier, Irving, Metropole or Astor hotels; they were all "full up." The Vancouver Athletic Club's Black trainer George Paris came to the rescue and took the couple home with him.

Johnson spent his first evening in Vancouver as the guest of the Railway Porters' Club where he entertained the members with stories of the ring and "sat in on a couple of quiet games." The next morning he and his companion were driven around Stanley Park and at noon kept "a date with a movie man at the dock" where they had landed from the *Makura* the day before. The film was a reenactment of their arrival.

Johnson was scheduled to box at the Vancouver Athletic Club on the evening of March 10. Three six-round bouts were on the card, with the champ to appear in the final match fighting Denver Ed Martin. It was Vic McLaglen, however, who had to face Johnson; Martin "had been unexpectedly called away to Seattle." Perhaps it was a matter of discretion being the better part of valour. McLaglen, the substitute from Tacoma, took a solid left straight to the solar plexus in the first minute of the fight, and only through Johnson's good will and restraint managed to stay on his feet for the full six rounds of the exhibition bout. As the *Province* reported, "Johnson had to take the best of care not to do any damage, and it must be admitted he succeeded admirably."

McLaglen had a future, but it wasn't in boxing. Son of an English rector, McLaglen had come to America where he spent time as a ranch hand, a prospector, and as a boxer. He wasn't particularly successful in the New World and returned to Britain where he went on to establish himself in the theatre, particularly as a music hall performer. In 1920 he first appeared in film.

His success in British movies encouraged him to return to the United States where he appeared in both character leads and as a two-fisted supporting actor. His best remembered silent film is *What Price Glory* (1926), and his two hit talkies were *The Lost Patrol* (1934) and *The Informer* (1935). He won the Academy Award for Best Actor for his role as the dull-witted turncoat Gypo Nolan in *The Informer*. In his long career he played opposite many leading ladies, including Marlene Dietrich, Mae West, and Shirley Temple. He was the dashing Sergeant MacCheney in the all-time great adventure film *Gunga Din* (1939) and Maureen O'Hara's bullying brother in *The Quiet Man* (1952.) McLaglen died in Hollywood in 1959. Perhaps it was his fight with Johnson in Vancouver that helped him decide the fight game wasn't for him.

After the exhibition match Johnson "was tendered a banquet by a number of his coloured admirers at the Bismark Café." In actual fact not all 40 guests were Black, and in his words of thanks at the close of

dinner Johnson said he was "glad to see the two races sitting together at the festive board." And speaking of the fight game he said, "Be my next opponent yellow, grizzly, gray or black, I will fight him with the same courage and determination that I have shown in the past …. Let me say of Mr. [Tommy] Burns, a Canadian and one of yourselves, that he has done what no one else ever done, he gave a Black man a chance for the championship. He was beaten, but he was game."

Johnson and his companion left Vancouver the next afternoon, travelling via the CPR's Soo Line to Chicago, and from there they went on to New York City. Professional boxing was at best an uncertain source of income, and all his life Johnson lived on something of a financial roller coaster. As he waited in New York for a fight to develop, he signed up for a 30-week vaudeville tour which opened at the Gayety (sic) Theatre in Brooklyn on April 12, 1909. Between 1909 and 1915

World Heavyweight Champion Jack Johnson and his beautiful travelling companion arrived in Vancouver from Sydney, Australia aboard the new T.S.S. Makura *on March 9, 1909. They are both fashionably and expensively dressed; Johnson liked style in both clothes and women.*

Johnson successfully defended his title seven times before he lost it to Jess Willard on April 5, 1915 in Havana, Cuba.

While he had managed to hold on to his title from 1908 to 1915, Johnson had lots of problems to face along the way. Almost immediately upon becoming the first Negro world heavyweight champion, the popular novelist and newspaperman, Jack London echoed popular White feeling when he called for former champion Jim Jeffries to "remove the golden smile from Jack Johnson's face." Not only the fact that he was Black, but also his "in your face" lifestyle made him unpopular with both fight promoters and fans alike. Even in his Galveston days his gold fillings glittered, his shaved bullet-shaped head shone, and his sheer size set him apart. Johnson's motto might have been, "If you've got it, flaunt it." He liked nothing better than a beautiful White woman on his arm, fast expensive cars, the best champagne, cigars, and fashionable clothes. Many Whites made no bones about it; they found having a "Negro" champion difficult to stomach, and "Great White Hope" tournaments were staged to find a White boxer who could successfully challenge Johnson for the title.

Jim Jeffries, the chosen "Great White Hope" of Jack London and many others, had held the world heavyweight title from 1899 until 1905 when he retired from the ring. After much persuasion Jeffries finally agreed to come out of retirement to fight Johnson. The bout took place on July 4, 1910 in Reno, Nevada and Jeffries lost badly. His only consolation was the $117,000 he had been guaranteed by the fight's promoter, Tex Rickard.

Jack Johnson loved fast and expensive cars and was an early auto racing enthusiast. In October 1910 he lost two races to Barney Oldfield. His reckless driving repeatedly got him into trouble with the law, as did his brawling and use of foul language in public. His June 1911 marriage to a White socialite Etta Duryea didn't win him many friends either. Etta committed suicide September 1911. Along the way Johnson had opened a restaurant called *Café de Champion* in Chicago. As it happened, he played a passable blues and jazz bass fiddle.

Far more serious than the various reckless driving charges he repeatedly faced was the 1912 charge in which he was accused of violating the Mann Act, a law that banned the transport of women across state lines for immoral purposes. He was found guilty in 1913 and sentenced to one year plus a day and fined $1,000. He appealed the conviction, but before a ruling could be handed down Johnson fled the country. After spending time in Europe, South America and Mexico, he returned to the United States where he gave himself up to the authorities and went to prison. Many scholars today are of the opinion that Johnson was unjustly accused and convicted. Having served his time, Johnson continued boxing throughout the 1920s, 30s and 40s. In the last two decades all his fights were exhibition bouts. Jack Johnson's final matches took place on November 27, 1945 when the

Regularly scheduled passenger service between Australia and Canada was inaugurated in 1893. The New Zealand Shipping Company's new Makura *entered the service in 1908, and from 1912 to 1924 partnered the* Niagara *to provide a monthly trans-Pacific service. The* Makura *was replaced on the run by the* Aorangi *in 1925.*

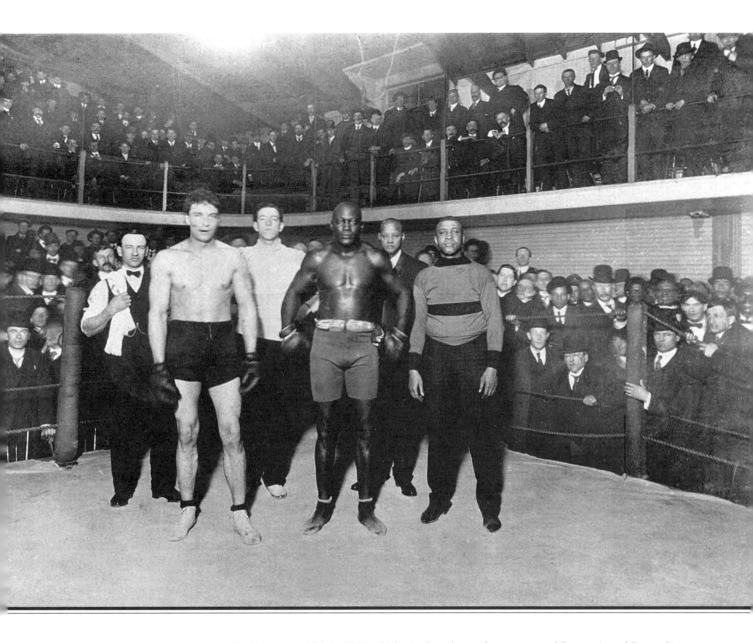

The Vancouver Athletic Club, which stood on the northwest corner of Dunsmuir and Beatty Streets, was the setting for Jack Johnson's March 10, 1909 exhibition bout with Victor McLaglen. While McLaglen didn't have a prayer, Johnson went easy on him and he managed to stay on his feet for the full six rounds. McLaglen later had a much more successful career as a film star.

67 year old was featured in two one-minute rounds as part of a New York City war bond rally.

Johnson died as he had lived—spectacularly. The end came on June 10, 1946 when he was killed in an automobile accident caused by speeding and carelessness. His life had a kind of postscript when in 1970 a fictionalized biopic based on his life and career appeared. The movie was entitled *The Great White Hope* and starred James Earl Jones. The film made a plea for racial understanding and tolerance.

The Seamen's Institute stood next to St. James' Church, facing Gore Avenue. Its architect may very well have been Thomas C. Sorby, a prominent early Vancouver architect who was an active member of St. James' and chairman of the Institute's building committee. While the building didn't have much by way of style, someone had taken the trouble to see that the windows matched those in the church.

The Mission to Seafarers is an important and well-established fixture on Vancouver's water front and rightly so; it has been serving the seafaring community for over a century. It all began when Father Clinton the rector of St. James', Vancouver's first Anglican church, felt that something should be done to provide visiting sailors an alternative to the saloons and unsavoury dance halls of Water Street. The problem was literally on St. James' doorstep. The original church had stood on the waterfront until it was destroyed along with the rest of the city in the Great Fire of 1886, and the new church built after the fire at Gore and Cordova was still only blocks away from the city's docks and wharves. With Clinton's blessing, his curate the Rev'd Henry Edwardes established St. Andrew's Waterside Mission in 1889. Unfortunately money was in very short supply and the enterprise was short-lived.

St. James' second attempt to provide for the needs of visiting mariners ultimately met with lasting success. The rector the Rev'd Henry Glynne Fiennes-Clinton, with the support of his parishioners, established what was known as the Seamen's Institute.

Fiennes-Clinton, or Father Clinton as he was commonly called, was one of those sons of the English aristocracy who went into the church. His father was also an Anglican priest as well as domestic chaplain to his first cousin the Duke of Newcastle. Young Fiennes-Clinton attended Keble College, Oxford and came away not only with what would have been called a high church theology but also with a highly developed sense of social responsibility and missionary zeal. Although never robust he persisted throughout his life in meeting every challenge that came his way head on. He had originally wanted to serve as a missionary to B.C.'s Coastal Indians, but his delicate health convinced the bishop of New Westminster that he should serve in the community that was about to become the city of Vancouver. Father Clinton has been characterized as seeming "to have crystallized the positive elements ... of imperialism and mysticism into a fortuitous blending of personal magnetism and compelling spirituality."

It was in the late 1890s that Father Clinton decided time, money and energy must go into establishing a Seamen's Institute. It has been estimated that by the end of the nineteenth century something like three million men sailed the seven seas, and of that number well over half a million were British seamen. While the Seamen's Institute was always open to all mariners regardless of race, nationality or faith, initially it was primarily a concern for the British sailor away from home that led to its founding.

Records are sketchy at best, but it seems it was in 1897 that Father Clinton finally had enough money on hand to erect a building in which to house the Seamen's Institute. Built on the vacant lot that was to the north of the church and facing Gore Avenue, the Seamen's Institute was well laid out. On the first or ground floor there was space for a billiard room and a gymnasium. On the second floor there was a reading room or library and a much larger room with a platform at one end that served as either a dance hall or a concert hall as occasion demanded. On the third or attic floor there was a classroom where instruction in seamanship was offered to young apprentice mariners.

The Institute tried very hard to be a home away from home, particularly for the very young seamen who were in fact just teenagers. In addition to gym programs and social nights, regular services were held each day and instruction for those wishing to be Baptised or Confirmed was provided. It was not at all unusual for a lad to be prepared for Baptism in Vancouver and some other place like Honolulu, and then be baptized somewhere else like Hong Kong or Sydney.

Special events were celebrated at the Institute as occasion demanded. On the centenary of the Battle of Trafalgar, for example, there was a special seamen's service at which the mayor and council were in attendance. That particular service was followed by "a sumptuous repast." On another occasion the sailors aboard *H.M.S. Shearwater* and *H.M.S. Egera* were invited to afternoon tea at the Institute. For the event the parish lent its school room, and Sister Frances, Vancouver's first "visiting or district nurse" and social worker, allowed the tars to sit in the grounds of St. Luke's Home adjacent to the church "and kill the caterpillars with nicotine."

At the May 1903 Vancouver gathering of Episcopal clergy from the American Pacific Northwest and Anglican clergy from B.C., one of the study papers presented was entitled "Work Among Sailors." It was presented by the Rev'd the Hon. C. Cumming-Bruce, Seamen's Chaplain employed by the Mission to Seamen Society of London, England. He was stationed in Portland, Oregon. Doubtless the Americans would have been quite taken with this man who was the eldest son of Lord Thurlow. In his address Cumming-Bruce said among other things that, "At an early age, and before his character is formed, the young sailor is called to give up his home and his friends .... He has no choice of his companions, and his life is devoid of all privacy. Nor are things any better when he reaches port. [There] he meets vice in its cruellest forms .... It is to offer a counter-influence ... that the Mission to Seamen Society was led to establish branches on the Pacific Coast. Every ship should be met ... and the crew warned of the dangers and temptations that await them. A bright Institute should be provided and each evening an entertainment of some kind should be arranged. First in importance is the work done among apprentices [that are] bound to the ship for four years.... They respond most gratefully to any kindness that is shown to them. On the other hand, if they are left to themselves they have only the saloon and the dance hall open to them; and evil habits may be formed which will cling to them throughout life. It is our object, therefore, to win their confidence, to introduce them to friends, to provide innocent recreation and generally to make their stay in port a blessing and not a curse .... But for diversions of this kind the apprentices would loaf about the town spending their money in all kinds of sailors' hells ... where they might be stripped of every cent they possess."

Cumming-Bruce's words had an immediate effect; Father Clinton's work with sailors was finally recognized, and the diocesan executive committee granted him $10 a month "to assist him in employing a lay worker to visit steamers and ships." At the same time the Archdeacon of Vancouver Edwin Pentreath wrote that "the time has come to build a Seamen's Chapel near the waterfront and provide a chaplain who shall devote his full time to the work. It would then be a diocesan and not a parochial work." He then went on to say that the Diocese of New Westminster "shall not be able to provide a chaplain without help from England."

It seems that in 1904 some sort of relationship between the Seamen's Institute in Vancouver and the world wide Mission to Seamen was established. While the nature of the relationship is uncertain, one thing is clear: Father Clinton felt he had to give up his work with the Institute. Archdeacon Pentreath sent off an appeal to be published in English church papers asking individuals and organizations to make a gift of £100 a year to help support the work of a seamen's chaplain in Vancouver.

Pentreath's initial appeal must have fallen on deaf ears because in 1907 he was writing to the British Columbia and Yukon Church Aid Association in London, asking if it could help the diocese establish a seamen's chaplaincy in Vancouver. In his letter he mentioned that it had been hoped the "great and noble Society, the Mission to Seamen, would be able to supply a chaplain but ... their revenues [did not] justify them in under-taking the full burden of his maintenance."

While the Mission to Seamen was prepared to meet the full cost of chaplains in foreign ports where there were few British citizens, it logically and justifiably was not prepared to bear the full cost of a chaplain in ports like Vancouver where the British population should have been quite able to share the financial burden. The B.C. and Yukon Church Aid Association agreed to pay

£100 a year, which meant of course that the Diocese of New Westminster had managed to rob Peter to pay Paul; it got money from one British missionary society to subsidize the work of another! There was an overseas Anglican mentality that saw aid from the "old country" as both indispensable and justified since many of their number had come as immigrants from the mother country. This Anglican mind set didn't completely disappear until the beginning of the Second World War.

Once financial arrangements had been finalized, the work of Vancouver's Seamen's Institute was taken over by the Mission to Seamen. In time the full cost of the chaplaincy and program were met locally. Today the Mission to Seafarers, as the organization is now called, draws its financial support from corporations associated with the shipping industry in the Port of Vancouver, from Anglican parishes from grants, and from individual donations.

In its centennial year Vancouver's Mission to Seafarers chaplaincy staff visited 3,069 ships and hosted 22,987 seafarers at its Flying Angel Club. The Society and its seafarers' club operate out of the 1905 waterfront heritage building which started life as the Hastings Mill office building. It was presented as a gift to the local branch of the Mission to Seafarers' Society in September 1981 by the National Harbours Board, which had been using it to house its own offices since 1930.

Today the Mission to Seafarers continues to do what Father Clinton's Seamen's Institute set out to do in 1897, that is, provide seafarers with a safe and welcoming place to spend time away from their shipboard homes.

Through the windows in the Seamen's Institute's attic classroom can be seen the outline of the Dominion Building. Its easy to imagine how hot the room must have been in summer and how cold it must have been in winter. The classes were probably intended for young apprentice seamen who were a special concern of both the local Institute and the world-wide Mission to Seamen.

The Fraser Canyon

A ROAD TO REMEMBER

For a number of years Cunard Steamships advertised that "getting there is half the fun." While the statement may or may not have been true for those travelling the seven seas, it certainly wasn't true for anyone travelling through British Columbia's Fraser Canyon in the 1850s or 60s. Actually, until well after the Second World War there were rumoured to be Prairie drivers that made the trip to the Coast by car, using the "all Canadian route," only to drive home over American roads. A one-way trip through the Fraser Canyon was enough. And while they may be purely apocryphal, there are also tales of Prairie folk who sold their cars in Vancouver and took the train back to the flatlands! Given the formidable task that road construction must have been some one hundred and fifty years ago, why was a road put through the Canyon in the first place? The answer is: gold and the flag.

In the early 1850s Thompson Indians had found small quantities of gold which they traded to the Hudson's Bay Company. Since hordes of men coming into the territory seeking gold would destroy the company's vast game preserve and effectively end its valuable fur monopoly, the company tried—unsuccessfully of course—to keep the discovery of gold secret. As always, although people may respect confidences, they invariably share secrets far and wide; by 1858 the news was out and the gold rush was on. It was along the banks of the Fraser River between Yale and Lytton that gold was found in quantity. Knowing that gold was to be found was one thing, however, getting to it was quite another.

Those trying to make their way to where the gold was being panned had to take one of two routes out of Yale, which was at the head of navigation on the Fraser. They could follow aboriginal trails along precipitous ledges across the rock face of the canyon, making their way up and down ladders made of roots and vines and poling log rafts around sheer cliffs where no footing of any sort could be found. Or they could use the old brigade trails of the fur traders. These routes generally followed the height of land and meant climbing 1800 feet between Yale and Spuzzum then descending to the Fraser, crossing to the river's east bank by whatever means were at hand and climbing again, this time to over 2000 feet to get to the upper reaches of the canyon. Either route required exceptional stamina and not a little nerve. It

soon became apparent that a trail, if not a decent road, was badly needed since men were bound and determined one way or another to get to the diggings.

In 1858 the governor of the mainland colony of British Columbia, Sir James Douglas, brought into being what came to be known as the Harrison-Lillooet Trail. The route involved travelling by boat up the Fraser, then into the Harrison River and on to Port Douglas at the top of Harrison Lake. From Port Douglas a trail was cut through to Lillooet on the upper Fraser River, a distance of approximately 100 miles. To build the road, if it could be called that, Douglas hit upon an ingenious plan. He recruited 500 miners newly arrived in Victoria from California, divided them into 20 companies, provided them with free transportation to where they were to work, and gave them food and lodging while they worked on the trail. As was to be expected he was wise enough to collect $25 as security, to be repaid in provisions at Victoria prices when the job was finished. While it was completed in record time, and therefore reduced the cost of food at the diggings near Lillooet, it was really of no use to the men working claims down river between Lytton and Yale.

By 1860 Douglas was reluctantly convinced that money had to be spent improving the makeshift trails that the miners in the Fraser Canyon were using. The men had even built a ferry of sorts to get across the river at Spuzzum. In June 1860 a contract worth $22,000 was awarded to Frank Way and Josiah C. Beeby to build a mule trail from Yale to Spuzzum, a distance of thirty miles. Two months later a similar contract went to William Powers and Hugh McRoberts to build that part of the trail that ran between Spuzzum and Boston Bar. The trail was to be stable enough to allow a mule carrying a 250-pound load to pass safely over it. The Royal Engineers under Sgt. Major George Cann built the most difficult, and consequently least profitable, sections along the route.

Douglas's mule trail was completed in October 1860. Since Britain expected the colony to be all but self-supporting, the only way the governor could finance the trail was to make it a toll road. While there was a schedule of rates for animals, goods and wagons of various sorts, travellers on foot were allowed to use the road without charge. Any men that didn't pay the toll for their pack trains were treated as smugglers and liable to have their animals and goods confiscated by the Crown.

The Royal Engineers built the most difficult sections of the Cariboo Road, including this piece at Great Bluff, 88 miles above Yale. This picture was taken between 1867 and 1869 by a very early photographic enthusiast, Rear-Admiral George F. Hastings, Commander of the Royal Navy's Pacific squadron, after whom Vancouver's Hastings Street was named.

By 1861 many men were making their way 400 miles farther north to Williams Creek in the Cariboo where much richer strikes were being made. The mule trains that carried supplies north for these miners were usually made up of anywhere from sixteen to 48 of these sure-footed beasts, each able to carry a 400-pound load. They plodded along behind a lead bell-animal that was more often than not a white mare. There was a man for each eight animals, and a pack train could be more than 100 feet long. The most difficult part of the route was the section between Yale and Lytton; on average a pack train took seven days to travel the 57 miles between the two points.

In late 1859 Walter Moberly, a civil engineer reported to Douglas that what was really needed was a wagon road not a mule trail to the Cariboo, and that it should follow the canyon rather than the Harrison-Lillooet route. Taking Moberly's advice, Douglas had the Fraser Canyon carefully examined in 1860 for what was properly known as The Great North Road, but popularly called the Cariboo Road. Governor Douglas believed the new road would do a number of things. First of all, it would bring an end to the exorbitant prices miners had to pay for supplies. It would also lessen the chance of people being trapped over the cold winter in what was at the time largely uninhabited territory. While in the first years of the Cariboo gold rush a few prospectors did choose to stay over the winter, most preferred to make their way to a more attractive climate.

Probably more important to Douglas than any other consideration was what he saw as the need to keep the mainland colony of British Columbia firmly British. Already the vast majority of miners and their camp followers were American, and Douglas knew that where Americans were the stars and stripes were soon to follow, unless the flag of some other country was already firmly planted and that nation's sovereignty established beyond dispute. Along with the Dewdney Road that ran from Hope to Similkameen, and the Douglas Road that cut through the woods from New Westminster to New Brighton on Burrard Inlet, Douglas believed the Great North Road to the Cariboo would not only funnel commerce through New Westminster rather than allow it to be sifted off into American cities, but also let it be seen that British Columbia was not some empty and ungoverned territory awaiting American annexation.

Perhaps surprisingly, given that this was the 1860s, it was also thought that the Great North Road might some day be extended across the Rockies, linking the colony by road with the rest of British North America.

The Cariboo Road was officially closed in 1891, although for some time it had been impassable for anything other than foot traffic as the construction of the CPR had left stretches of the road unusable by wagons or any other wheeled vehicles.

Douglas decided to use both military and civilian labour to build the wagon road to the Cariboo The new road was to be wide enough for two teams to pass—18 feet—widening to between 22 and 44 feet on difficult curves to allow trains of wagons to make their way around the sharper ones. As it turned out, the section between Yale and Spuzzum could only be 16 feet wide, narrowing to 15 at some points. Just as they had build the most difficult sections of the mule trail, the Royal Engineers built the most difficult sections of the wagon road. In May 1862, under Captain John Marshall Grant they started work on the six mile section of road between Yale and Chapman's Bar, and on a second stretch along the Thompson River near Spences Bridge. Both pieces of road called for extensive blasting of rock face and construction of trestles and long stretches of cribbing. The cribbing supported the roadbed at those places where there was no choice but to build the road out over the water. Names associated with the building of the Cariboo Road were to become familiar to every school child in the province; Joseph Trutch (Chapman's Bar to Boston Bar), Thomas Spence (Boston Bar to Lytton), and Walter Moberly (northward from Lytton to join up with the section being built southward from Alexandria in the Cariboo by Gustavus Blin Wright). Trutch was also responsible for bridging the Fraser at Spuzzum. Bridging the Fraser Canyon is a story in itself. Work began on the Yale to Lytton portion of the road in May 1862, and incredibly was finished in the fall of the same year. By 1863 stage coaches and freight wagons were using the new road to the gold fields even though the Great North Road wasn't officially finished until the following year.

The Cariboo Road through the Fraser Canyon had a life of less than a quarter century. Incredibly, between 1888 and 1927 there was not so much as a passable wagon road connecting the interior of the province with the Coast. How so? Railroads! First the Canadian Pacific and later the Canadian Northern. It could be said that technology won the day. After all, giving up a dirt and gravel wagon road would have been seen as a small sacrifice to be made if the trade-off brought the long awaited transcontinental railroad a step closer to completion.

As it built its line through the Fraser Canyon the CPR's track snaked back and forth across the road 26 times, creating what could only be described as a series of hopelessly *unlevel* crossings! As well, one four mile stretch of road was completely wiped out. It could be said that the CPR used the wagon road so long as it served its purpose, then simply abandoned what was left of it when it was of no further use to it, or to anybody else; it did this of course with the tacit approval of the provincial government. In 1882 the government itself had given a fair indication of its level of concern for the upkeep of the road by handing over its maintenance to private contractors. When in 1887 responsibility for maintaining the road through the Canyon was returned to the government, the road was impassable to all but foot traffic or those riding horseback. Neglect and indifference led to the official closing of the Cariboo Road in 1891. After that date those who used the road did so at their own risk. As a kind of footnote, in 1910 the cables supporting Alexandra Bridge were cut. Although the bridge had been damaged by flood waters in 1894—one of its cable anchors was partly dislodged—it was still safely used by horses and riders. The cables weren't cut for safety's sake, though, but because the damaged bridge was considered a potential hazard to downstream navigation!

Coincidentally, it was in 1910 that there was a rekindling of interest in the Cariboo Road. This interest was expressed in different ways in different quarters. The Canadian Northern Railway, which was building the western end of its transcontinental line through the Fraser Canyon to Vancouver, applied to the Board of Railway Commissioners in Ottawa "to interfere with and wipe out the Cariboo Road where it [was] adjacent [to the railroad's right of way.] On July 6, 1910 the provincial minister of public works advised the federal government that the province did not intend to rebuild either the old wagon road or the bridge at Spuzzum, and that the CNR could destroy whatever portions of the road were in its way. Interestingly, on November 30 of the same year Premier McBride suggested that his Conservative government was in fact interested in reopening the Cariboo road. It seems that Eastern Canadian motoring clubs and enthusiasts were asking why there was no coast to coast road of any sort in Canada. McBride was nothing if he wasn't politically sensitive, and the very next year he went after the CPR for compensation for the damage it had done to the Cariboo Road. The road it seems had cost $1 million to build, and the provincial government estimated it would cost $87,000 to restore the section between Yale and Spences Bridge, not including a replacement span at Spuzzum. Negotiations dragged on for sixteen years, at the end of which the CPR paid the province $45,300 as full and complete payment.

It was on October 11, 1924 that tenders were at last called for the rebuilding of the Cariboo Road from Yale to Spences Bridge. Of the three separate contracts signed, two ended up with cost overruns of more than 100 percent; the government had to meet the unexpected cost of retaining walls, stabilizing embankments, and so forth to protect the CPR's trackage! As well, the government had to meet the costs incurred by the CPR in relocating sections of track in a number of places.

The rebuilt road was now the Cariboo Highway. The section between Yale and Lytton was opened to traffic in 1924, and the portion between Lytton and Spences Bridge was completed in 1929. The toll on the new highway—collected at Spuzzum—was a dollar per vehicle. In 1929 tolls were collected from 11,523 motorists, and by 1936 the number of paying tolls had increased to 23,997. This was a significant number because there were fewer than 100,000 automobiles in the whole province in 1936. Until 1936 the new road was open each year from only May 1 to November 15; in the depth of the Depression the government could not afford to keep the road open over the winter. Incidentally, the Cariboo Highway was a toll road until 1947.

Surprisingly the new highway was only 16 feet wide, whereas the old wagon road for the most part was at least 18 feet wide. Newer doesn't necessarily mean better. Lest the word 'highway" conjure up visions of

asphalt or concrete, let it be known that the new Cariboo Highway was either dirt or gravel all the way from Hope to Prince George. Even at that, the section between Yale and Ashcroft alone cost nearly $3 million to build. Road building has never come cheap in British Columbia.

It was not until the 1930s that paving got underway. Even then, distances, terrain, and the need to keep traffic moving over the narrow road made it a slow process. And the process got even slower during the years of the Second World War when priorities directed manpower and money elsewhere. On April 25, 1950, however, things took a turn for the better. That was the date when the Fraser Canyon Highway officially became an integral part of the Trans Canada Highway. A continuous upgrading program has meant that those travelling through the Canyon today no longer have to think of sharp curves and unseen perils, incredibly narrow sections where it was all but impossible for two vehicles to pass, of bone-shaking bumps and potholes. Instead, for today's travellers the route through the Fraser Canyon is "A Road to Remember" only because of the incredible beauty that marks the route as unique in Canada, if not in all of North America.

As this photograph taken 18 miles above Yale clearly shows, the Cariboo Highway of the late 1920s left much to be desired. Tires cut by sharp bits of gravel, engines overheating to the boil, and never being quite sure how far it was to the next gas station made the road through the Fraser Canyon a road to remember.

THE "RAINBOW" COMES TO CALL

On Wednesday, November 23, 1910 Mayor L.D. Taylor and the city's aldermen, resplendent "with their civic top hats polished to a nicety," together with notable military personages sailed forth from the Gore Avenue wharf aboard what *The Province* referred to as "the city's state barge, to wit, the waterworks launch with Steve Madison at the Wheel." Their destination was *H.M.C.S. Rainbow* which had dropped anchor in Burrard Inlet at 2:00 p.m. The day had been long in the planning, and the delegation eagerly looked forward to welcoming Commander J.D. Stewart, his officers and crew to Vancouver.

The *Rainbow* was one of Canada's first two warships, and had been commissioned for the Canadian Navy at Portsmouth on August 4, 1910. The ship left the British port on August 20 for a 15,000-nautical-mile trip to Esquimalt, arriving on November 7. With the passage of the Naval Service Act, the Royal Canadian Navy had been established only a few months earlier on May 4. The Act called for the creation of a small navy under federal control. The government could in an emergency, however, place the Canadian Navy at the disposal of the British Admiralty.

The new Canadian Navy became a reality when the federal government bought two obsolete British cruisers—one for each coast. These vessels were to serve as training ships for the five additional cruisers and six destroyers that the Liberals intended to acquire. The tired British warrior sent to the West Coast was the *Rainbow*, a cruiser of the Apollo class bought for £50,000. It was one of sixteen similar vessels built under the Naval Defence Act of 1889. Launched at Jarrow-on-Tyne in 1891, it was 300 feet long with a 44-foot beam, and drew 18 feet of water. The ship managed a very respectable 19 knots over a measured mile, and was able to maintain a cruising speed of 18.1 knots when necessary.

The *Rainbow*'s steel armour varied in thickness from 2 to 5 inches. While the ship carried 23 guns, twin 6-inch guns were its chief armament. Shells fired from the two big guns were theoretically capable of penetrating 18-inch plate at a range of over a mile. Newspaper reports of the day also mentioned that "forward [it had] two torpedo tubes, two others having been removed when [the ship] was placed in service for the Canadian Navy."

The civic dignitaries aboard the *Rainbow* for the reception on November 23, 1910 were received by a guard of honour. Speeches of welcome were delivered, and the visitors were shown over the cruiser. After refreshments in the ward room they were returned to shore aboard "the civic barge." *The Province* in its coverage of the event said of the civic dignitaries that they "returned impressed with the feeling that the *Rainbow* will provide a valuable training medium for the youth of Canada who wish to enter the service."

When the ship arrived on the West Coast it had a crew of 189, all British. Some were men who had completed their 20 years of service in the navy and had become members of the Royal Fleet reserve, others were young men of the British Navy who had volunteered to enter the Canadian service on a permanent basis, and 32 were men of the Royal Navy who had been specially selected and

The Vancouver Daily Province *cartoonist captured the city's mood as it welcomed the* Rainbow. *Canada's first naval ship on the Pacific Coast, on Wednesday, November 23, 1910.*

THAT WELCOME TO H.M.C.S. RAINBOW TODAY

H.M.C.S. Rainbow *rides at anchor in Burrard Inlet awaiting the visit of Vancouver's civic dignitaries. It remained in port for a week recruiting would-be-sailors. While it was "new" to Canada, the light cruiser was nearly 20 years old.*

loaned to the Canadian government for two years to serve primarily as instructors. The only Canadian recruits aboard the *Rainbow* when it arrived in Vancouver were a blacksmith, a stoker and a wireless operator.

There were other sailors aboard the Rainbow, and they were youngsters between twelve and fourteen years of age, who had been transferred from British Navy League training ships. These boys were described by *The Province* as showing "how the British naval man is obtained. He is caught young, trained, and worked hard, and in the end stands alone as the best sea-fighter in existence. Deep-chested, healthy, active and clean in morals … he makes friends wherever he goes." Reading that paragraph today, we might wonder if the writer is talking about training young sailors or bulldogs!

Recruiting in Vancouver was not without its problems. It seems that while there had been a number of applicants, most had failed to pass the British medial test. However, by the end of its week's stay in port a total of 23 boys had joined up. These "young Canadians [were] to be taken aboard the *Rainbow*," said *The Province*, " and trained in British naval style that they might uphold the traditions of the race."

Not long after it returned to Esquimalt the *Rainbow* was caught in something of a political storm. It seems that the Liberals' 1910 move to establish a Canadian Navy was not only opposed by the Conservatives who felt that Canada should be supporting one strong imperial navy under the control of the British Admiralty, but also by French Canadian nationalists. They opposed the creation of a Canadian Navy because they believed it would involve Canada more closely in imperial affairs. Sir Wilfrid Laurier, the Liberal prime minister, was in a no-win situation and consequently he lost the election of 1911 to Sir Robert Borden's Conservatives.

The change in government brought about a drastic reduction in the naval budget, and there was no more talk of building cruisers and destroyers. Throughout 1912 and 1913 the *Rainbow* was limited to harbour training exercises with only an occasional short trip to sea for the sake of its engines. In 1912 Borden agreed—after consulting with the First Lord of the Admiralty, Winston Churchill—to provide $35 million for three "dreadnaught" battleships. Although the bill passed in the Commons, it was defeated by the Liberal majority in the Senate.

The *Rainbow's* situation changed on July 9, 1914 when the ship was ordered to go north for three months. The purpose of the trip was to patrol the seal fisheries. In 1911 Russia, Japan, the United States and Great Britain had signed a Convention that prohibited the hunting of pelagic seals north of a certain line. The ship's slender if not skeletal crew was strengthened by the transfer of 76 men from the *Niobe* in Halifax, and the vessel itself was dry-docked for cleaning and repairs. It was, of course, replenished with stores and food.

At the centre of the picture are Mayor L.D. Taylor and Commodore J.D. Stewart, the Rainbow's *commander. They are flanked by aldermen, ranking officers of the city's military establishment, and ship's officers.*

As things turned out, the *Rainbow* never did go north on seal patrol. Instead it was dispatched to Vancouver on July 19, 1914 to escort the *Komagata Maru* from Burrard Inlet. The Japanese steamer had been riding at anchor in the harbour ever since it arrived in May 1914 with 400 East Indians aboard; Canadian Immigration had barred their entry into the country. The would-be immigrants refused to leave, and having taken control of the ship were defiantly staying put. On July 18 approximately 175 local police and immigration officials had tried to board the ship in order to transfer the Indian passengers—by force if necessary—to the CPR's *Empress of India,* which would take them to Hong Kong. The men trying to board the *Komagata Maru* were greeted with a hail of missiles. Lumps of coal, firebricks and pieces of scrap metal were rained down upon them.

Although it would be an oversimplification to say that the arrival of the *Rainbow* had brought an end to the siege, its presence certainly was a factor in speeding up negotiations that resulted in the *Komagata Maru* leaving Vancouver. On July 23 the warship saw the Japanese vessel safely though the Strait of Juan de Fuca and out to sea.

Having returned to Esquimalt, it was not long before the *Rainbow* was being prepared for war. On August 1 the British Admiralty had signalled Canada to be ready to protect the West Coast. The German's *Leipzig,*

one of the ships in Admiral Graf von Spee's Pacific Squadron, was known to be off the coast. The First World War broke out on August 4, 1914 and although the *Rainbow* would have been no match for the much newer and better armed *Leipzig*, the presence of the Canadian ship on the coast at least reassured the local population, offered some modest protection, and guarded the very important shipping lanes that converged in the Strait of Juan de Fuca. Particularly during the first weeks of the war, the cruiser's presence had a positive effect on morale. Regarding the *Leipzig*, the *Rainbow's* potential problem was resolved when the German warship left the Coast and headed into southern waters. The defeat of Graf von Spee's Pacific Squadron at the Battle of the Falkland Islands in December 1914 removed any threat to the British Columbia coast that may have existed.

By 1917 the *Rainbow's* crew was needed on the East Coast to man patrol vessels, and on May 8 the ship was paid off. The West Coast's cruiser was recommissioned, however, on July 5 to serve as a depot ship in Esquimalt. Paid off again on June 1, 1920, the *Rainbow* was sold for scrap to a Seattle shipbreaker.

In 1910 *The Province* had written of the twelve to fourteen year olds aboard the *Rainbow*: "These fine, manly well developed little tars...who will be trained on [this] trim little warship are worth watching." One hopes they were not just watched, but well watched over as they went to sea in the war that was to end all wars.

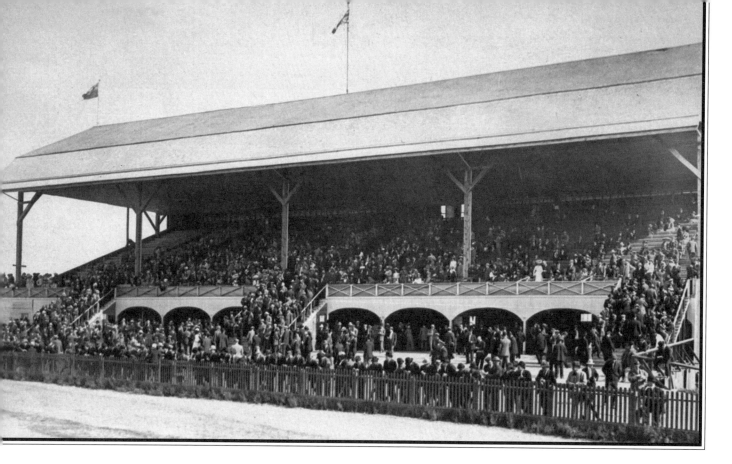

There were very few women making their way to seats in the new grandstand at Minoru Park in 1909. At the time racing was still very much the sport of Kings, gentlemen, and perhaps, more than a few rogues and ne'er-do-wells.

Richmond

MINORU PARK

Horse racing first came to Vancouver on June 25, 1889 when a point-to-point race took place on Howe Street. A grandstand was built on what is now the lawn in front of the Art Gallery, and people lined both sides of the street for this Vancouver "first." It was also the "last." Howe Street really didn't lend itself to horse racing, and in 1890 a track was cut out of the forest at Hastings Park.

In 1909 a second local track came into being; it was a one-mile oval on Lulu Island. The principal shareholders were H.E. Springer, F.B. Springer, C.M. Marpole, A.E. Suckling and Charles Lewis. Their track was built on land belonging to Sam Brighouse.

The name chosen for the race track was Minoru Park, and it was very much of its time. *Minoru* was the name of the horse that had just won the Derby at Epsom Downs on May 26, 1909. And *Minoru* was no ordinary racehorse: the animal was carrying the royal colours of

purple, scarlet and gold, and was owned by the King himself. While Edward VII had won the Derby twice before when he was Prince of Wales, there was nothing to equal *Minoru*'s win of 1909. The King had been in poor health for some time and there was much public concern. The win was the occasion for an outpouring of popular loyalty and support for the ailing monarch. The crowd at Epson went wild with thousands of spectators enthusiastically and spontaneously singing "God Save The King." Even the bobbies on duty threw their helmets in the air, and joined in the chorus of "Good old Teddy! Teddy boy! Hurrah! Hurrah!" Edward epitomized for the British everything they admired about themselves. In the far corners of his empire the King was loved and admired as much as "at home" by those who had left the Old Country for new lands. At the time nothing could be more logical than to demonstrate love and loyalty by naming a new racetrack after the King's winning horse.

In 1909 there wasn't much in Richmond to block the view! Part of the Fraser River delta, Lulu Island encompassed superb agricultural land. At a time when clear action shots were still a rarity, the unknown photographer who took this picture at Minoru Park deserved high praise.

Minoru Park opened on August 21, 1909 with over 6,000 seated in the new grandstand. In less than three months the grandstand, a mile of stabling, a clubhouse and the track itself had sprung into being on what had been a farmer's field of oats. The facts that building codes are not what they are today, that no time-consuming environmental impact studies were required, and that few if any planning officials had to be satisfied with the design, doubtless made it relatively easy to build quickly. However, hastily built structures are not necessarily always sound structures. The opening day was marred somewhat when two hours before the first race was scheduled to take place a 60,000-gallon water tank on the back stretch collapsed. Without water the track could not be dampened down, and there were times when the clouds of dust obscured part of the track from view. In time, however, Minoru Park's track came to be regarded as the finest racing surface on the Pacific Coast. Interestingly, nearly 90 percent of the horses racing at Minoru were American-bred and owned.

Events other than horse racing took place at Minoru Park. Perhaps the track's chief claim to lasting fame lies in the fact that it was the site of the first Western Canadian flight. On March 25, 1910 a Californian, Charles Hamilton, demonstrated his Curtiss biplane. As part of his exhibition he flew past the stands at a breathtaking 55 miles per hour. He also raced against a thoroughbred, *Prince Brutis*. Hamilton erred in giving the racehorse too much of a head start, and it won the race!

With the outbreak of World War I in 1914 Minoru Park closed. It reopened in 1920 under new management as Brighouse Park. While a second Lulu Island race track, Landsdowne Park, had opened in 1924, Brighouse remained popular and profitable until World War II. After 22 seasons of racing, however, Brighouse was forced to close forever in 1941. With so many away from home in the armed forces, shift work in war industries, and gas rationing, there simply weren't the crowds going to Lulu Island for racing. Those that did go to the races were generally only prepared to go as far as Landsdowne. Brighouse, on the southwest corner of Number Three Road and Westminster Highway, was a mile farther down the road, and people were not prepared to go "that extra mile" for horse racing.

Today the old track is buried under a shopping centre's concrete and asphalt. Minoru and Brighouse only exist as local place names commemorating something of Richmond's past.

Following its banner and band, the Salvation Army is marching west on Hastings toward Main. It may well be on its way to Hastings and Carrall, a favourite corner for evangelistic rallies in the years before the First World War.

Vancouver

"ONWARD CHRISTIAN SOLDIERS ..."

Colourful though the image is, in its early days Vancouver wasn't quite the godless frontier town pictured in today's Gastown tourist brochures. It is quite true that Water Street had saloons aplenty, but in their midst stood the community's first church erected by the Methodists in 1876. Although the Methodist Church supplied the minister, the 16- by 30-foot building had an interdenominational board of trustees: four Anglicans, two Methodists, and one Presbyterian. The church seems to have been ecumenical out of economic necessity, rather than any desire to show forth an interdenominational spirit. By the time the first train arrived in 1887, not only had the Anglicans, Methodists, and Presbyterians all built their own churches (leaving the old building to become a feed store), but the Baptists and Roman Catholics had erected

their own places of worship as well. Such was the ecclesiastical landscape when the Salvation Army first appeared, both literally and figuratively, on the streets of Vancouver.

In their uniforms, carrying their banner, and marching through the streets, who were these high profile "Salvationists," as they were often called? The Salvation Army was one of a half dozen or more denominations that grew out of the nineteenth century Holiness Movement in Great Britain. Their members believed that the initial salvation experience in an individual's life must be followed by a further sanctification experience in which the process of becoming holy was completed. For the most part, those who joined these churches were disaffected Methodists who longed to recapture the fervour of the early followers of John and Charles Wesley

Even the Salvation Army was not without its status symbols. In 1907 Commissioner Combs announced that the Vancouver band was to have "a full set of the best silver-plated Instruments," and that the Junior Corps would get the old brass instruments, becoming "the first to have a brass band in the territory."

when sanctification and holy living were the identifying marks of the Methodist movement.

The founder of the Salvation Army, William Booth, was in fact a Methodist minister who had been caught up in the Holiness Movement. It led him to set out, in the company of others who shared his perspective, to bring the Gospel to the alcoholics and prostitutes of the London slums. By 1878, when he published in minute detail the quasi-military organization, dress, and directions for daily living in his *Orders and Regulations for the Salvation Army*, his movement had caught the imagination of like-minded souls who wanted to give a practical face to evangelism. While it may not always be obvious to outsiders, even today its concern for meeting social needs has in no way displaced the Salvation Army's paramount goal, which is to win souls for Christ.

The fervour spread quickly and by 1882 the Army was at work in Ontario. It wasn't long before the troops reached the West Coast. Victoria was "invaded" in June 1887, and six months later the Salvation Army drum and tambourine were first heard in Vancouver. Those with a particular interest in the women's movement will find it worth noting that the first officers to unfurl the Salvation Army flag in Vancouver were all women: the "Hallelujah Lassies" of local legend— Captain Mary Hackett and Lieutenants Iverack, Tierney and Lynes. They held their first open air meeting on the corner of Carrall and Cordova on December 10, 1887. Once a crowd had gathered, the women then marched it off to Frank Hart's Opera House for their first indoor

service. Hart's "opera house" was, by the way, nothing more than a ramshackle hall that had started life as a roller rink in Port Moody. Hart demolished the 60- by 120-foot building, moved it, and re-erected it at the False Creek end of Carrall Street. Two hundred and fifty pair of roller skates came with the building. The Salvation Army was able to rent the building only when it wasn't being used as a theatre or skating rink.

The four women worked hard, and their effort met with success. The mission was so successful that in 1889 Vancouver was made a divisional headquarters, and a male officer was sent to the city to take charge as Commander! In the same year new quarters were rented in a building on the northeast corner of Water and Abbott Streets. The building backed onto the beach, and the barracks (as the bare room was called) was up a flight of stairs over Oscar Brown's fruit store. Upward of 75 people could be accommodated for services. It seems that any place was considered better than Hart's Opera House.

It was only a very few years before the barracks was relocated to a larger and better upstairs meeting hall, just off the southwest corner of Water and Carrall Streets. There the headquarters remained until 1906, when temporary space was rented on Hastings Street to serve as headquarters while the Army built its own building. Even though the Salvation Army was housed in rented "barracks" until 1907, it had already bought a building that could serve as a men's hostel. In 1898 the Stag and Pheasant Hotel with accommodation for fifty and a popular bar and poolroom was reincarnated as The Anchor, the Salvation Army's first local shelter for men.

This 1943 picture is of Mrs. Hannah Elizabeth Greatrex. As the yet unmarried Lt. Hannah Lynes, she came to Vancouver in December 1887 as one of the city's first four Salvation Army officers.

The hotel-cum-hostel stood at 160 Water Street, and had been erected in 1886, immediately after the Great Fire. As well, it seems that some time along the way, the Army had also bought two lots on Dupont (later Pender) Street near Cambie for future development.

Apparently there were reservations about the Pender Street site, for in 1906 property on the northeast corner of Hastings and Gore was purchased as the site for the new headquarters (or Citadel as it was to be called) and for a new men's hostel to be known as the Hotel Welcome. The buildings were officially opened on Sunday, June 23, 1907 by Commissioner Combs, the Salvation Army's chief officer in Canada, who came from Toronto for the dedication of the new facilities.

The buildings were of "brick and stone handsomely interlocked." The name of the architect remains unknown, but the Army's official gazette *The War Cry* for July 20, 1907 does say that the buildings were planned on the basis of "years of experience which officers have had in other cities," and " the Army makes no experiments in the way of construction [and while] there are improvements certainly … the main features

have been settled years ago." Since both the citadel and the hostel looked more like they were designed in the nineteenth rather than the twentieth century and lacked a "made in Vancouver" look, there is a good possibility that their plans were taken from a well-used design manual that had been around for some time at headquarters in Toronto.

Regardless, the interior layout of both buildings was certainly functional and well thought out. On the ground floor of the citadel there was a 600-seat auditorium with a sloping floor. On the second floor were the offices for both the provincial headquarters and for immigration staff, as well as "a commodious room capable of accommodating … a hundred and twenty persons." Also on the second floor "at the back [was] a beautiful suite of airy, healthful living rooms for the officers of the corps." The third floor provided space for the Junior Hall with seating for 300 children and for additional officers' living quarters. There was a floor between the Junior Hall and the auditorium by design.

The adjoining Hotel Welcome, facing onto Gore Avenue, could accommodate over 100 men. Offices, a reading room, and a number of small rooms were on the first floor. It wasn't many years before these rooms housed the Army's labour bureau and social service department. The second and third floors accommodated lodgers at prices from a dollar and a quarter per week and upward. On each floor were "splendid lavatory arrangements, with shower baths and other conveniences."

Regarding showers, *The War Cry* also made a point of mentioning that "the basement … will be utilized for men from lumber camps and such places, who need a little trimming up and fixing before they take ordinary hotel accommodation. The basement possesses a separate entrance with magnificent bathing and crematorium facilities." Crematorium facilities? While "cremation" in contemporary English refers exclusively to the process whereby human remains are reduced to ashes, the word once had a broader meaning. It referred to the burning of any unwanted refuse. The Salvation Army's new crematorium today would be called an incinerator. Doubtless many men arrived at the Hotel Welcome with their clothes crawling with vermin; before they were allowed into the hotel proper, they would have been sent downstairs where they bathed and their infested clothing was burned in the crematorium. Clean and hopefully free of lice, fleas, or other little passengers, and supplied with fresh clothing, the men could then move into the hostel above.

Since 1907 was a year of particularly high unemployment in B.C., the new facilities were not opened any too soon. The number of out-of-work loggers, miners, seamen, fishermen, cannery workers and construction men

arriving almost daily was so large that for the first time the city itself had to take action. It not only provided meal tickets but also turned the old disused city hall on Powell Street into a men's dormitory. Along with secular and other church-related agencies like the Central City Mission, the Strathcona Institute for Sailors and Loggers, the Canadian Camp Brotherhood, and the Seamen's Institute, the Salvation Army also did what it could to assist the destitute. Fortunately the design for the new "Hotel Welcome" anticipated possible enlargement, and almost immediately after it opened an additional storey was added, increasing accommodation by one-third.

By 1948 the citadel and hostel buildings needed replacing and were torn down to make way for a modern concrete temple, a building that was very much in the popular style of its day. This structure still stands, though it is now home to a Buddhist congregation, the Army having relocated its headquarters to Burnaby in 1982.

This is not to say that the Salvation Army has deserted the city's downtown east side. Together with the Union Gospel Mission, St. James' Social Service, the Franciscan Sisters of the Atonement, First United Church, and a number of other religious and secular agencies, the uniformed men and women of the Salvation Army continue to be visibly at work in that part of Vancouver where the Hallelujah Lassies began their work over a century ago.

Vancouver
POWER!

The Vancouver Electric Illuminating Company was incorporated on January 20, 1887, and on August 6 in the same year, the city's electric lights were turned on for the first time. Electric power was supplied by a small coal-fired steam plant. In 1888 there was talk of the need for a street railway, and by 1889 the Vancouver Street Railway System was laying track. Six streetcars—each able to carry 35 passengers—arrived from New York, and on June 26, 1890 the first trial run was made along Westminster Avenue (now Main Street). On April 26, 1896 the lighting and street railway companies joined forces and were incorporated as the Vancouver Electric Railway and Light Company.

Unfortunately the depression of the 1890s spelled disaster, not only for the Vancouver firm, but also for utilities in Victoria and New Westminster. Through the efforts of Frank Barnard and Robert Horne-Payne, $2.25 million was raised to buy up the assets of the Vancouver, New Westminster and Victoria street railways and electric power companies. A new company, the British Columbia Electric Railway Company, was formed on April 3, 1897. Horne-Payne became chairman and Barnard took on the job of managing director. To provide day-to-day management for the new public utility, Johannes Buntzen was appointed general manager and Henry Sperling was made general superintendent.

The Mainland's first hydro-electric plant was built on the North Arm of Burrard Inlet. Known as the Lake Buntzen Power House, it went into operation in 1904. It was not many years before the building was doubled in length to accommodate a total of eight 3,000 H.P. generators. It is the enlarged powerhouse that is pictured.

The new Westminster Avenue (now Main Street) substation seemed to be surrounded by a veritable forest of power poles when it was built in 1903-04. The pair of smoke stacks visible above the new building belonged to the old steam-powered electric generating plant that was maintained for some years as an emergency back-up facility.

Horne-Payne had a particular interest in the development of hydro-electric power and his enthusiasm moved Barnard to take a look at its practicality. He concluded that hydro-electric generators made good sense, so they decided to build a hydro-electric power plant the first of its kind on the Pacific Coast at Goldstream on Vancouver Island. Located 15 miles out of Victoria, it went into operation in 1898 and was an immediate success.

The two men were not slow to build on success. In 1898 the B.C. Electric incorporated a subsidiary—the Vancouver Power Company—to build a hydro-electric development on the North Arm of Burrard Inlet, using water diverted from Coquitlam Lake by way of Lake Buntzen. On June 3, 1904 hydro-electric power was delivered to Vancouver's first substation from the Lake Buntzen Power Plant over 20,000-volt transmission lines. *The Province* reported that at the substation "one large rotary transformer capable of handling about 800 horsepower was turned on, [and] the steam plant as usual

[furnished] … another 700 or 800 horsepower …. The transformer is an immense affair, fed with … wires half as large as your arm. It is an expensive device, … manufactured by the Westinghouse people."

Since initially only one of the two main transformers was operational, the old steam plant continued to supply power until the second Westinghouse unit was put into service. As well, smaller transformers were installed in the new substation to provide AC power for electric lighting. It seems that the larger units were to provide DC power for the street railway system.

The Westminster Avenue substation was built by the firm owned by alderman Edward Cook. The steel-framed brick building had large windows that gave passers-by a clear view of the awesome machinery it housed. And being a power plant, its electric lights were on day and night. The architectural firm that designed the vaguely neo-Classical building was that of William Blackmore & Son. The building permit for the $32,000 structure was issued on August 26, 1903.

The new substation didn't get built without incident. On August 4, 1904 Joseph Bays, a mason's helper, was sweeping the floor when somehow his hat was knocked off his head and fell across a nearby electric cable. Bays, who had been warned earlier to stay clear of any wires, must have automatically if thoughtlessly reached over the wire to pick up his hat and was electrocuted.

Today's media is often accused of being insensitive, invasive, and sensational. *The Province* reported that "Bays' body was an awful sight. His right leg was burned off clean, below the knee. His body both front and back, was torn and burned as if flayed with red-hot irons. Even his head and arms were blackened and bruised, and the body looked for all the world like one that had been dead for a month." It cannot be said that today's writers and broadcasters are any less sensitive than were newsgatherers of old! Doubtless Bays' unfortunate death forcefully reminded those working with high voltage power lines of the immense potential danger associated with their jobs.

The plant continued in operation until after the Second World War when it was replaced by the Murrin substation, which stands at Main and Georgia.

As the new high voltage hydro-electric power came on line, the delivery of electricity throughout Vancouver was affected. Voltage in primary circuits was raised from 1,000 to 2,000 volts, and in secondary circuits from 50 to 100 volts. All city homes had to be equipped with new meters, and all lamps and light fixtures had to be altered to accommodate the new Edison screw base light bulbs that are like the ones still in use today. On the street corners the old 32-candle-power incandescent bulbs, popularly called "glow worms," were replaced by the much brighter arc lamps.

The Westinghouse transformers stepped down the 20,000 volt power that came into the substation over the transmission lines from Lake Buntzen to a level that could be used to operate the city's lighting system and run the street railway. Interestingly, even in a building as obviously utilitarian as a substation, the architect couldn't resist including at least a little elegant detailing like the balustrade in the foreground.

Across the road, beyond the "Hollow Tree," a display of photographs and an advertisement for Fricke and Schenck can be seen. This postcard was produced by the European Import Company, a firm that shared Fricke and Schenck's premises at 162 West Cordova in 1911 and 1912. It is reasonable to assume that the picture was taken by Fricke and Schenck.

Vancouver

ALIENS IN THE PARK

When newcomers or visitors arrived in Vancouver 75 or 100 years ago they expected to see the mountains, the ocean and the trees. And when it came to trees, a top attraction was Stanley Park's "Hollow Tree," located on the Park Driveway between Prospect and Ferguson Points. While the attraction today would more aptly be described as the "Hollow Stump" than the "Hollow Tree," what remains does give some idea of what must have been an impressive sight in earlier days. The stump has a circumference of nearly 18 metres (60 feet) and as countless photographs attest, the cavity within the trunk is large enough to accommodate buggies and open touring cars.

While present-day visitors may wonder why the tree was not preserved for posterity, the fact is that its life was already nearly over when white settlers first discovered it. Rot begins in the centre of western red cedars, and spreads outward. By 1900 age had already created the huge hollow chamber that made the tree a unique attraction. Not surprisingly, the "Hollow Tree" became a popular spot for amateur photographers wanting to snap pictures of family and friends. It had also become an attractive site for commercial photographers who were willing and able to produce pictures for those who did not have cameras of their own, yet wanted a snapshot to show to the folks back home. Soon, in fact, there were too many professionals vying for business at the "Hollow Tree" and no one was doing all that well financially.

In 1908 one of these enterprising photographers suggested to the Parks Board that the exclusive right to take and sell pictures in the park become a concession, and that it go to the highest bidder. Naturally amateurs

It was not at all unusual for a stop at the "Hollow Tree" to be included in the civic tour accorded visiting dignitaries. Lord Strathcona, second from the left, poses for the obligatory snapshot. Strathcona was principal shareholder in both the Hudson's Bay Company and the Bank of Montreal, and made the C.P.R. possible through his financial backing. He was unquestionably the most influential Canadian of his day.

As this picture of three young men at the "Hollow Tree" clearly indicates, in their day the phrase "wearing one's Sunday best" was more than a figure of speech. Bowler hats, walking sticks, high starched collars, and waistcoats would have been worn by every adult male "of any consequence" seen strolling in the park.

would still be able to take pictures to their hearts' content. The Parks Board liked the idea and called for tenders. Two firms bid, one being King Photo Studio owned by Valiant Vivian Vinson and the other Fricke and Schenck who got the contract and the right to call themselves the official Stanley Park photographers. They were given permission to build a studio "in harmony with the surroundings" and to put up a sign. Their request to add a chimney to their shed was refused.

The agreement signed in 1908 between the Parks Board and Fricke and Schenck was for five years. The lessees were to pay $750 in the first years, with annual increases until they were paying $1,000 in the fifth year. Business was never as lucrative as anticipated and in each year there were adjustments and rebates. Nevertheless, Fricke and Schenck's work must have pleased both the general public and the Parks Board since their lease was renewed in September 1912 for two further years, and again in June 1914. This lease was to run until the end of May 1916, and allowed the firm to operate concessions at Brockton and Prospect Points, as well as at the "Hollow Tree." The photographs were to be marked "Stanley Park, Vancouver, Canada."

The years between 1914 and 1916 were unfortunately not particularly kind to Fricke and Schenck. Not a great deal is known about George

Not many Vancouver families would have travelled in the style of the one pictured in front of the "Hollow Tree" in a rather elegant landaulet. In its day, this town carriage would certainly have been one of the finest in Vancouver. It is tempting to assume that the woman holding the infant is the child's nanny.

Owning a horse and buggy of any sort would have been beyond the financial reach of most Vanouverites. While the rig pictured backed into the "Hollow Tree" looks rather ordinary, it was obviously sufficiently impressive to allow its owner to have a girl on each arm!

Christian Fricke and George Schenck other than that by 1904 they had found their way from Germany to Vancouver where they opened a photographic business at 61 West Cordova. The business moved to 162 West Cordova in 1910 where it remained until 1913. From 1913 until 1915 it was located at 524 Granville Street. Not only did the company move a number of times, but in addition to "Fricke and Schenck," it operated under three other names. From 1909 to 1912 it was also know as Camera Workers, from 1908 to 1911 as Stanley Park Photographers, and from 1915 to 1917 as the Granville Studio. While we do not know exactly how many people were employed by the partners, we do know that a young

man by the name of Garfield A. King was working with them from 1908 to 1911. In 1911 he became a partner in the firm. Perhaps photography wasn't for him after all, or he simply saw greater opportunities elsewhere, but for whatever reason by 1912 he was articling with the law firm of MacDonald, Parkes & Anderson. In the 1915 city directories King is identified as a barrister with his own firm. Given what was to come, Fricke and Schenck were probably quite happy that their partner had decided to become a lawyer.

On May 12, 1915 the members of the Parks Board passed a resolution which stated, "the Superintendent be instructed to enquire of the Chief of Police

as to the nationality of the Big Tree Photographic principals, and in the event of said lessees being Germans or Austrians, the necessary legal 14 days notice be given cancelling such lease." It's hard to believe that all the members of the Parks Board were not well aware of Fricke and Schenck's country of origin long before they asked the police chief to investigate. Even though anti-German feeling was running high in 1915, they were carefully covering their political and legal butts as they reflected the public feelings.

At the time H.H. Stevens, a local member of parliament, was quoted in *The Sun* (May 27, 1915) as saying that it is "government policy to intern all [German and Austrian] aliens. It is being done at a rapid rate … all that is necessary when one hears of alien enemies is to notify the police department and their case will be looked after at once." And it was as simple as that. The British Columbia Provincial Police, under the War Measures Act, could round up anyone—naturalized or not—that they felt might be a threat to the country or community. The B.C. Manufacturers' Association was quoted in the same edition of *The Sun* as being "of one mind and favours (sic) internment of all alien enemies." Whether or not Fricke and Schenck were naturalized Canadians wasn't mentioned in the article. The newspaper, however, did report that "it was alleged that conversations at the big tree since the outbreak of the war

Although there have been many weddings under the trees, and even a few in cars, there probably haven't been too many in a car inside a tree. The ceremony is taking place in a 1903 Franklin runabout parked in the "Hollow Tree." The air-cooled Franklin was a fine and expensive car.

were distasteful to British ears and could no longer be tolerated." The two men doubtless spoke English with a pronounced German accent and quite probably on occasion spoke to each other in their native tongue.

It was when they lost their lease, after the police department had urged the Parks Board to cancel it, that Fricke and Schenck were probably very glad that Garfield King, their former partner, had indeed become a barrister. On May 26, 1915 King wrote on their behalf to the Parks Board requesting that the lessees be permitted to assign their lease, subject to satisfactory arrangement being made between the assignee and the board. In response the board allowed Fricke and Schenck "to assign the lease to anyone suitable to the commission who is a British subject."

And what happened to Fricke and Schenck? Who knows. They disappeared from the city directories as though from the face of the planet. At the end of it all Vancouverites certainly must have slept easier, knowing that there were no longer aliens near their Hollow Tree!

Chilliwack

A MOVING STORY

The second St. Thomas' Anglican Church—as did the first much smaller church—stood at Five Corners, Chilliwack's principal intersection. This view looks southwest along Westminster Avenue (now Old Yale Road).

Sorry! The temptation to entitle an article about Chilliwack's St. Thomas' Church "A Moving Story" is irresistible. After all, there aren't that many Anglican parishes that have moved not one but two church buildings from one site to another.

The story begins in Port Douglas at the north end of Harrison Lake where a church was built by the sappers of Colonel Moody's Royal Engineers. The building was paid for by Baroness Burdett-Coutts, an Englishwoman who devoted much of her fortune to "church planting" in British Columbia. The little church was dedicated to St. Mark on May 18, 1862 by the bishop of British Columbia, the Rt. Rev'd George Hills of Victoria. Although the governor of the mainland colony, Sir James Douglas, favoured the Harrison/Port Douglas/Lillooet route to the gold fields of the Cariboo, the miners far preferred the route through the Fraser Canyon that was completed and opened in 1864. That road, via Yale, Spuzzum, Boston Bar and Lytton, was so popular that by 1872 Port Douglas was all but a ghost town.

In 1873 Bishop Hills offered the disused Port Douglas church to the small congregation that had come into being in the growing town of Chilliwack in the Fraser Valley. The Anglicans in Chilliwack gladly and

St. Thomas' was moved in the summer of 1909 to its present much larger site. The building has a surprising architectural sophistication for a small town Fraser Valley church of the period.

quickly accepted the bishop's offer of a church building. The little church was soon taken apart, loaded on to six Indian canoes and floated down to Chilliwack Landing by way of Harrison Lake, Harrison River, and the Fraser River, from whence the pieces were transported a mile overland to where they were reassembled. The site for Chilliwack's new Anglican church was a parcel of land at Five Corners, the centre of the new town. The angular four-fifths of an acre site, which was bounded by Wellington Street and the Old Yale Road (known at the time as Westminster Street), was donated to the congregation by Issac Kipp, an ardent Methodist who was one of the town's co-founders. The church was reconsecrated by Bishop Hills on November 6, 1873, this time to St. Thomas. When a resident priest was appointed to the parish in 1878, a vicarage was built next to the church. The house was 14 feet by 26 feet and contained four rooms.

Chilliwack was growing, and so was its Anglican congregation, which by 1897 had decided that a new and larger church had to be built. An architect, R.P. Sharpe, designed the new building, which was erected on the Five Corners site where the little old church had stood. Within a decade it was realized that the site, although central, was too limiting; there was room for neither an adequate size parish hall nor a larger rectory. Something had to be done.

In March 1909 the Church Committee voted 21 to two to buy a larger piece of land (that had been located and was considered suitable), move the church to the new site, and sell the Five Corners property. Five Corners was prime real estate, and it was sold within a month to W.H. Hodgins for $23,000—a very large amount of money in 1909. The terms were that $5,000 was to be paid to the parish within three months, and the balance was to be paid in instalments at six percent interest. For its part, the parish was to have the church building moved off the Five Corners site within four months.

The present church property, a two-acre triangle of land bounded by First Avenue, Gore Avenue and Nowell Street, and known as the Mountain View property, was bought from Melbourne H. Nelems and David E. Stevenson for $3,000. The parish hired Samuel Calbrick, a local carpenter, as contractor. He agreed to move the church for the sum of $975, to be paid upon completion of the work. The church was to be moved off the old site by July 8, and be on the new site ready for occupancy by August 9. Should the work not be finished by the stated deadline, Calbrick was to pay the parish ten dollars per day as liquidated damages. The parish for its part was to pay for the removal and replacement of such power and telephone lines as was necessary.

The last service held in St. Thomas' on the Five Corners site was on Sunday, July 4, 1909. The rector Canon Joshua Hinchcliffe noted in the "Remarks" column in the parish service register on Sunday, July 18 that the church was on the street in front of the Dominion Hotel. Since parish records make no mention of mishaps, delays or difficulties, it can be assumed that the move went according to plan. The building was raised, placed on short peeled log lengths that acted as skids, and then slid along parallel squared timber tracks, which doubtless were greased. The horsepower needed to move the building was of course just that—horse power!

In the same year that the church was moved, a new parish hall and a new rectory were built on the Mountain View site. As it happened, the move from Five Corners not only provided St. Thomas' with a much larger piece of land and money for a new parish hall and rectory, but made it possible for the parish to assist two new and struggling neighbouring congregations. It seems that by 1911 the purchaser of the Five

Corners lot, Mr. Hodgins, owed a balance of only $10,000 on the mortgage. From these proceeds, St. Thomas' congregation voted to give $5,000 to St. John's in Sardis, and $4,000 to St. Peter's in Rosedale to help meet the cost of church buildings.

Given all that the good people of St. Thomas' were able to do with the income from the sale of their Five Corners site, this tale can quite justifiably be called a moving story!

The church as it first appeared when relocated to its new site. To the east can be seen a corner of the new parish hall. It wasn't to be long before parishioners volunteered their time, talent, and horses to get the grounds in shape. New breaking can be seen in the foreground.

A CAPTAIN AND HIS SHIP

There are famous ships and famous men, and there are many times when the two are found together. It would be difficult to write about either the Dominion Government Steamship *Quadra* or Captain John Walbran without reference to the other.

The federal government's 265-ton lighthouse tender/fisheries patrol vessel *Quadra* was one of the finest ships to see duty on Canada's west coast. Named after Juan Francisco de la Bodega y Quadra, the late eighteenth century Spanish governor of Nootka, the *Quadra* was built in Fleming and Ferguson's Paisley shipyard in Scotland. Built of steel, the ship was 174.5 feet long and 31.1 feet wide. Capable of 12 knots, the vessel sailed from Greenock under the command of Captain John T. Walbran on October 15, 1891 and arrived in Victoria on January 4, 1892. It was built at a cost of £15,000 to replace the aging lighthouse tender, *Sir James Douglas*. Coal-burning, the new schooner-rigged steamship travelled much of the way to British Columbia under canvas to save fuel.

As a lighthouse tender, the *Quadra* had a certain responsibility for the well-being of sailors up and down the coast. As there were few light houses north of Nanaimo, big acetylene-fuelled light buoys marked many harbour entrances and dangerous passages. The crew also had to check regularly to be sure that the lights were in working order and that none of the buoys had been either damaged or set adrift in winter storms. There were many occasions, of course, when the *Quadra* came to the rescue of ship-wrecked crews, particularly along the west coast of Vancouver Island where so many vessels have foundered over the years.

Since the government had no dedicated fisheries patrol vessels in the 1890s, the *Quadra* also had to keep an eye on salmon runs, halibut fishing, and sealers operating off the coast. The need to enforce regulations often brought Captain Walbran into conflict with the

John T. Walbran was captain of the Quadra *for nearly twelve years. It was during his years on the coast that he began writing about the origin of coastal place names. His initial research eventually led him to prepare his definitive "British Columbia Coast Names, 1592-1906" for publication in 1909 by the Geographic Board of Canada.*

Built in 1891, the Dominion Government Steamship Quadra *looked more like a millionaire's yacht than a lighthouse tender and fisheries patrol vessel. Even though its crewmen were all civilians, its Captain, John Walbran, ran his ship like a British man-of-war.*

masters of both Canadian and American sealing schooners. The *Quadra* travelled as far north as the Bering Sea when patrolling the sealing grounds. Since Walbran was not only captain of a lighthouse tender and a fisheries inspector, but also a magistrate, on the spot justice was the order of the day. And "the spot" was more often than not the deck of the *Quadra;* poachers and other miscreants were dealt with swiftly. Should problems arise, his crew was fully trained in the use of the ship's twelve Martini-Henry rifles. As well, Walbran often carried a constable on board when he knew ahead of time that he would be holding court.

There were also times when the lighthouse tender cum fisheries patrol vessel served as an hydrographic ship, surveying yet uncharted portions of the coast. Interestingly, the British Admiralty named both Walbran Island near Rivers Inlet in 1890 and Walbran Rock off Lama Point in Fisher Channel near Bella Bella in 1894 after the *Quadra's* captain. Walbran Point on Loretta Island was so named in 1898 by the Geographic Board of Canada.

Captain John Walbran was as famous as the ship he commanded from 1891 until 1903. Born in 1848, he was a Yorkshireman who attended Rippon Grammar School and received his naval training aboard the school frigate, H.M.S. *Conway.* The *Conway* was a training ship for boys intending to become officers aboard merchant ships. Already on the West Coast in 1891 as an officer aboard the Canadian Pacific Navigation Company's ships, Walbran was appointed master of the yet to be built *Quadra.* He sailed for Britain and acted on the government's behalf while the ship was being built.

The *Quadra* wasn't a naval vessel, but the fact that it was a government ship was reason enough for Walbran to see that it was kept looking like one of the finest vessels in the Queen's navy. Even though all his crewmen were civilians, they wore the classic sailor's uniform of the day. Walbran, himself, wore a frock coat and gleaming naval sword. His sword wasn't the only thing aboard that gleamed; the well-trained and disciplined crew took as much pride in their ship as did

On February 26, 1916 the Quadra *was rammed by the CPR's* Charmer *in heavy fog at the entrance to Nanaimo's harbour, and sank in shallow water just below Gallows Point lighthouse.*

its captain. It always looked as though it had just been freshly painted, and its brass fittings shined like gold. On Sunday mornings following roll call, the captain would officiate at Morning Prayer.

There were occasions, particularly when dealing with aboriginal peoples, that Walbran and many others felt it was important to show the flag in the very best light. Certainly the *Daily Province* agreed, writing on July 24, 1897 that "we learn … that the annual grant for uniforms of the officers and crew of the *Quadra* is not to be allowed this year. A Government steamer and no uniforms! … If economy be the motive, we must point out that this is the falsest of false economy. The *Quadra's* duty lies largely in dealing with Indians and uncivilized people and uncivilized people are proverbially no respecters of persons divested of the outward and visible sign of authority represented by uniforms." Regardless of how we may feel about the perspective reflected in the 1890s newspaper article, the writer did reflect the popular point of view of the day.

It would seem that as early as 1894 Walbran was collecting information relating to the names of places he was visiting up and down the coast. He came ashore in 1903, doubtless to have more time to work on his labour of love, his "British Columbia Coast Names–1592-1900–Their Origin And History." He was actively encouraged in his research and writing by the federal minister of marine and fisheries, the Hon. L.P. Brodeur. Walbran's book was published in Ottawa in 1909 by the Geographic Board of Canada, and sold for two dollars a copy. In spite of its age, "British Columbia Coast Names," with its biographical and anecdotal bits and pieces sandwiched between dates and facts, is not only a first-rate source of information but great fun to read as well. And to his credit, the accuracy of his account has rarely been found wanting; although the book has been reprinted a number of times, it has never been re-edited. Walbran died in 1913.

The *Quadra* still had a few years left to go. Its work load had been lightened somewhat in 1909 when

The Quadra *was raised with little difficulty by a derrick barge. The barge was manoeuvred into place by the* Eva, *which is best remembered as a sometime cannery tug on the Skeena River. The damage to the* Quadra *was such that the federal government thought it wiser to sell the 25 year old vessel than spend money on repairs and refurbishing.*

the 50-ton *Newington*, a former British North Sea and Icelandic steam trawler, was bought by Ottawa for west coast service. Still later the *Estevan* and the *Berens*, based in Victoria, served the southern coast, while the *Alberni* and the *Alexander Mackenzie*, sailing out of Prince Rupert, served the northern coast.

It was at the entrance to Nanaimo's harbour on February 26, 1916 that the *Quadra's* days as a lighthouse tender and fisheries patrol vessel came to an end. In a dense fog the *Quadra* was rammed by the CPR's *Charmer*, which was entering the harbour as the *Quadra* crossed its bow. Quickly an attempt was made to beach the stricken vessel, but the attempt failed and it sank close enough to shore that its funnel and masts remained above water even at high tide.

Once the vessel had been refloated it seems that, given the ship's age, the government didn't feel it was worth the cost of repairs. The damaged ship was sold to Britannia Mines to be adapted for use as an ore carrier. It transported zinc concentrate from Howe Sound to the company's smelter in Tacoma. This second career ended in 1924 when the *Quadra* was chartered by rum runners who used the vessel to transport illicit cargoes of liquor to points off the American west coast.

The *Quadra* could carry 22,000 cases of liquor. It was met offshore by smaller vessels that took the prohibited booze into port. The *Quadra's* third career was short-lived. Within the year the U.S. Coast Guard cutter *Shawnee* seized the ship and towed it into San Francisco. Tied up for a number of years while Canadian and Californian lawyers argued about rights and ownership, the rusting derelict eventually sank at its mooring. What was left of Captain Walbran's "spit and polish" *Quadra* was finally sold for scrap for $1,625.

SHOPPING ON GRANVILLE

Vancouver's first suburbs were well established by 1900. Mount Pleasant, Fairview and Kitsilano were immediately to the south of False Creek, and only a relatively short streetcar ride from the city centre. Farther away were places like Kerrisdale, Grandview, Cedar Cottage and South Vancouver. Still, a ride on either the streetcar or interurban would have shoppers downtown in less than an hour. Not that all shopping had to be done downtown. Each of Vancouver's suburban communities had its block or two of stores, which might include a grocery store, meat market, pharmacy, dry goods store, barber shop, shoemaker, hardware merchant and bakery. More often than not there would be that childhood mecca: a confectionery store with its seemingly endless variety of penny candies. In the days before refrigeration, let alone frozen foods, meeting daily needs meant a daily walk "to the store" for most housewives. Going "to the store" actually meant visiting not one but a number of merchants along the local shopping street.

Far more interesting than going to the store, though, was going downtown! Perhaps at this point we need to be reminded that until after the Second World War shopping was something that women, more often than not, did on their own. Certainly until after the First World War the six-day work week meant that most men had little opportunity to do much more than work, eat and sleep. Even until the end of the Second World War working conditions weren't that much better. Men (and working women, of course) had to put in a five and a half-day work week, with Saturday afternoon and Sunday off. And annual holidays were two weeks long at most.

There were surprisingly few changes in the look of Vancouver between the two world wars. A few significant structures like the Marine and Medical Dental buildings, the Royal Bank at Granville and Hastings, the present Hotel Vancouver, and one or two other "skyscrapers," all dwarfed today by their newer and taller neighbours, were about it. Anyone who had left Vancouver in 1914, not to return until 1945 would immediately have been right at home, and felt as though nothing much had changed in the intervening years.

Almost by definition, "going downtown" would have included seeing all there was to see along both sides of Granville Street between Hastings and Georgia. While there were many good stores along Hastings, Granville was a cut above. Granville's cachet wasn't accidental; it owed its status as the city's premier shopping street to the CPR. The railway had anchored Granville at its north end with its monumental 1899 harbour-front station. The building was an early example of the chateau style that in time would become something of a Canadian railway trademark. And if the station didn't establish Granville Street's primacy, the company's Hotel Vancouver and opera house four blocks up the street certainly did. As well, the Bank of Montreal with Lord Strathcona as its president, and numbering among its directors CPR men like Sir Thomas Shaughnessy, R.B. Angus, and G.R. Hosmer, built its delightful Scottish Baronial regional head office on the northeast corner of Dunsmuir and Granville. It was a building that would not have been out of place in Victorian Glasgow. The Hudson's Bay Company, another old CPR friend, had relocated from Cordova Street to the northeast corner of Granville and Georgia in 1893. The fact that Lord Strathcona was the company's Governor until his death in 1914 just *might* have influenced the Hudson's Bay's decision to build its new store diagonally across the street from the Hotel Vancouver. Two other banks, the Merchants Bank and the Bank of Quebec, were also on Granville. On and near the southeast corner of Granville and Pender, they were directly across the street from the main post office. (It was not until February 1910 that the *new* post office at Granville and Hastings first opened for business.)

Along Granville on a summer's day, say sometime between 1907 and 1914, there would be many women out shopping. All, of course, have changed from their housedresses to their afternoon frocks and donned complementing hats and gloves for the trip downtown. Since Vancouver was still a relatively small city in those days, and *everyone* went downtown, shoppers would be sure to meet old school chums, former and present neighbours, or friends from church. While there were always such serendipitous meetings, many women met downtown by plan. And where better to meet than in one of Granville Street's many tea rooms. They might have chosen "The Old Country Tea Rooms," "Ye Little Brown Inn," or "The Queen Tea Room," all in the 600 block between

The year is probably 1907, and this picture is looking north on a summer's day at Granville and Georgia. The Hudson's Bay's awnings protect the window displays from the hot afternoon sun, and the street has been watered down to settle the dust.

Georgia and Dunsmuir. Farther down the street "The Tea Rooms" shared their premises with Mary Walker, the dressmaker, at 569 Granville.

Not only could news and views be shared over lunch or tea, but also talk about the prices and bargains of the day. The shopper on Granville before the First World War could choose or at least admire jewellery at Birks, O.B. Allan, or Todd and Manning. And gorgeous furs could be seen in the windows of J. Boscowitz & Sons, just down the street from the Hudson's Bay. Both diamonds and furs might be the stuff that dreams are made of, so the average shopper was much more likely to be looking for something a little less luxurious and considerably more practical: a new fall outfit, for example. She might drop in at Ladymore, the Parisian Ladies Tailoring Shop, More & Wilson's Ladies' Wear, or I.L. Kostman's Famous Ladies Tailoring Company. Interestingly, *The Famous* became much more famous when it moved around the corner to Hastings Street. However, if the shopper preferred to make her own clothes or her limited budget forced her to do so, she could select an appropriate fabric at Saba Brothers Fancy

Goods or at one of the other fabric shops or in the yard goods department of either the Hudson's Bay or Gordon Drysdale's Department Store. It may have been that she was well along with her dressmaking and her purpose in being downtown was to stop in at Smith's Button & Pleating Works to drop off enough material to have tailored buttonholes and matching covered buttons made for her new outfit. At the same time she could call in at the Singer Sewing Machine Company's store to pick up some extra bobbins; both shops were in the 600 block on the west side of the street.

If the main purpose of the day was to window shop, there was much to see on Granville Street. Pianos were big in every way, and they could be seen at Kent Piano, Fletcher Brothers, and at Mason and Risch, which was just across the street from the Hotel Vancouver. All these stores did well in a day when it seemed that everyone played the piano. By 1914 all the music houses had added phonographs to their line. Shoppers could also admire the latest furniture styles at the Gardner Browne Company, across from the Hudson's Bay. Fine china was sold at R.G. Buchanan's, and oriental goods, which were very popular at the time, were the specialty of Benjamin Newstead's Vancouver Curio Store.

Of special interest to women in those far off days were a number of businesses that no longer exist. At a time when ostrich steaks are more in fashion than ostrich plumes, it is not surprising that the South African Plume Shoppe is no longer with us. Similarly, in an age when letting it all hang out is the order of the day, the demise of the Spirella Corset Company and later the Marion Brown Corset Shop, which was discreetly just off Granville on Dunsmuir, was inevitable. Changing fashions have also all but signalled the end of hat shops like The Patrick Company, which stood at 652½ Granville. While Vancouver had 23 milliners in 1909 and 48 in 1914, today there is a handful at most. Changing fashions have also spelled the end of linen shops like the Irish Linen Store, and later, Dalls on Granville. There was a time when every bride looked forward to receiving at least one or two damask tablecloths and matching dinner napkins. But then, how could linen shops expect to survive in an age of TV trays, permapress, and plastic placemats?

While the streets may have been full of women shoppers "back then," none of the foregoing is to suggest that there weren't many men on the street. Although the husbands of most women rarely had an opportunity to go shopping with them at any time other than a Saturday afternoon, there was always a small army of men to be seen on the downtown streets any day of the week. They were the white collar workers—from office boys to company executives—employed in the hundreds of downtown offices. And their needs were met by a number of Granville Street shops that catered to them. There were, for example, three tailors and six men's clothiers. Among the shops selling men's furnishings was Edward Chapman—a firm that is still operating—as well as W.S. Charlton (later Charlton and Morgan) and Arnold and Quigley, both of which survived into the 1950s. Other gentlemen's needs were met by the Hudson's Bay Company's Liquor Department and by A & B Liquors, both in the 600 block, and by the four barber shops that were waiting to serve them. In Charles Hermann's shop customers wouldn't have waited long. His shop, which was located in the basement of the Rogers' Building at Granville and Pender, had sixteeen chairs! As well, in the four blocks between Georgia and Hastings there were six cigar stores. In all probability the four drugstores in the same four blocks also sold cigars and cigarettes. Two of these drugstores, the Georgia Pharmacy and the Owl Drug Company, continued on into the years after the Second World War.

Rather surprisingly there were six shops in the four blocks between Georgia and Hastings that sold photographic supplies. A number of them also functioned

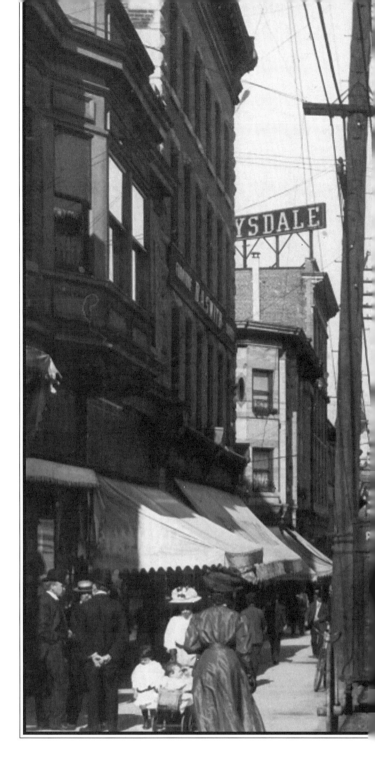

as portrait studios. Both men and women were caught up in the photographic craze of the day. The publication of Princess Louise's photographs, which illustrated *Our Railway to the Pacific* (1886), a book written by her husband the Duke of Argyle who had been Canada's Governor General, and *Queen Alexandra's Gift Book*

This 1907 photo looks north along Granville past the corner of Dunsmuir. The Bank of Montreal's Scottish Baronial head office is seen just beyond the intersection, and farther down the street the Bank of Commerce at Granville and Hastings is under construction. The ad attached to the cow catcher on the Davie Street car announces the fall opening of the Imperial Roller Rink at English Bay.

featuring her "Photographs from my Camera," doubtless helped make photography an acceptable and respectable hobby for women as well as for men.

Then as now, photography and travel went together naturally. It's easy to imagine shoppers of long ago stopping to look at the pictures of fine steamships and of exotic places or even of "the old country" in the windows of passenger agents like D.E. Brown, or Hope & Macaulay Limited who identified their location as "opposite the Bank of Montreal" in their advertisements. The partners were the ticket agents for the Allan, White Star, Cunard, Holland America, Red Star, and Union

Granville and Hastings looks busy on a warm summer day in this 1906 photograph. Beyond the maze of poles and wires, the new post office is under construction. Partly obliterating the view of the CPR train station, three banners are strung across Granville Street. Two of them invite prospective patrons to take in Saturday's lacrosse game at Recreation Park, while the third suggests an "Afternoon Sea Trip" aboard the CPR's Joan.

Castle lines, as well as for a host of other steamship companies. In those days, however, there was no asking "Where will we go this year?" for 99 percent of the population. In fact it was only a relatively small segment of the population that could even hope for a once-in-a-lifetime travel adventure, let alone an annual vacation very far away from home. Nearer the CPR station were passenger agents for the Grand Trunk System, White Pass & Yukon Railway, Donaldson Line, Pacific Coast Steamship Company, and the Royal Mail Steam Packet Company. Perhaps among the many shoppers there were a few who stopped in at the steamship ticket agencies to pick up an assortment of brochures. They may have been dreaming of the trip to the old country that in their heart of hearts they knew would never take place. Or possibly they were wondering what it would cost to bring family members from home to join them in the new life that could be found in Canada and in Vancouver.

Even 50 years ago a trip downtown was still something to be enjoyed. After all, Granville Street was still vital and vibrant with things to see and things to do. Today, though, with more and more people working in suburban business parks, shopping in conveniently located satellite town centres, and finding entertainment in one-stop mega-malls, its hard to imagine anyone willingly going downtown to shop. The sheer desolation that is now Granville from Georgia to Hastings—empty lots, boarded up buildings, and a pedestrian zone that has consistently failed to attract significant foot traffic—has turned the street into little more than an avenue of memories for those who admit to being old enough to remember happier days on Granville Street.

AGASSIZ: WHAT'S IN A NAME?

There was a time when all Fraser Valley and Lower Mainland communities like Port Coquitlam and Haney on the north side of the Fraser, and Port Kells and Cloverdale on the south side of the river had a life of their own. Today, however, these centres and others like them have become in large measure Vancouver's bedroom communities. The West Coast Express and commuter bus routes that fan out across Delta, Surrey and Langley have meant that places as far out of Vancouver as Mission, Abbotsford and White Rock have many residents who are no more than "part time."

Today, it is only in the upper reaches of the Fraser Valley, that is, above Abbotsford and Mission, that there are towns and villages that continue to exist largely beyond the shadow of what is now called the Greater Vancouver Regional District. One of these towns is Agassiz, which is at the heart of the well-defined Harrison-Agassiz Valley, and is approximately 75 miles east of Vancouver and 20 miles west of Hope. This valley of some 14,000 acres, located on the north side of the Fraser River, is sheltered by surrounding mountains that rise to between 3,000 and 10,000 feet. The community's history of White settlement goes back nearly a century and a half.

White settlers first arrived in the Harrison-Agassiz Valley in December 1858, less than a year after the Mainland had become the Crown Colony of British Columbia. On February 14, 1859 Governor James Douglas set out the conditions governing the pre-emption of Crown lands. Essentially the regulations stated that an applicant had either to reside on the property being pre-empted for six months in each of

In this springtime photograph circa 1910 "traffic" is held up waiting for a CPR freight train to pass. On the right can be seen the freight shed that was a part of Agassiz's station built to replace the original one, which burned down in 1893.

three succeeding years and make certain improvements, or have someone else reside on it and make the improvements before the land pre-empted could be purchased for one dollar an acre. A number of would-be settlers or homesteaders came to the valley in the early 1860s, but most stayed only for a short time then left, letting their pre-emptions lapse.

An early settler in what was to become the Harrison-Agassiz Valley was Lewis Nunn Agassiz. Just who was he? It's difficult to say very much about him with absolute certainty. As is so often the case, extracting facts from family tradition isn't all that easy. With the passage of time, in all families the purely apocryphal has a way of becoming the gospel truth. Sifting through the stories, however, it seems that the Agassiz family was of Swiss origin, and had emigrated to England in the early eighteenth century. Lewis Nunn Agassiz was born on December 24, 1827 at Bradfield in Essex. His family was both well-off and well-connected, and his father was a friend of King Frederick William IV of Prussia who offered young Agassiz a commission in his army. The sixteen year old wanted, however, to join the British army, and the king generously bought him a commission in the Royal Welsh Fusiliers. On August 20, 1844 he joined the regiment as a second lieutenant, and on April 16, 1847 he became a first lieutenant.

Lewis Nunn Agassiz

When Agassiz was 24 his regiment was stationed in London in Canada West (now Ontario), and it was there he met and married Mary Caroline von Schram. His bride was of United Empire Loyalist stock, and her family was relatively well-off. By the time of their marriage on March 24, 1852, it seems that Agassiz had tired of military life, sold his commission, and left the army. The newlyweds moved to a large well-equipped farm on Prince Edward Island. Agassiz's father had bought it some years before for two of his other sons (he had eleven sons and four daughters that survived to adulthood) but when one of the boys drowned, and the other returned to England to take Holy Orders, the place was vacant. Agassiz knew next to nothing about farming and it wasn't long before

he admitted defeat, returning with his wife and infant son Arthur to London where he involved himself in a series of unsuccessful commercial ventures. Lewis Agassiz seems to have been no better suited to business than he was to army life or farming.

In 1858 Agassiz left his wife and four children with his in-laws and set off for the gold fields of British Columbia. He made his way to Victoria by way of Cape Horn and San Francisco. In Victoria he became one among 30,000 men making their way to the Cariboo.

As one of his daughters reported in her memoirs, "after three years of unsuccessful mining, he sent for mother and the children" who left London in March 1862, travelling via New York, the Isthmus of Panama, and San Francisco to Esquimalt. Agassiz met his family in Victoria from whence they travelled on the *Otter* to New Westminster where they stayed with Charles S. Finlaison who—with Agassiz—had built a hotel in New Westminster at an earlier date. Unfortunately it had burned to the ground and they lost all they had put into the venture.

From New Westminster the family made its way to Yale. It was Agassiz's intention that they should go on to Williams Lake where he wanted to try his hand at ranching. But the trip to Yale had been more than enough for his wife who wisely and firmly refused to take one step further into the hinterland! Being a positive and practical woman, Mary Caroline more or less marched Lewis off to see the highest local official in town about a job. The "highest official" was the stipendiary magistrate E. H. Saunders, an Englishman who had served as an officer in the Austrian army. As it happened, the position of Chief Constable and postmaster was open in Hope. Since Agassiz had the right accent, the right manners, and in both the geographical and genealogical senses, the right if distant connections, he got the job. Doubtless the Agassizs were considered to be a welcome addition to the small community by the English-born and self-appointed gentry of Hope. The Agassizs fitted in well. It was they who entertained and accommodated visitors like Governor Douglas, Chief Justice Begbie, Edward Dewdney, Clement Cornwall (later a Lieutenant

Governor of the province) and Forbes Vernon after whom Vernon in the Okanagan was named.

Although Agassiz's wife and children enjoyed living in Hope, he was not content to remain there forever. He had always wanted to own land and he had seen the ideal property. On November 25, 1862 Agassiz pre-empted 160 acres in what would in time come to be called the Harrison-Agassiz Valley. While he had set the wheels in motion, he seems to have been wise enough not to expect Mary Caroline to move onto the land until a lot more than the basic "improvements" required for pre-emption had been made. He arranged to have John Walker and Crispen Taylor, who had pre-empted neighbouring lands, take up residence and not only make the qualifying improvements to their land, but for a price improve his land as well, while he and his family continued to live in Hope. It wasn't too long, however, before he employed a man named Maxwell to manage and operate his farm. He paid him $60 a month, and gave him a Chinese boy to help with the work. The lad was paid $10 a month.

Agassiz also arranged to have a house built on his farm. The first member of the Agassiz family to live on the property was his eldest son Lewis Arthur who was known as Arthur. Even though he was only in his early teens when he moved onto the property in 1866, he took to farming like the proverbial duck to water. The family took up residence in 1867 and named the farm Ferny

Coombe, a *coombe* being a little valley. Life wasn't easy for the Agassizs but they survived, and largely through the efforts of Arthur the farm was a success.

By 1875 Arthur had virtually assumed full management of the farm, and just as well, too, for in the same year Lewis Agassiz left his wife and ten children—who ranged in age from 22 years down to 2½ years—to visit his mother in England for a few months. Being Lewis Agassiz, he decided that since he was going to be halfway around the world anyway, he might just as well take five years and travel back to British Columbia by way of the Continent, the Near East, India and Asia! He had just visited a brother in Constantinople and gone on to Asia Minor for some hunting, when on July 24, 1880 he died of the effects of sunstroke and was buried at Acre in Syria.

Lewis had died but life went on at Ferny Coombe. In view of his extended travels, the family had probably long since learned to get along without him. No doubt there were days that were difficult, but the family was never hard up. To begin with, there was what one of his daughters described as "a small remittance from England each year." Probably the amount was more

The 300-acre Dominion Experimental Farm occupies a site purchased from the Agassiz family. Work had started on the farm in 1888 even though title to the property did not pass to the federal government until September 19, 1889.

In this pre-Great War picture, Agassiz's Pioneer Street looked like it could be one of two things, mud or dust, depending on the weather. The little building in the foreground is the post office and the larger building farther down the street is the Bella Vista Hotel.

substantial than the words "a small remittance" might suggest. There was always money to employ help. In Hope, for example, Indian women were hired to do the washing and scrubbing, and the family employed an indentured Chinese houseboy who was "bound for two years." Agassiz also had enough money to go on buying up land in the valley of his dreams until he owned 1,600 acres or roughly one-tenth of the arable land available. As well, gifts and bequests from England, varying in amount from £300 to £1000, arrived from time to time to make life easier.

It was fortunate that while her late husband was both unrealistic and self-indulgent, Mary Caroline had both feet planted firmly on the ground and was concerned only for the welfare of her children. She was fortunate in having Arthur to manage the farm so she could devote her time to the upbringing and eduction of her younger children. Then, too, Mrs. Agassiz had many friends among the colony's politically and socially significant. In fact it was one of the Agassiz's friends, Joseph Trutch, who named the little community in which they lived in their honour.

As the story goes, Trutch—who was acting for the Dominion Government overseeing that the CPR was meeting all of its contractual obligations—happened to be staying at the Agassiz home and was joking with two of the girls: Mary Louisa (known as Minnie) and Constance. He playfully suggested that the new CPR train station and village that would spring up around it could perhaps be named Minne-apolis after Minnie, or Constant-inople after the other daughter, Constance. Then it seems he said, "No, the place should be named *Agassiz;* that way we can honour the whole family."

The coming of the CPR in the 1880s was the first of three developments that determined the future of the new town. Construction of the section of the railway between Emery Bar, which is just below Yale and Port Moody, began in 1882. The $2.68 million contract was signed with Onderdonk and Mills who completed the job on April 22, 1894. They built from both ends and the two lengths of track were joined at Nicomen. Even though it was not until July 4, 1886 that the first transcontinental passed through Agassiz, service between Ruby Creek (which is ten miles east of Agassiz) and Port Moody began almost immediately. For many years a local train carrying passengers and produce made the daily run. Although this "milk run" was slow, stopping at every town along the way, the service meant that communities like

Agassiz were no longer isolated, and for them the days of the pioneer were over.

Arthur Agassiz was one of the small gathering of people who witnessed the local and very informal "last spike" ceremony at Nicomen. He was probably there not only out of curiosity, but because train service was going to make a big change in at least one aspect of his life. He had been the local postmaster since September 1884 when the community was still known as Ferny Coombe, and continued to be Agassiz's postmaster until July 1893. Not only would he still be meeting river boats, delivering and receiving sacks of mail, but with the coming of the CPR he would also be meeting trains from both the east and west.

The second event that changed the lives of those living in Agassiz was the November 1,1886 opening of the St. Alice Hotel, five-and-one-half miles away at Harrison Hot Springs. In the years before the First World War Harrison Hot Springs were valued primarily for their curative powers, real or imagined. Advertisements of the day claimed the waters to be efficacious "in treating rheumatism, kidney and liver diseases, etc." The hotel's publicity also noted that there was "a resident physician in attendance." The St. Alice burned down in July 1920, and it was not until May 1926 that a new Harrison Hot Springs Hotel opened. By then the recuperative powers of the springs were no longer being emphasized. Instead, Harrison was promoted as a resort, a place for fun and relaxation. The hotels on Harrison Lake, both the old St. Alice and the new Harrison Hot Springs, meant steady employment for the people of Agassiz and business for the local shops and services.

The third development that added a dimension to life in Agassiz was the establishment of the Dominion Experimental Farm in 1888-89. The purpose of the farm and others like it across the country was twofold: "to facilitate the work of the agriculturalist and to place farming upon a profitable basis." Until 1911 the farm at Agassiz gave most of its time and attention to fruit growing and horticulture. After 1911 there was an equal, if not larger, emphasis on animal husbandry, with dairy cattle, hogs, poultry and workhorses each having a place in the program.

The site selected by the federal government for the Dominion Experimental Farm was a 300-acre portion of the Agassiz farm. It is tempting to wonder if, in the words of the Director Dr. William Saunders, the land was selected solely because "of all the farms visited, none appeared to combine so many advantages." It is not unreasonable to wonder if political friendships had a bearing on the selection of land owned by the Agassizs. One of the criteria that was to be taken into account in selecting a site stated that the land was to be in "a central location which would be fairly representative of the farming lands in the Coast climate." Looking at a map, its difficult seeing Agassiz as central to anything!

Regardless, the railway, the hot springs, and the experimental farm have provided Agassiz and the Harrison-Agassiz Valley with a basic economic stability. By 1910 the town itself not only had a school and four churches but also an Oddfellows Hall and a Good Templars Hall. There were also telegraph, telephone, express and post offices. As well, there were three hotels, three general stores, a butcher shop, sawmill and two blacksmiths. It also had a mining recorder collector and coroner, all in the person of the Justice of the Peace, Arthur Agassiz. Interestingly, Agassiz did *not* have a real estate agent and that perhaps says something about the stability of the community.

Like many towns in the Fraser Valley, Agassiz's salad days were the years before the First World War when belief in the inevitability of continuing progress and growth was still an article of faith for most people. While naturally enough there was ongoing change after the war, the community experienced little real growth after 1914. Still, who today is going to argue that by definition bigger is always going to be better. Not the people who choose to live in Agassiz, that's for sure.

Lewis Arthur Agassiz

Vancouver

CONSECRATION DAY

It was on August 4, 1914 that Great Britain and consequently all the parts of the Empire including Canada were at war with Germany and Austro-Hungary. In Canada the initial response to the declaration of war united Canadians in a patriotic fervour. The first contingents recruited were easily filled by recent British immigrants. When war broke out Canada was in the throes of a growing economic depression, and those who formed the ranks of the unemployed, whether Canadian or foreign born, were almost as quick to join up. By the end of 1914 the Canadian Expeditionary Force numbered 50,000, and by the summer of 1915 there were 150,000 men in uniform. At the same time, however, it was becoming obvious to both government and military leaders that men were no longer rushing forward to volunteer for King and country at anything like the numbers that were required. At Ypres in April 1915 the 1st Canadian Division had suffered 6,036 casualties. The bloom was off the rose; people were coming to realize that it was going to be a tough long fight and that men were dying in battle in unprecedented numbers. They may have also been thinking that perhaps the fighting and the dying could best be left to other people in other places. At any rate, the federal government and the country's military leaders knew that something had to be done to strengthen waning popular support for the war and to encourage a re-invigorated volunteer recruitment program.

One of the ideas generated called for a day of patriotic re-dedication that would help rebuild public enthusiasm for the war and boost recruitment. The date suggested for this "Day of Consecration," which was to be held in cities and towns throughout the country, was Wednesday, August 4, 1915, the first anniversary of Britain's declaration of war. Vancouver's civic leaders responded to the idea with energy and enthusiasm and were able to stage a hugely successful event that produced what appeared to be a spontaneous and popular response to the call for a renewed and strengthened patriotism. In reality there really wasn't very much about the day that was in any way spontaneous. The public merely responded to a carefully orchestrated program that led them inevitably to make the renewed commitment that was wanted. None of this is to say that those

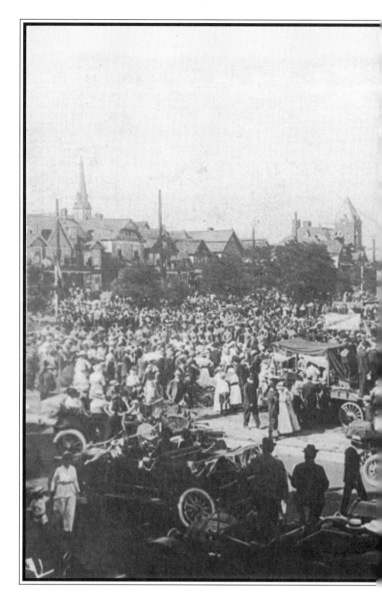

organizing and staging the "Day of Consecration" didn't believe wholeheartedly in the cause they were endorsing, or that they would for a moment have seen themselves as manipulating people's minds and emotions. The fact that the *Vancouver Sun* was able to say *before* the event took place that "the following resolution will be offered and carried by a show of hands: 'That, on this anniversary of the declaration of a righteous war, this meeting of the citizens of Vancouver records its inflexible determination to continue to a victorious end the struggle in maintenance of those ideals of liberty and justice which are the sacred and common cause of the allies'" does perhaps make the response *that had yet to be made* seem just a little contrived.

The parade of 12,000, most of whom marched from Main and Hastings, and the program which attracted 50,000 to the Cambie Street Grounds came off without a hitch. The mayor had declared the afternoon a

Although estimates of the number of people overflowing the Cambie Street Grounds for "Consecration Day" were as high as "nearly the entire population of Vancouver," the more likely number was between 50,000 and 60,000.

half holiday, and all shops and businesses were encouraged to close. Special streetcar and interurban service was arranged, and routes altered to avoid interfering with that to be taken by the parade. All the arrangements for the parade were the responsibility of Chief of Police M.B. McLennan. The major denominations had arranged for special services to be held in the early afternoon in their downtown churches. Those taking part in the parade were reminded that there were to be no automobiles and that all would proceed on foot "and in their ordinary everyday street attire ... it not being an occasion for any display excepting that of patriotism and stern determination to prosecute the war to a successful conclusion." Not all the sermons were preached in church! As it happened many of the recent recruits in the parade were not in uniform for the simple reason that they had not yet been supplied with them. However they were, as *The Sun* reported, "enthusiastically applauded as with

erect bearing and rifle in arm they stepped forward in service of their King and country."

Following in order were mounted city police, military units, men and women from each of the city's eight wards followed by representatives of South Vancouver, North Vancouver and Point Grey. Then came the Orangemen, Sons of England, Boy Scouts, Mechanics Institute volunteers, the Japanese Societies, and finally other Japanese. The Vancouver businessmen's battalion joined the parade at Hastings and Burrard at 2:15 p.m. This "unit"—60 strong—included not only veterans of the Boer War and the Riel Rebellion but "the medalled defenders of their country, the only time it was invaded in this generation": white-haired men who had fought the Fenian raiders. Their oldest comrade was former prime minister Sir Mackenzie Bowell, aged 92.

The Sun pointed out that "Union Jacks, Canadian ensigns and the flags of the allied nations were in evidence all over the city …. Vehicles flew the flag 'that had braved a thousand years the battle and the breeze' and which is destined to wave for at least another thousand as the emblem of justice and liberty …. Men, women and children carried miniature flags in their hands and the whole scene was one radiating patriotic enthusiasm." As it happened *The Sun* had been selling a $4.00 flag kit for some days before "Consecration Day" which could be purchased through the newspaper for only $1.48.

Since in 1915 there was no way a crowd of 50,000 was going to be able to hear speakers at an outdoor rally, those planning the day came up with the idea of having six platforms set up around the perimeter of Cambie Street Grounds. At each stand or rostrum there would be a chairman, a clergyman and six speakers. Prayers and addresses would run simultaneously at the six sites so everyone would have a reasonable chance to hear something of what was said, and the whole crowd would only join together for the singing. Each speaker was strictly limited to ten minutes. Those invited to deliver the addresses were prominent civic political and business leaders. At Rostrum"B", for example, the chairman was Mayor L.D. Taylor; the cleric, Bishop dePencier; and the speakers were Sir Mackenzie Bowell, Dr. McKay, H.H. Stevens, B. Schock and Colonel Worsnop.

The proceedings opened with "God Save the King" after which the clergy at each of the rostrums offered prayers. Then followed the singing of "O Canada." The resolution mentioned earlier was read out and as was to be expected endorsed unanimously. The national anthems of the Belgians, Russians, French, Japanese and Italians were sung between the addresses that followed. The program closed with the singing of "Rule Britannia" and for the second time "God Save the King." Perhaps the organizers felt the Lord might not have heard it the first time it was sung!

As would be expected, all the speakers said much the same thing. It was reported "they were in good form as earnestly and fervently they told of Britain's need and appealed to the young men to prove worthy of their fathers and their citizenship by taking up arms in liberty's cause." Reeve Edward Gold of South Vancouver, for example, reminded his audience that "in this empire of ours we are free men and our duty and responsibility is clear and it is upon us to awake to the call of Kitchener, 'men and more men.' Can we forget and must we not loudly proclaim the good and noble work [of] the brave women and mothers whose heads

are bowed in sorrow, but like the injunction of the Spartan mothers of old to their sons [say], 'Son go forth, return with your shield or upon it.' We appeal to the patriotism and manhood of every physically fit young single man … and we invoke the blessing of the Lord … in all things until Victory is perched upon the banner of Britain and her allies." Strong stuff this, calculated to send any hesitant youth off in a hurry to the nearest recruiting depot.

Another speaker Judge S.D. Schultz told his audience that "The empire's escutcheon is undefiled—it still gleams refulgent with the white light of honor (sic) and glory. The consciousness that we are battling for a just cause in the interests of humanity already presages victory … [and] we must not relax our efforts to guard the liberties of our Empire … the issue is between liberty and oppression, between might and right." And in his address George Morden, editor of the *North Shore Press,* told the crowd that "the noble response of Canada's sons, whether by birth or adoption, whether of a few generations or of a few years upon Canadian soil, stained the war scarred fields of Flanders as a voluntary sacrifice of love, for the vindication of British honor (sic) and the maintenance of British justice and liberty."

Summing up "Consecration Day," *The Sun* reported that "Never before in the history of the city has such a gathering of citizens been witnessed as that which congregated [for the event.] Every individual … in whose veins runs the blood of the Anglo-Saxon, appeared anxious to publicly consecrate themselves in the Empire's service. Not only is this true of Britishers resident in Greater Vancouver but it is also true of the citizens of those countries allied with our men. The Italians and the Japanese were out in large numbers. Of the other nations fighting with us there are not many citizens in Vancouver, but what there are, were present."

And being Vancouver, the newspaper's fulsome and glowing account of "Consecration Day" had to end with a typical West Coast weather report, reminding readers that the day they had all experienced was "ideal, bright and not too warm!"

The Vancouver Sun offered an impressive flag kit for only $1.48. It included a 3- x 5-foot Union Jack, rope halliard, a 6-foot joined flagstaff with ornamental ball end, and a metal staff holder or window bracket. For mail orders postage was 7¢ if the destination was within 20 miles of Vancouver, and 15¢ to other parts of the province.

AFTER A YEAR OF WAR
The Flag Is Still Flying

Show your loyalty and faith Today
to commemorate a year of war

Loyalty is the knightliest attribute of mankind—be loyal to yourself today by securing the means of showing your loyalty to your altars and your hearth. Be among the first to come—don't let others set the example; above all, don't miss this opportunity which has cost the press of your country yeoman effort to bring about.

This is not a stiff muslin flag PRINTED with Ink—but Is a beautiful soft cotton bunting that with ordinary care should last a lifetime. The colors are DYED in guaranteed fast colors, with canvas heading and grommets.

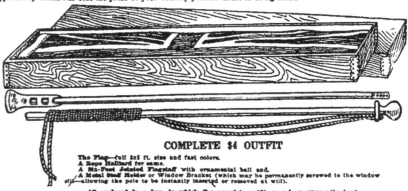

COMPLETE $4 OUTFIT

The Flag—full 3x5 ft. size and fast colors.
A Rope Halliard for same.
A Six-Foot Jointed Flagstaff with ornamental ball end.
A Metal Staff Holder or Window Bracket (which may be permanently screwed to the window sill—allowing the pole to be instantly inserted or removed at will).

All enclosed in a box, in which the complete outfit may be permanently kept in compact space when not in use (size box, 3½ inches square by 3 feet long).

THIS $4 FLAG AND OUTFIT FOR ALL OCCASIONS
$1.48 FOR THE $4 OUTFIT; OR THE FLAG ALONE FOR $1.10

You will need the flag for every patriotic event for years to come—for every one of those great victories that you positively KNOW are sure to come! You can use it constantly for decorative purposes in public and private sociables, in the school house, in the church, and—best of all—in the home.

Get it from This Newspaper by Presenting the Coupon Printed Daily in Another Column

ARRANGEMENTS HAVE BEEN MADE WITH THE BURNS DRUG COMPANY, 732 GRANVILLE STREET, TO ASSIST IN THE DISTRIBUTION OF THESE FLAGS.

A B.C. Salvage Company vessel has run lines to the Spokane, *which was steered to shallow water after submerged rocks holed its hull. The ship had been caught in a riptide in Seymour Narrows and forced off course because of the captain's negligence.*

On The Coast

"THE TOTEM POLE ROUTE"

British Columbians are inclined to assume that maritime traffic in the heyday of coastwise passenger service was the exclusive preserve of Canadian companies like Canadian Pacific, Grand Trunk Pacific (later CNR) and the Union Steamships. Not so. There were a number of American companies sailing regularly between state-side and Alaskan ports in the years before the Second World War.

One of these American lines was the Pacific Coast Steamship Company with a fleet of ten vessels, four of which could carry over 500 passengers each. The line provided a regular passenger service between Seattle, Portland, San Francisco, Los Angeles, and San Diego, and between Seattle and Skagway. As well, it scheduled fourteen-day luxury cruises with ships stopping at Victoria going north, and on the way south calling at Vancouver. The company advertised the route as "The Totem Pole Route" and rather amazingly claimed in its brochures to have "discovered the famous Inside Passage!"

One notable Pacific Coast Steamship was the 2,277-ton *Spokane*. Built in San Francisco in 1902, it was a luxury excursion steamer designed to give its 239 affluent passengers, who were looked after by a crew of 31, "a fortnight's pleasure in a floating hotel." The company's brochure mentioned that "as incidents of the perfect equipment, a Ladies Maid, watchful and attentive is provided; a Stringed Orchestra aids in the entertainment, … a Barber-shop caters to the comfort of the tourist, [and] a well fitted Dark Room is furnished for photographers." Lest anyone think that family fun was the name of the game, the brochures also pointed out that "while young children are not excluded from the ship, it is recommended that they be left at home, as their care is sometimes a hindrance to full enjoyment of the cruise." To underscore what was said, it was also made clear that "full rates must be charged for children of any age occupying a berth."

The Pacific Coast Steamship Company knew that in spite of all the ballyhoo written about comfort, luxury, and "proceeding calmly northward," prospective passengers would still want to know something about safety at sea. To put their concerns to rest, publicity materials pointed out that the *Spokane* was "designed especially for the Alaskan service, [with] a watertight double bottom, and bulkheads that insure safety."

There was one occasion in the *Spokane*'s years of service when safety didn't seem all that well "insured"! It was in June 1911, when the ship took an unplanned and—as it were—in-depth look at one small portion of the B.C. coast. With both Captain J.E. Guptill and the pilot Captain R.D. MacGillivary on the bridge, the steamer reached Seymour Narrows above Campbell River at about 2:00 p.m. on Thursday, June 29. Rather than wait for slack water to run the ship through the narrows, it was decided to proceed on the ebb tide which didn't seem to be all that fast-moving. The *Spokane* moved quickly and safely past Ripple Rock. Suddenly, however, the vessel veered toward the steep rock wall on the east side of the narrow channel. Caught in an unusually strong riptide, there was no way the ship could avoid the rocks at the foot of the bluff. The steel hull on the starboard side was badly holed. The impact and noise of grinding metal set the passengers scrambling from their staterooms.

The captain had no choice but to beach the vessel which was in obvious danger of foundering. At full speed ahead, the *Spokane*, which was sinking bow first, made the two miles to the beach at Plumper Bay in 40 minutes. By the time the ship was grounded the Chief Engineer and his men were waist deep in water. It was their courage that saved the ship and the lives of those on board.

And, those on board anticipated the worst. Screaming passengers were terrified when the vessel rolled from side to side as it was being beached. Many were fighting their way to the lifeboats on the higher port side when suddenly as the ship settled into the mud it finally rolled to starboard. Fearing the ship was about to capsize, many passengers jumped overboard. Those that couldn't swim to shore were picked up by lifeboats. The survivors, after spending the night on the beach, were rescued and looked after by the Grand Trunk Pacific's *Prince George* until the arrival later in the day of a southbound American steamer that took them to Seattle. Incredibly only two passengers were lost, both women; one was trapped in her flooded stateroom and the other suffered a fatal heart attack during the rescue.

Even though the *Spokane* was submerged over its main deck at high tide the vessel was successfully salvaged. Patched up and refloated by the British Columbia Salvage Company, the ship was escorted back to Seattle for permanent repairs and refurbishing.

Captain Guptill had his license suspended for 60 days. It was found that he should have waited for the slack tide before taking his ship through Seymour Narrows even though he was "following a custom admittedly practised by many other capable and experienced pilots."

The *Spokane* continued to sail the coast until 1932, though from 1922 it did so as the *Admiral Rogers*. (In 1916 the Pacific Coast Steamship Company had been bought out by the rival Admiral Line.) After having been laid up from 1932 to 1946, the ship was sold to a group of Seattle businessmen who planned to convert it into a floating hotel. The plan didn't materialize, and in 1948 the 46-year-old vessel was broken up in the yards of the Puget Sound Bridge and Dredging Company. The former flagship of the "Totem Pole Route" was no more.

The Spokane *is berthed alongside the CPR's wharf in Vancouver. Although it cost more to keep the hull gleaming white than it would have had it been painted a darker colour, the owners knew that white not only enhanced the ship's appearance, but suggested luxury and class as well.*

COEUR-DE-LION'S MEMORIAL

was described as depicting "the spiritual rather than the material aspect of those who died in the Great War of 1914–1918."

It wasn't to be long before those who died in the conflict, popularly described as "the war to end all wars," were memorialized in carved stone and cast metal from one end of the country to the other. Not only were city councils, veterans groups, service clubs and churches soon erecting monuments to the fallen, but many businesses as well were commissioning the creation of memorials to those of their employees who had so recently given their lives (or had them taken from them) in this "Great War." The CPR's monument was one of Vancouver's first 1914–1918 memorials. Of its 11,602 employees who had enlisted, 1,100 died in the war. As well, 370 of the company's men won decorations for bravery, two of which were Victoria Crosses. The railway not only commissioned three bronzes from MacCarthy's design but also placed commemorative plaques in its offices in London, Liverpool and New York, and in many of its stations across Canada.

On Saturday, April 29, 1922 all three memorial statues described as showing "a soldier being borne to his reward beyond death by an angel [holding] aloft the laurel wreath with which he will be crowned" were unveiled simultaneously. In Vancouver the event took place at noon within the framework of a simple yet moving service. A crowd of over 5,000 gathered at the southwest corner of the CPR's station (the memorial's original location) for the dedication. The lieutenant governor, the Hon. Walter C. Nichol officiated, with Bishop A.U. de Pencier pronouncing the benediction. Hymns were accompanied by the band of the 72nd Battalion, Seaforth Highlanders of Canada.

Platform guests included Premier John Oliver, Mayor C.E. Tisdall, and local officials of the CPR, including the general superintendent of the B.C. district F.W. Peters, who delivered a short address. Local military men, in whose number were four generals—J.M. Ross, R.G.E. Leckie, A.D. McRae, and Victor Odlum—were also among the special guests. Particular attention was of course paid to the relatives of those employees who had died in the war. They first assembled in the station's waiting room before taking their places in special seats reserved for them. Each of the three memorials was

I f one were searching for a sculptor to create a war memorial it would be hard to overlook an artist whose given name was Coeur-de-Lion, that is, *the lion-hearted*. In fact the design submitted by the Montreal sculptor Coeur-de-Lion MacCarthy was the one chosen by the Canadian Pacific Railway for three identical bronze war memorials that were to be erected by the company in Montreal, Winnipeg and Vancouver. Coeur-de-Lion, by the way, probably didn't think his name at all odd given that his father was Hamilton Plantagenet MacCarthy. The design chosen by the CPR

unveiled by a man who had lost a son in the war. In Vancouver the man chosen was C.S. Maharg, who like the son he had lost, was an employee of the railway.

While some may question the memorials' aesthetic merit, and others will debate the politics of war, one can neither argue with the motivation of those who erected them nor with their purpose which was, as is recorded at the base of each statue, "to commemorate those … who … left all that was dear to them, endured hardship, faced danger, and finally passed out of the sight of men by the path of duty and self-sacrifice, giving up their own lives that others might live in freedom."

The Canadian Pacific Railway's First World War memorial is of bronze and is mounted on a granite pedestal, the whole being 18 feet in height. Dedicated on April 28, 1922, the Great War memorial is pictured at the moment of unveiling, which took place exactly at noon.

Vancouver

"A REALLY BIG SHOW"

The idea for Vancouver's first Horse Show originated with the local Stock Breeders' Association which invited the members of the Hunt Club to become joint sponsors of the event. The idea caught on quickly and soon the Vancouver Horse Show Association had come into being. The year was 1908, and the first show was scheduled for March in the Beatty Street Drill Hall. The Association had hoped there might be as many as 400 entries, but the total number exceeded 700! Good as the show was, the Drill Hall had drawbacks: the ring was 50 feet short of the ideal length, and the space for spectators was severely limited.

The members of the Vancouver Horse Show Association held their first annual meeting on December 1, 1908. At the meeting they planned the erection of a suitable building to be ready in time for the 1909 Horse Show, which was scheduled to take place in late April. The general meeting agreed to purchase all the land that was available in the block bounded by Georgia, Gilford,

and Alberni Streets; it was only the Chilco or western end of the block that could not be acquired. The land was bought for $26,000. Of the eleven designs for a horse show building submitted to the Association, two had been set aside for serious consideration.

Such was the situation when a new and enlarged board of directors came into being. Their number included Jonathan Miller, D.C. McGregor, E.R. Ricketts, Dominic Burns, and Victor Spencer. They were not a group of men who were going to let any grass grow under their feet, and they quickly chose the design submitted by Warren H. Milner of Seattle, Washington. His plan called for a frame structure with a steel truss roof. The building was to cover four-fifths of an acre, cost $49,000, and provide—as the Association's purpose stated—for the "exhibition of horses and the housing of a multitude of spectators."

The building was well designed. It had a ring 75 by 200 feet with a floor of solid timber surfaced with tan bark to a consistency as near firm sod as possible. The

Built in 1909, Vancouver's Horse Show Building burned to the ground on March 18, 1960. Two years earlier Stanley Park's Superintendent urged the Parks Board to acquire the property, demolish what was by then the very ugly Stanley Park Armouries and add the acreage to the park.

Even though this "artist's impression" is overly imaginative, it does successfully suggest that the Horse Show Building was very large. When built, it was the largest enclosed space in North America, other than New York City's Madison Square Garden.

turns at the ends of the show ring were banked slightly "to form a continuous drive." Circling the ring were 100 private boxes, the floors of which were two feet above the show ring. Although boxes in arenas and stadiums are now taken by business corporations, in the days of the Horse Show Building they were leased by well-known (and well-heeled) people in the community. The list of box holders included names like Marpole, Tees, Tupper, Farrell, Spencer, Mahon, Trapp, Ceperley, Trorey, and Hendry. Ten feet above the boxes was "the visitors' gallery benching back to the outside walls with a clear sight line of seventy-five percent of the ring." At the back of the first four rows of seats there were posts at 30-foot intervals. *The Province* reporter suggested that since the show was a moving one, the posts would be of no real concern to those sitting in the rows behind them. At the ends of the building extra galleries extended up to the roof. Altogether, there was seating for 3,500 people. When the building was used for rallies or conventions there was room on the main floor for an additional 2,500 seats. The building's first capacity crowd gathered in 1910 to see and hear Sir Wilfrid Laurier who was electioneering.

There was a certain pride in the fact that the entire building was lighted by electricity. The newspapers mentioned that the show ring was to be lit by sixteen arc lamps. As well "Incandescent lamps [were to] light up every nook and cranny throughout the rest of the building, with red globes on all exit lights." Readers were also told that the entire building was "guarded against fire by five large lines of pipe with hose valves and firehose on every floor" and "six large and convenient exits leading directly to the street."

The building was designed in such a way that all the rigs and horses for stabling entered by way of a 20-foot doorway on Gilford Street. The horses and equipage first arrived in the 40- by 100-foot hitching room. From this hitching room the horses were sent down easy inclines to the stables below. Arriving on the stable floor, the horses were cleaned up at one of four wash racks and then taken to their stalls. Each horse stood with its back to the strong light, and none was near an open window. In a pinch there was enough room for 196 horses.

The various carriages and wagons, which had been left in the hitching room, were moved off to one of the wash racks where they were cleaned. After cleaning, they were sent into one of the wide carriage rooms that went along either side of the show ring, behind the wall at the back of the boxes.

The show had three judges who were Canadians of international standing and "their names [were] such as command the respect of every admirer of the horse." Each had a field of expertise; one judged heavy harness horses, saddlehorses and hunters, another judged light harness classes, and the third judged heavy stallions and draught horses. The ring master, W.J. Clements, and his four assistants were all liveried for the show.

The first show in the new building ran from Wednesday, April 21 through Saturday, April 24, 1909, and had entries in 126 different classes. These classes included draught teams, pairs drawing broughams or victorias, high steppers, trotters, four-horse teams, both single and double city delivery horses and wagons, and Hackney mares. As well there were categories for pairs pulling a phaeton driven by a lady, Shetland ponies, saddle ponies ridden by boys or girls, ponies drawing gigs driven by boys or girls, four-horse teams drawing brakes, three-horse teams, pairs drawing landaus, military horses ridden by officers in uniform, ladies' saddlehorses, high jumpers, and on and on and on! Entries came from Washington, Oregon, the Prairies, as well as from all over British Columbia. An interesting entrant was J.W. Considine of Seattle, one of the owners of the Orpheum vaudeville circuit, who entered eight horses and "nine equipages of the very latest and most modern fashion."

The show in the main ring was well worth watching, but the city's society matrons doubtless found the show in the boxes equally entertaining. After all, the Horse Show was *the* fashion event of 1909. On the day following the opening of the Horse Show, the great unwashed could read about the "many handsome gowns...seen at the opening yesterday afternoon and again in the brilliant audience last night." In the afternoon, for example, the mayor's wife wore "a gown of dark mauve, with a black turban trimmed with jet ornaments and two long black plumes." She reappeared in the evening "in a rajah silk dress with a lace bodice and a black hat." In the evening Mrs. Considine "was much admired in a beautiful gown of heavy Italian lace, trimmed with deep bands of ermine and an imported hat covered with immense paradise plumes."

For those patrons who felt in need of refreshment, there was the Tea Room operated by volunteers from the Anti-Tuberculosis Society. And for other needs "the comfort of all visitors [was] provided for by ample retiring rooms and toilets."

The First World War brought an end to elaborately staged horse shows, with all their glitter and glamour. By the time the war was over there were few calling for the revival of the colourful shows of pre-war days. The automobile had virtually taken over the streets in the intervening years, and fewer and

fewer city dwellers kept horses; automobile shows were the coming thing. In fact, as early as 1913 when the Vancouver Exhibition Association opened its 300-foot long Transportation Building, built to display the latest automobiles, the handwriting was on the wall. The Horse Show Building only saw intermittent use

This picture of box-holders, their guests, and patrons seated in the front rows of the visitors' gallery could justifiably be entitled "Elegance in the Afternoon." As can be seen in the photo, the partitions between the boxes could be folded back, making it possible for a single larger space to be created. Admission to gallery seats was 50¢ for adults and 25¢ for children, except on Saturday when the entrance fee was 25¢ for adults and 10¢ for children.

during the 1920s, and it was eventually sold to H.O. Bell-Irving.

In the early 1930s the federal government proposed leasing the Horse Show Building with a view to using it as a depot for some of Vancouver's military units. The trustees of the Bell-Irving estate spent between $5,000 and $6,000 repairing the neglected property; and after a five-year lease was signed, the department of national defence spent a further $25,000 to create what it considered to be a modern drill hall. Its principal tenant was the 65th L.A.A. Regiment of the Irish Fusiliers; however, a Signal Corps division, the 11th Machine Gun Battalion, and the non-permanent 11th Squadron of the R.C.A.F. also used the building.

The end came on March 18, 1960 when the Stanley Park Armouries (as the building was then called) burned to the ground. The fire was first noticed at 4:00 a.m. The old wooden structure was destroyed in no time at all. Only ten minutes after the first of three alarms went in the roof collapsed, and within an hour the structure was nothing but a smoldering ruin.

How the fire started remains a mystery. Given that the Irish Fusileers had been partying until 1:00 a.m., it being St. Patrick's Day and all, there were suspicions. But as the fire chief said at the time, "It will be extremely difficult to establish the cause, and then it will only be suspicion. I doubt we will ever be able to prove a cause."

Sadly, but not surprisingly, few people regretted the building's destruction. It never was a thing of great beauty. Somewhat defensively the executive board had reported in 1909 that it had "wisely expended the funds at hand, by making the interior second to none in the country rather than in a gorgeous or monumental display on the exterior." While the exterior was anything but gorgeous or monumental, it was attractively painted in lemon chrome with white trim. Above the black roof rose the rather squat towers where visitors could look out over Coal Harbour and the city. Colourful flags and pennants flew from 22 roof-top flagpoles for the duration of each year's Horse Show and for special events.

By the time the building burned in 1960 it was obvious that it had seen better days. Its bright yellow and white exterior had long since been painted over, and its dull drab brown government paint job was doubtless considered more serviceable. The remains of a concrete foundation wall can still be seen on the south side of Georgia Street, west of Gilford. They are all that is left of the Horse Show Building which in its day was the setting for one of Vancouver's premier annual social events.

In fashion, the Edwardian period was unquestionably the era of the hat. Just as the hats came in all shapes and sizes, so did the women wearing them. The Province's *cartoonist undoubtedly saw the 1909 Horse Show from a seat that was not in one of the boxes!*

The North Arm

WIGWAM INN: DREAM AND REALITY

t the top of Burrard Inlet's North Arm stands Wigwam Inn, a relic of the past with a story to tell. Although the old resort is less than 20 miles from downtown Vancouver, it is probably safe to say that very few present day Vancouverites have ever laid eyes on the place, if for no other reason than it is only accessible by boat.

Wigwam Inn was the brain child of Benjamin Franklin Dickens. Dickens had come to Vancouver from Belleville, Ontario in 1898 and got a job as advertising manager with the *Daily Province*. It was not long before he left the newspaper to set up his own advertising agency, the first in Canada. For Dickens, an avid outdoors man, the North Arm which he later promoted as "Indian Arm," had a special appeal. He dreamt of building a summer resort at the head of the inlet that would not only attract Vancouver's elite, but people from all over the world. In 1906 he decided to turn dream into reality, and began the development of what he called Indian River Park. Ads which always featured an architect's sketch of a stylishly elegant resort hotel appeared in the 1907 Vancouver papers. Self-owned cottages were to share the site with the luxury hotel that was to be the resort's centrepiece and focal point.

Dickens had bought 200 acres which were divided into 50- by 150-foot cottage sites. The sites were offered for sale at $200 to $300 each, depending on location. The lots did not sell well, and by 1910 his Vancouver Springs Indian River Company was in trouble. Help was just around the corner, however, in the person of Gustav Constantin Alvo von Alvensleben, one of the sons of Prussian Count Werner von Alvensleben. The personable 27-year-old Alvo, as he was called, arrived from his native Germany by way of South America in May 1904 with little more than energy, intelligence, and extremely good connections. Within four years he was a millionaire, having set himself up as a broker, promoting real estate and using the stock market to his advantage. Working with his brother Werner who remained in Berlin, Von Alvensleben is credited with attracting over $60 million in German capital to British Columbia before the First World War.

In 1910 von Alvensleben became involved with Wigwam Inn. He took over ownership of the inn which by then was under construction, while Dickens retained ownership of the surrounding acreage and became general manager of von Alvensleben's Indian River Park Company. Somehow the rumour got around that mineral

Inaccessible by road, Wigwam Inn at the head of Indian Arm is encircled by magnificent scenery. Even though it is only 12 kilometres from downtown Vancouver, it somehow gives the feeling that it is far more remote than it actually is.

An ad appearing with this picture in the 1907 Vancouver newspapers told the reader that "a firm of local architects have made the preliminary sketches for the 'Wigwam' Inn, a building in harmony with the surroundings, with its quaint gables and old-fashioned chimneys and fireplaces ... plans will be rushed so as to get the hotel well under way this season." The dream was rather different from the ultimate reality.

springs that contained healing properties for a wide range of disorders had been discovered on the property. Given German faith in the therapeutic powers of such springs, it was not surprising that investment quickly came from people like Emma Mumm of the champagne family and General (later Field Marshal August von MacKensen) and other European investors.

The inn, which featured hot and cold running water, electric light, and steam heat, had 32 bedrooms. They were furnished with iron bedsteads and felt mattresses—the last word in luxury. Typical of the day, bathrooms were "down the hall." The dining room could accommodate over 100, with room for additional diners being provided outdoors on the adjacent wide covered verandah. A "commuters'" boat service was advertised, the idea being that one could holiday at Wigwam Inn and continue to go to the office in town each day. While vistas of "mountains, sea and river" were referred to in the inn's advertising, no mention was made of the fact that the resort's closed-in location allowed for very few hours of sunshine, or that the local glacier-fed waters were perishingly cold!

The planned opening date was May 24, but unforeseen difficulties meant that the resort hotel could not be officially opened until June 2, 1910. For the grand opening the company chartered Captain John Cates' stern-wheeler, *Baramba*, to take 600 invited guests to Wigwam Inn for the day. Of course, the hope was that many would be moved to buy cottage sites. Although the inn was well appointed and had a certain rustic charm, it was a far cry from the picturesque lodge that the promotional materials would have led one to believe existed at Indian River Park. When the disparity was mentioned, it was suggested that the newly built inn was to become an annex for the much grander building that would be built in the future. The buildings and grounds which Dickens originally intended to reflect an Indian theme ended up looking more like an alpine resort where Alvo von Alvensleben would have felt at home.

The grounds were redesigned to allow space for a German beer garden, and both stone-walled terraces and alpine summer houses were built. An *oom-pah-pah* band played in the beer garden during the afternoon, and for open air dancing in the evening. From 1910 until 1914 Wigwam Inn and Indian River Park succeeded in being a money-making luxury resort. Men like John D. Rockefeller and John Jacob Astor were among the prestigious guests who spent holiday time on the North Arm.

As luck would have it von Alvensleben was in Germany when war broke out on August 4, 1914. Knowing that he would be interned if he returned to Vancouver, he made his way back to Seattle, Washington instead. His Canadian assets, including Wigwam Inn, were seized and turned over to the federal Custodian of Enemy Property. The Inn was sold to E.J. Young, an American who owned the Vancouver Lumber Company and had logging and lumbering interests that stretched along the West Coast from Oregon to Alaska. Dickens sold his "town-site" property to Young in 1917. Not surprisingly the German alpine theme disappeared rather quickly and was replaced by the Indian theme that Dickens had originally favoured. Appropriate "legends" were created to enhance the appeal of local natural attractions, and a sixteen-page booklet recording these "ancient" tales was produced for sale to visitors. The new owner hired a manager for the hotel and ran it in conjunction with Captain H.S. Hilton's Harbour Shipping Company, which provided a daily sailing to Wigwam Inn between June and September. The excursion fare was one dollar, and the weekend rate at the hotel including meals was five dollars. Day trippers could get lunch for fifty cents. On Thursday evenings a dance cruise left the Gore Avenue wharf in Vancouver at 7:15 p.m., returning to the city at midnight. In 1920 a new firm, the Harbour Navigation Company, owned by Captain J.D. Stalker, bought out the Harbour Shipping Company for $16,000. Stalker's "flagship" was the 68-foot *Scenic* which had been built in Bremerton, Washington in 1908. It served all the settlers along the shores of the North Arm as well as visitors travelling between Wigwam Inn and the city. Stacker ordered a new vessel from Vancouver Ship Yard Ltd. in 1924. In appearance it looked for all the world like any one of the newer West Vancouver ferries. The new ship was built on the strength of Edward Young's assurances that the further development of Indian River Park would go ahead. When Young's plans didn't pan out, the new *Harbour Princess*, as the ship was called, became a day excursion boat available for charter. Although few people will remember Wigwam Inn, many will have happy recollections of the *Harbour Princess*. Over the years it carried thousands of children from all over Vancouver to the company's grounds at Belcarra Park for their annual Sunday School picnics.

In the mid-1920s Harbour Navigation took over the Wigwam Inn lease—Indian River Park was still owned

The Wigwam Inn that opened in 1910 was very different from the building featured in earlier ads and promotional brochures, but it nevertheless attracted wealthy visitors from near and far. At $3.50 a day for accommodation and meals it was considered to be an expensive luxury resort hotel.

by Edward Young—and employed a most capable Irish woman, Margaret McAuliffe, as manager. She ran the place wonderfully well until she retired at the end of the 1941 season. As would be expected, the number of hotel guests was limited during the Depression years; nevertheless, day visitors and what overnight guests there were did make it possible for Wigwam Inn to stay in business.

Business picked up in the 1940s, gas rationing and the fact that there was more money around made holidays at places like Wigwam Inn both practical and attractive. To accommodate his thriving excursion business, Stalker bought the *Hollyburn* from West Vancouver Ferries in 1945. In 1951, after 30 years in business, Stalker sold out to a trio of owners—Louis Lawson, Fred Mitchell and Peter Cowan—the first two being Harbour Navigation employees. Soon after the new owners took over Edward Young died, and they bought Wigwam Inn from his estate. The three men spent a lot of money renovating and upgrading the property, and the North Arm resort continued to attract guests throughout the 1950s. They sold out at the end of 1960

and were the last owners of Wigwam Inn to make money; the automobile was creating holiday options that were much more attractive than anything Wigwam Inn had to offer. Successive owners tried to recapture the rustic charm of earlier years that had made the resort so popular, but to no avail. A firm which called itself Wigwam Inn Holdings Limited bought the resort and operated it in a rather different way. On June 29, 1962, the RCMP raided the inn. The police had been watching the place for some time and knew that a full-blown gambling casino was in operation. Fifteen were arrested.

The courts named a receiver to protect the interests of Harvey Cain who held a $38,000 mortgage on the property, and ruled that a guard should be employed to protect the property. A caretaker was hired, but he only stayed on until the end of December when it seems the owners could no longer afford to pay him. With the return of good weather in the spring of 1963 weekend boaters cannibalized the unprotected property, helping themselves to furniture, china, glassware and just about anything else worth stealing. Vandalism went

The dining room at Wigwam Inn could accommodate 100 guests. Another 100 could be accommodated on the wide covered verandah if necessary. Given the hotel's remote and natural setting, caged birds in the dining room do seem somewhat incongruous.

From the 1920s on into the 1950s most visitors would have travelled to and from Wigwam Inn aboard one of the Harbour Navigation Company's ships—the Harbour Princess; the Scenic; and after 1945, the Hollyburn.

hand-in-hand with theft, and what wasn't taken was smashed, broken or defaced. From time to time hippies camped in the derelict building, ripping up doors, hardwood flooring, banister and anything else that was handy for firewood. As if all this wasn't enough, a film crew further devastated the place by tearing out supporting walls in order to create the kind of set they needed for their movie, a picture which, incidentally, was never finished!

The empty and decaying building was bought by Tony Casano in 1972. He and occasional helpers laboured to restore the building. While he did get it to the point where it was weatherproof and free of rot, after seven years on the job he had to give up; he simply didn't have the funds to carry on with the work. In December 1979 the property once again had new owners—Western Pacific Resorts Inc. The company did manage to get the place rehabilitated to the point where it could re-open at the end of the 1980 summer season. Actually the firm had bigger plans for the property, hoping to get it rezoned to either commercial or recreation commercial so that

buildings could be put up and then sold on a "time share" basis. Given that the parcel of land comprised 155 acres, one third of which are flat and suitable for development, and that there are over 6,400 feet of waterfront, the concept seemed practical to its promoters. Plans called for the construction of 40 two bedroom condominiums, new tennis courts, a swimming pool, Jacuzzi hot tub, sauna, and other recreational facilities. It is enough to say that nothing came of the scheme and the property was once again sold in 1986. It passed into the hands of the Royal Vancouver Yacht Club which uses the restored facility as a popular outstation for its members. Such is the situation at Wigwam Inn as the twenty-first century begins.

As a kind of historical footnote, its interesting to know that not long before he died in 1963, Alvo von Alvensleben had one final look at Wigwam Inn. He is reported to have said to his host as he looked over the property for one last time, "Art, I must have been crazy." Quite possibly a number of those who followed after him, trying hard to make a near impossible dream come true, might have ruefully agreed with his self-assessment.

Burnaby

THEIR LUCKY DAY

Some photographs almost seem able to tell their own story, and the picture opposite is one of them. It was taken in 1912 on a summer day when the paperboys had time to admire a new line car and talk to its crew.

At any other time of year the boys would have hurried straight from school to pick up their papers so they could be delivered as quickly as possible. In those days the late arrival of a newspaper too often meant a customer complaint, and a fine for the paperboy. The couple of younger boys in the picture, kid brothers perhaps, may well have being tagging along just to have something to do.

The picture was taken on Edmonds at Kingsway in Burnaby, with the Edmonds Development Company's new Building in the background. Edmonds and Kingsway was an important intersection in 1912. Burnaby's new $25,000 municipal hall and police headquarters were just around the corner on Kingsway.

In July 1911 it was announced that a gentlemen's club was being formed and hoped to occupy the two upper floors of the new building. The proposed club, which was to have given "sixteen excellent rooms for gentlemen, besides ample accommodation for billiards, smoking, reading rooms, etc." never became a reality, and the building's upper floors were rented out as offices.

The intersection was the end of the line for New Westminster's two streetcar lines. From Edmonds one track ran down Kingsway/Twelfth Street to Columbia Street and on out to Sapperton. The other track went along Edmonds to Sixth Street, down Sixth to Fourth Avenue, from whence it zigzagged over to Queens Park and on down to Columbia Street. This line was part of the original 1891 interurban route into New Westminster from Vancouver. Even when this picture was taken special trams were still using the trackage to carry lacrosse fans to and from Queens Park.

As the boys in the photo would have known (kids know these things) line car "L4" was one of two new work cars built in the B.C. Electric Railway's New Westminster car shops in 1912. The other car, "L5", was shipped to Vancouver Island for service in Victoria. Car "L4" would have been at work on Edmonds in 1912 in connection with the upgrading of the original tram line. New 60-pound rail was being laid along the entire length of the route, and where necessary the system of overhead trolley wires would have been upgraded at the same time. All had to be ready for December 2, when a new and improved New Westminster streetcar schedule was to come into effect.

But December 2 was still off in the future when the picture was taken. On the day of this photo, not only did the boys get to explore the mysteries of the new line car, but they got to talk with the men that worked on it. Imagine, *actually* talking to guys that wore spikes strapped to their legs, and who not only got to climb electric poles but got paid for doing it! Talk about the ideal job. Maybe, just maybe, after seeing all that was to be seen, and talking with the lucky men who got to

When the Edmonds Development Company's building opened in late 1911 it provided space for stores on the ground floor and for suites of offices on the two upper floors.

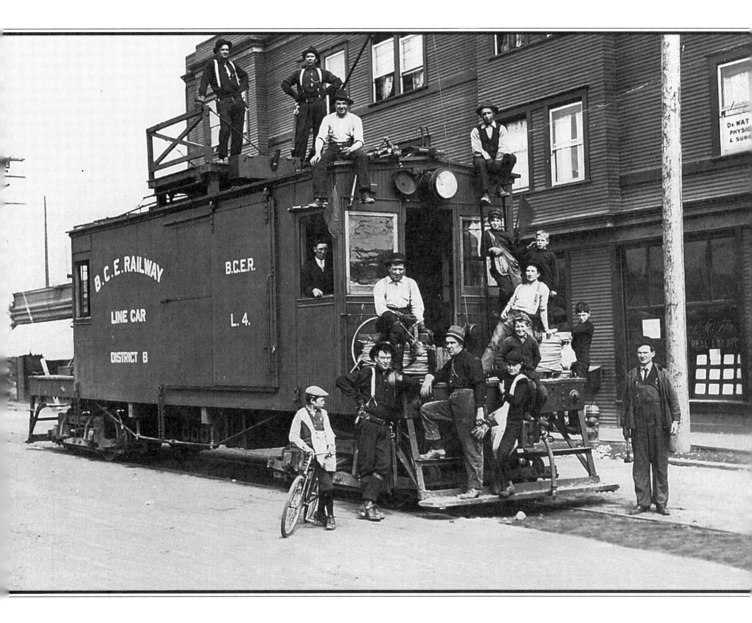

work on the lines all day, the kids got a piece of trolley wire, a bolt, or a clamp of some sort to take home. It was their lucky day. Life didn't come much better.

Doubtless just two or three years later some of the young linemen in the picture would have found themselves in far-off Flanders. In the times of endless waiting that was a reality of trench warfare, perhaps now and then their thoughts wandered back to their days as linemen, working at Edmonds and Kingsway. They, too, might have agreed that life didn't come much better than it was in the summer of 1912.

What kid could resist having a good look at a brand new line car? We'll never know who snapped this picture taken in front of the Edmonds Development Company's new $14,000 block at Edmonds and Kingsway in 1912.

ALEXANDRA BRIDGE

When in 1861 the governor of the mainland colony of British Columbia, James Douglas, decided that a wagon road was to be built through the Fraser Canyon, it was well understood that the terrain was such that the road would have to cross the Fraser River. As early as 1858, in connection with the mule trail that had already been built through the canyon, a ferry had been operating below Chapman's Bar, which is approximately two miles above Spuzzum. The ferry was really nothing more than a glorified raft, guided by hemp ropes that were attached to the rock face on either side of the river. Those using the ferry either poled or pulled their way across the fast-flowing water.

In October 1861 Governor Douglas sent Sgt. William McColl, R.E. with a party of sappers to select a site for the bridge that would have to be built. McColl recommended locating it a mile below Chapman's Bar at a spot where the river was less than 255 feet wide, and where the approaches on both banks would be relatively easy. On February 2, 1863 an agreement was signed with Joseph W. Trutch to build a suspension bridge across the Fraser River at the recommended site. The bridge was to be called the Alexandra Bridge in honour of the Princess of Wales. Trutch was already well known to both Governor Douglas and to Colonel Moody when he was awarded the bridge contract. But who was he?

Joseph William Trutch was born to upper middle-class parents in Somerset, England, in 1826. Following the usual stint at boarding school he served a five-year engineering apprenticeship with Sir John Rennie, one of the leading civil engineers of the day. Rennie had built London Bridge, and when Trutch entered upon his apprenticeship Sir John was building the Great Northern Railway from Liverpool to Edinburgh. Upon completion of his apprenticeship and after working for a short time for the Great Western Railway, Trutch sailed for California in 1849. He soon discovered that it was not to his liking and moved to Oregon where he found both a wife and professional success. In 1856 the couple moved to Illinois where work was not only plentiful, but so was winter snow! After only two years in the American mid-West, Trutch returned to London in 1858 to apply in person at the Colonial Office for a surveyor's appointment in the colony of British Columbia. It has been suggested that

an urge to resume life under the British Flag, together with the appeals of his brother John who was already in B.C., moved him to seek suitable employment in the mainland colony. John was Assistant Surveyor General of Washington Territory when he decided to move to B.C. in 1857. As it happened, it was during his stay in London that Joseph Trutch first met Colonel Moody. The resulting friendship did his career nothing but good.

Trutch was successful in his job hunting, and on July 25, 1859 Sir James Douglas awarded him a $10,000 contract to survey a large portion of the lower Fraser River delta. In 1860-61 he went on to bid successfully for Harrison-Lillooet trail construction contracts worth £10,000. Trutch next contracted for $75,000 to build the 12-mile section of the Cariboo Wagon Road that was to run between Chapman's Bar and Boston Bar. He was the man who was to build the suspension bridge across the Fraser.

G.S. Andrews described Trutch as "well educated … professionally qualified … and very British in decor and loyalty," but he was no snob, being both willing and able to appreciate the training and accomplishments of those who did not share his social or academic background. He seems to have been particularly impressed by the pioneering and successful work of John A. Roebling, the man who developed the suspension bridge as we know it. Trained at the Polytechnic in Berlin, Roebling had emigrated in 1831 from his native Germany to the United States where in time he became an American citizen.

In 1844 Roebling built his first suspension bridge, which carried a barge canal over the Allegheny River. In 1847-48 he built the Delaware Aqueduct, a suspension bridge that carried the Delaware & Hudson Canal. His work successfully demonstrated the value of the suspension system for supporting heavy loads, and its superiority over conventional masonry-arch or timber-truss bridges. Trutch had seen Roebling's impressive Niagara River Bridge near the Falls, an 821-foot span that carried a single track railroad on its upper level and a carriage way on its lower level. Doubtless Trutch was not only impressed by the immensity of the structure, but also by the fact that it was built at approximately one tenth the cost of a conventional span. Just by way of an aside, Roebling's greatest

This photograph, of the first Alexandra Bridge comes from the album of Rear-Admiral George F. Hastings, after whom Hastings Townsite was named. It was taken between 1867 and 1869.

accomplishment and lasting memorial is New York City's Brooklyn Bridge, built to his design in 1883, and still going strong.

While Trutch's Alexandra Bridge was no Niagara River Bridge, it was built on the same principle, and in its own way was just as significant and successful. Construction began on June 16, 1863 and was completed on September 1 in the same year. The bridge itself was fully described in the Victoria *British Colonist* of September 12, 1863. To quote, "The timber for [Trutch's Wire Suspension Bridge] was cut in the forest near the spot, and all the sawing was done by hand. The tower timbers are each 20 inches square. Supporting the cables are 16 of these sticks, each 26

feet 6 inches long, 4 sticks being framed together by means of 14 girth timbers and 17 1¾-inch wrought iron bolts, … coming together at the top, forming a pyramid, of massive timber. On the summit is fitted a heavy cast-iron saddle, covering the whole of the timbers, and keeping the cable which rests on it in position … there being in all four [of these pyramids], two at each end of the bridge."

The same article goes on to say that "the cables, of which there are two, are each 4½ inches in diameter, 528 feet long, and are composed of 1,264 wires, laid up in linseed oil, and protected externally by a coating of tar, pitch and oil boiled together … each of these cables weighs 12 tons. They were completely finished before

being put over the towers; they were manufactured at a point half a mile from the bridge and transported to the bridge on 25 trucks built for that purpose. Attached to the cables and platform direct, and on each side of the bridge, is an arrangement of diagonal bracing, very light in appearance, forming an effective truss, and rendering the bridge perfectly rigid. From the platform four wire guys are fastened to the rock in each bank; thus by means of the truss and guys, all undulation or oscillation is entirely prevented. The distance between the cables is 14 feet, thus giving ample room for all the traffic likely to pass over it." The span between the towers or "pyramids" was 268 feet when the bridge was completed; by way of a final test, a four-horse team with a load of three tons crossed over it and the deflection was calculated to be less than a quarter of an inch.

Financially Trutch's excursion into bridge building served him well. His contract with the colonial government allowed him to collect tolls for seven years. The tolls ranged from one-third of a halfpenny per pound of goods, upward to eight shillings four pence for vehicles drawn by four or more animals. Those travelling on foot were allowed to use the bridge without charge. It has been estimated that Trutch made something

Sir Joseph Trutch, K.C.M.G., one of the contractors who built the Cariboo Road and the builder of the first Alexandra Bridge, went on to become successively B.C.'s commissioner of lands and works, surveyor-general, and a member of the executive council. In 1870 he led the delegation to Ottawa that negotiated the terms of union between British Columbia and Canada. In 1871 he became the first lieutenant-governor of the new province.

Though no longer in use, the second Alexandra Bridge may still be seen from the present realigned highway and bridge. It is a reminder of the days when travel was not and could not be rushed!

between $10,000 and $20,000 a year from tolls. Whether credit for the bridge's design rightly belongs to Joseph Trutch or to A.S. Hallidie of San Francisco remains uncertain. Hallidie was the subcontractor hired by Trutch to build the bridge, and he was also on site for the time it took to build it. Regardless, it has to be acknowledged that Trutch was the man with the vision and the ability to see the project through to successful completion.

Alexandra Bridge lasted longer than the Cariboo Wagon Road of which it was an integral part. The road was officially closed in 1891 since construction of the Canadian Pacific Railway through the canyon in the 1880s had made it all but impassable. It could fairly be said that the road was kept open only long enough to allow the railway to use it for moving supplies to its construction camps. Once the rail line was finished, there was little interest in maintaining the wagon road.

In 1894 flood waters partly dislodged one of the bridge's cable anchors, making it unsafe for vehicular traffic. The damage was not so severe, however, that those travelling by foot or on horseback couldn't continue to use the bridge. The bridge remained in limited use until its cables were cut in 1910, by which time it was seen as a potential hazard to downstream navigation.

The story of Alexandra Bridge is a little like a play in two acts with a seventeen year intermission! Even as the first Alexandra Bridge was being dismantled, interest in reopening the Cariboo Road was being expressed by relative newcomers on the scene—the growing number of motorists.

While there was talk of reopening the road, nothing really happened until after the First World War by which time there had been a change in government. John Oliver's post-war Liberals were as road-conscious as Richard McBride's pre-war Conservatives had been railway-oriented. On October 11, 1924 contracts for the rebuilding of the road between Yale and Spences Bridge were signed, and the construction of what was to become known as the Cariboo Highway began. Of necessity, the construction of a bridge above Spuzzum had to be undertaken if there was to be a road of any sort put through to the Cariboo.

The new, or second Alexandra Bridge had a 277-foot span, and its deck was 12 feet above high water. The old bridge was unfortunately only 9 feet above high water. The new bridge's deck was 5 feet wider than that of the old bridge. While the second Alexandra Bridge was originally expected to cost $45,133.40, it ended up costing $92,340.64. The new bridge was originally designed to handle vehicles of 34,000 lb. gross vehicle weight. The limit was later increased to 40,000 lb. gross

Originally advertised to open on July 1, 1926 and to cost $45,133, the second Alexandra Bridge opened on May 24, 1927 with a final cost of $92,340. Overly optimistic government projections are nothing new.

vehicle weight when the original heavy plank surface was replaced by a steel grid decking.

The section of highway between Yale and Lytton of which the second Alexandra Bridge was a part, was opened on May 24, 1927. The reopened road linked the coast and the interior of the province that had been without a highway connection for seventeen years between 1910 and 1927.

In 1950 the Fraser Canyon Highway became a component part of the Trans Canada Highway. As part of an on-going up-grading program the second Alexandra Bridge was replaced in 1967 by a much less picturesque but much more functional crossing. The second Alexandra Bridge was not demolished, however, and remains as a memento of the past, and as a monument to the vision and courage of those who first made travel through the Fraser Canyon and on to the Cariboo both possible and practical.

Vancouver

VISITING VIPs

I t's easy to assume that interest in celebrities is some thing relatively new. After all, without *Oscars, Emmys,* or *Golden Globe Awards,* how could there possibly be celebrities! It's all a matter of definition. Although today's VIPs are film people, TV personalities, and highly visible (and highly paid) hockey or basketball stars, there was a time when things were different.

Its true that in the days before the First World War there were movie stars like Charlie Chaplain, song and dance men like George M. Cohen or Eddie Foy, and international personalities like Caruso or Melba, but they all had stiff competition for celebrity status. Although it is difficult to believe, the public was equally interested in both politicians and captains of industry. And it goes without saying that royalty

Sir Wilfrid Laurier is being greeted by Mayor L.D. Taylor in front of the CPR's second station in August 1910. A Quebec lawyer and politician, Laurier led the Liberal party from 1887 until 1919, and was the country's first French-Canadian prime minister. Serving in office from 1896 until 1911, he was very popular, and did much to unify the country. His government was defeated when it advocated reciprocity (free trade) with the United States. Laurier had come to Vancouver to open the city's first Exhibition at Hastings Park on August 16, 1910. The fair attracted 68,000 and was a great success, thanks in no small measure to Laurier's presence.

From September 18 to 21, 1912 Vancouver went all out to entertain a VVIP—a very very important person, that is. He was Canada's Governor General, the Duke of Connaught, who was visiting the city with his wife Louise and their daughter Princess Patricia. The city was decorated as never before (or since) for this visit by a son of Queen Victoria, who was uncle to just about everyone, including George V, William II of Germany, the Czarina of Russia, Queen Marie of Romania, Queen Maud of Norway, Queen Ena of Spain, and a host of lesser royals. On the duchess's left is E.R. Rickets, lessee and manager of the Vancouver Opera House. He was pressed into service by the city whenever any major visit had to be stage managed. The royal visit was unquestionably Rickets' greatest challenge and triumph.

had no trouble winning the celebrity sweepstakes hands down.

Vancouver's newspapers of the period fed the public's interest in the rich and famous. In 1907, for example, they told readers that Timothy Eaton was dying in Toronto; that Mackenzie King the federal minister of labour was in town; and that Queen Ena of Spain (a British princess by birth) had been safely delivered of her firstborn. One of the papers even ran a regular column entitled "In the Royal Courts of Europe" which, incidentally, featured a lot more romantic fiction than fact.

Write-ups were one thing, but people wanted to *see* the celebrities, or at least have pictures of the ones visiting Vancouver. There was a huge demand for photographs of visiting VIPs, a demand which the newspapers—for want of technical sophistication—were unable to meet. It was left to enterprising local photographers to publish postcards of the various worthies who passed through the city.

Their "snap shots" recording the relatively brief visits of celebrities to Vancouver unquestionably helped people feel closer to the news and events that were taking place in their community. It doesn't matter how we feel about the relative importance of long-ago visitors; that they were important to those who bought the photo-cards to send to their friends, or mount in their own postcard albums, is all that matters. And isn't it great that these postcards, tucked away in albums for 80 or 90 years, have survived to say something about those who were considered newsworthy in days long gone.

A WAR MEMORIAL AND MUCH MORE

The Japanese War Memorial which stands in Stanley Park was dedicated on April 9, 1920, and was the first outdoor war memorial erected in the city to commemorate those who had fallen in the Great War of 1914–1918.

A unique monument stands in Stanley Park. Located approximately one third of the way along the path that leads from the Pavilion down to Lumberman's Arch, it is the Japanese War Memorial, which was dedicated on April 9, 1920. It was in fact the first significant outdoor war memorial erected in Vancouver. It not only commemorates the 54 Japanese-Canadians who served in the Canadian armed forces in the First World War, but also lists the Japanese survivors who served overseas. Forcefully, if unintentionally, the monument also commemorates the struggle of a visible yet ignored minority for recognition, acceptance and respect.

Vancouver in the 1890s was a city populated almost entirely by people of British or continental European background. Although the First Nations were present, by and large they were treated as though they were invisible. Certainly they didn't intrude into the lives or thinking of the White population. The same could not be said for that other visible minority, the Asians.

The Japanese War Memorial story really began in 1887 when Gihei Kumo, a carpenter of the village of Mio in Japan's Wakayama prefecture made his way to Vancouver and on to Steveston. There he recognized the opportunities in the fishing industry that were awaiting his fellow villagers. He was not the first Japanese to arrive in British Columbia. In his initial report written in 1889 the Japanese Consul General said that there were about 50 Japanese in B.C., the first ones having arrived in 1877. He knew of 30 that were working in sawmills, ten in homes as domestics or cooks, and one who was operating a general store. These early arrivals had no influence on future events as did Komo, however.

Komo, like the others, had only been able to come to Vancouver because of the great changes that had taken place within the Japanese social structure during his relatively young life. In 1867 what became known as the Meiji period began; it was the time when Japan moved quickly from feudal state to imperial power, adopting as its model the Western industrial economic and social systems. Among other things, compulsory mass education and compulsory three years military service for men between the ages of 21 and 32 were introduced by the Meiji reformers. As in Europe and America, so in Japan rapid industrialization and urban growth had a downside. Life became miserable for many on the lower rungs of the newly built socio-economic ladder.

One of the positive changes that marked the Meiji period was the new freedom given Japanese citizens to study abroad and to look for business or work opportunities overseas. Theoretically those working overseas were required to return to Japan within three years. The ruling was intended to protect Japanese citizens from the kind of exploitation that was so often the lot of emigrant Chinese. Upon arriving in a foreign country from Japan, the immigrants were expected to register at their consulate.

Gihei Kumo returned home to Japan and told of his success on the Fraser. Many were quick to return to the New World with him. Not surprisingly it was not long before emigration companies, having received permission from the Japanese Foreign Office to recruit men in certain prefectures, were sending men across the Pacific to work in the Fraser River fishing industry.

Initially the Japanese came to the Coast intending to stay only for the fishing season, returning home when it was over; however, when the catch wasn't as good as it might have been, they saved money by wintering in Vancouver. Like the Chinese, most of the Japanese lived in their own particular part of town. Japtown, or Little Tokyo as it was sometimes called, developed where these first immigrants wintered along Powell Street—east of Westminster Avenue (now Main Street). In Japtown the newcomer could live life in what was virtually an exclusively Japanese environment. Incidentally, although the name "Japtown" is regarded today as racially demeaning, it was used by Whites of the day without hesitation and was intended to be derisive. Some took rooms in boarding houses off Powell Street, while others lived in what were called "cabins." These "cabins" were in fact single rooms in cheaply-built tenements and were more often than not shared by a number of men. With a wood and coal stove for heating and cooking and little else, these "apartments" were about as basic as accommodation could be. Excessive drinking and gambling in this *issei* community did nothing to improve its image in the eyes of the non-Asian population.

There were something like 2,000 single male Japanese in Vancouver and Steveston by the beginning of the twentieth century, but between 1901 and 1905 few young men were able to leave Japan. First off, they had to serve their time of compulsory military training, and then—as circumstances would have it—they had to fight in the Russo-Japanese War of 1904-05, in which Imperial Russia was defeated by the newly empowered Imperial Japan.

After the war when emigration resumed, many Japanese arranged to bring their families to Canada with them. Once settled, others who were not already married arranged to have their parents send them brides from Japan. As the Japanese continued to arrive on the Lower Mainland, they did so without any encouragement from the local White community. When Japan, an ally of Great Britain, defeated the imperial forces of Czar Nicholas

This building at 1365 Harris Street (now East Georgia) is listed in Henderson's city directories of the period as "Cabins." Although residents who were Asian in origin were rarely identified by name in early directories, it is relatively safe to assume that this tenement was occupied by Japanese.

II, it was a assumed in Japan that the status and prestige of overseas Japanese would be much improved. The Meiji victory had the opposite effect, however, and the Japanese came quickly, if unjustly, to be seen as "the Yellow Peril." In fact, as early as 1895 Japanese settlement in British Columbia was actively discouraged by provincial legislation that extended an earlier clause in the provincial elections act barring Chinese from voting to include Japanese as well. This legislation passed despite the fact that after three years' residency all immigrants, including Asians, could become naturalized Canadians.

Initially a very real incentive for Japanese to seek citizenship was the fact that only British subjects were eligible for fishing licenses. Even though the Japanese immigrants became British subjects, they were denied the provincial franchise and could not vote in federal, municipal, or school board elections. Why? Because the federal and local lists were taken exclusively from the provincial lists. They were also barred from occupations for which a qualification was having one's name on the provincial voters' list. The list of proscribed jobs included those in public works—no matter how menial—forestry including hand logging, and the post office. As well, they could not be called to the bar or serve on a jury, or serve on

any police force. They were of course eligible to pay taxes, and for conscription. In time the franchise became particularly important for the many Japanese who not only wanted to make Canada their permanent home, but also hoped to find fulfilling employment as something other than fishermen, sawmill workers, or running corner stores.

One Japanese did take action, hoping to have the discriminatory law removed from the statute books. In 1900 Tomekichi Homma, as a British subject, challenged the provincial law that denied him the right to have his name on the provincial voters' list and thereby have the same rights as White Canadians. While he won his case in the supreme courts of both British Columbia and Canada, he lost his case when the province appealed to the Privy Council in London. The Privy Council ruled that since the British North America Act gave the provinces exclusive jurisdiction over civil rights, including the right to vote, British Columbia was acting legally when it chose to deny Orientals the franchise.

Although White British Columbians did not distinguish between Japanese and Chinese, the local Japanese and Chinese didn't see themselves as brethren in a common cause in so far as anti-Asian discrimination was concerned. By and large the Japanese felt themselves to be superior to the Chinese.

After the Russo-Japanese War ended in 1906 immigration to Canada once again became a popular option for Japanese wanting to create a better life for themselves. The arrival of shiploads of Asians, including Japanese, occasioned White fear, anger and ultimately irrational action. In August 1906 Vancouver's Liberal

M.P. wired Prime Minister Sir Wilfrid Laurier, telling him that 4,000 Japanese had arrived since January and that 2,000 more were on their way. Matters were made worse in March 1907 when the United States imposed strict restrictions on Japanese immigration from Hawaii and Canada. The new restrictions effectually closed immigration into the United States. Locally the result was that between March 1907 and March 1908 over 7,600 Japanese arrived in Vancouver to take up residence on the Lower Mainland.

On August 12, 1907 Vancouver's newly-formed Asiatic Exclusion League stated that unless they were checked "the Japanese would ultimately control this part of Canada." The fact that *The Vancouver Province* of July 6 had reported that 300 Japanese were on their way to Vancouver to take up construction jobs on the Grand Trunk Pacific railway, that the province's exclusion Bill would probably be vetoed by Ottawa, and that "there is no way of stopping the rush of Orientals" didn't help matters. The same newspaper reported on July 13 that the steamer *Kumeric* was leaving Japan with 1,200 passengers bound for Vancouver, and on July 15 that five Tokyo emigration companies had agreed "to send 6,000 Coolies to the Province" made matters still worse. Finally, the influx of immigrants frustrated in their desire to enter the United States, and who were now intending to make British Columbia their home, was too much. Heightened anti-Asian sentiment that had simmered throughout the summer erupted into violence on September 7, 1907 when men of the Asiatic Exclusion League rampaged through Chinatown, where few Chinese dared appear on the streets to defend either their property or themselves, then moved on to confront the Japanese east of Westminster Avenue. To its surprise, the Japanese were on the streets ready to defend themselves and their property. The Japanese fought back with considerable success, and in consequence their property suffered relatively little damage.

One of the results of the riot of 1907 was that in 1908 a "Gentlemen's Agreement" was effected between Canada and Japan, restricting to 400 the number of Japanese that would be allowed to emigrate to Canada in any given year. Peace reigned, at least until 1914 when Yasuchi Yamazaki—president of the Canadian Japanese Association and editor of the *Tairiku Nippo*—reminded his compatriots of the unique opportunity the war had placed before them. By actively involving themselves in the war effort they could once and for all demonstrate their loyalty and commitment to Canada. Fighting in the Canadian army, he believed, could win them honour and trust, and break down the barriers of discrimination. He believed White Canadians would feel moved to remove the main barrier to Japanese-Canadian political and economic equality which was of course the long denied franchise.

In 1916 at a meeting of the Canadian Japanese Association, those present voted unanimously to form the Canadian Japanese Corps. This vote was in spite of the fact than when the Japanese-Canadians volunteered for service in the Boer War, their offer to fight overseas was turned down. The Japanese community appealed to its own for men and money to fund the new unit. The response was excellent, and a White reserve commander and a White sergeant-major were hired to train the recruits. In spite of the fact that the men were training at

This Philip Timms postcard captioned "Struggling for Admission, Vancouver B.C." may be picturing the arrival of the Kumeric. *The card is dated August 14, 1907, and the message reads, "Picture taken of transport with over 1400 Japs on board getting ready to land. These Japs come from Hawaii. All are very well dressed."*

Mr. K. Shimono, an early Vancouver Japanese-Canadian second-hand dealer, stands proudly in the doorway of his shop with a piece of furniture and a customer. Shimono's store was located at 138 East Cordova. He occupied the ground floor while the First Norwegian Methodist Church was on the floor above.

no cost to the government, Ottawa refused to accept the Japanese contingent into the Canadian army. The corps, which had attracted 227 volunteers, was forced to disband.

It was only later, when the government found itself unable to find men enough to keep the Canadian Expeditionary Force fighting in France up to strength, that Japanese-Canadians were accepted as recruits. Even then they had to make their own way to Medicine Hat, Alberta where they were inducted into the 13th Canadian Mounted Rifles. Of the 196 men who joined the army in hope that their show of patriotism would further the Japanese-Canadian community's struggle for equal rights, 54 died in battle and 93 were wounded. Even though the Japanese had voluntarily served King and country, and had fought and died for their adopted land, the government of British Columbia continued to deny those of Asian background the vote. It was not until April 1, 1931 that the legislature by a margin of one vote franchised those who had service in the Canadian Expeditionary Force. All other Japanese-Canadians had to wait until 1949 to be given the vote.

Not surprisingly the local Japanese community was much faster than the government of British Columbia to recognize the contribution of those who had served in the Great War. At the close of the war local Japanese Canadians gathered at the Empress Theatre at Hastings and Gore to pay tribute to those of

their community who had died in the war. It was not long afterward that members of the Canadian Japanese Association suggested a permanent memorial to those who had fallen should be erected. The idea was taken up enthusiastically and soon the fundraising began; an architect was hired, and a possible site had been selected. The site for the proposed monument was in Stanley Park, and on September 24, 1919 the Parks Board approved the erection of the memorial on the spot chosen by the Japanese-Canadian community. The $15,000 needed to meet the cost of the monument was raised in virtually no time at all.

The architect commissioned to design the monument was James A Benzie. Born in Glasgow in 1881, he was a graduate of the Glasgow School of Art and Anderson's Technical College. Arriving in Vancouver in 1910, he became a partner of A.A. Cox. In 1915 he opened his own architectural office, and from 1923 until his death in 1930 he was in partnership with William Bow. Benzie's reputation was such that he was elected president of the Architectural Institute of British Columbia in 1926.

The monument itself is a marriage of neo-classical and oriental elements. Its 12-foot base is divided into twelve sections which may, in the architect's mind, have been meant to suggest chrysanthemum petals. At any rate, each section bears the name of one of the twelve major battles in which the Japanese-Canadians fought. Capping a 34-foot Haddington Island white sandstone column is an attractive Japanese lantern in white marble. The lantern, with its pagoda roof of terra cotta, is lighted at night. Four bronze plaques are mounted on the column's pedestal; one bears the names of the 54 war dead, another names the surviving veterans, and still another bears the Canadian coat-of-arms, while the fourth plaque displays the Japanese Coat of Arms.

The war memorial was dedicated on April 9, 1920 and was unveiled by Alderman J.J. McRae, acting on behalf of the Acting Mayor Ramsay who was filling in for the absent Mayor Gale! Following prayers and addresses, McRae released the Union Jack that covered the lower part of the monument and accepted the memorial on behalf of the city. Music for the occasion was provided by the Great War Veterans' Association band. Captain R.T. Colquhoun, who had trained the original volunteers at their own expense, proposed a silent toast to those who did not return.

In responding to the toast to "The Returned Citizens," Captain Ian MacKenzie argued strongly that the Japanese veterans should be given the franchise which they deserved. Among other things, MacKenzie said of the Japanese-Canadian troops that "they offered and [were prepared to give] their lives in the fight for liberty and they are entitled to the freedom and enjoyment of the elementary rights of democratic citizenship." The master of ceremonies for the occasion Matamoshin Abe, president of the Canadian Japanese Association, reminded those present that the dedication was taking place on the anniversary of the battle of Vimy Ridge in which "Canadians of Japanese origin" took part.

When the monument was dedicated and unveiled it stood in solitary splendour at the centre of a broad expanse of lawn. It had a presence and appropriate importance. Unfortunately it now seems to be almost crowded off its pedestal by the ever-expanding Aquarium and its whale pools. Why sea creatures have to live in a forest, and why so much open space has to be given over to the Aquarium for its car park is anyone's guess. Perhaps the time has come to move the Japanese War Memorial to a more expansive and tranquil spot. It would be so much more appreciated if it once again could have the visual impact it had in 1920 when it was dedicated, and its lovely lantern lit for the first time. The Japanese monument in Stanley Park is indeed a war memorial and much more. It is a symbol of a people's struggle for recognition, respect and acceptance. As such, it deserves a prominence that its present location no longer affords it.

Built in 1906 as the Methodist's Japanese Mission, this building stood on the southeast corner of Powell and Jackson. During the Second World War and beyond it served as a depot for the United Church of Canada's Welfare Industries. It served as the Japanese Buddhist Church from 1956 until the late 1970s when it was torn down.

DIGGING DEEP

Given that many Canadians believe their federal government to be prehistoric in its ways, there is something appropriately humorous about Ottawa naming one of its ships the *Mastodon*. Fantasizing for a moment, a whole fleet of government vessels named after long extinct creatures can be imagined. We could have ships named the *Woolly Mammoth, Brontosaurus, or Tyrannosaurus Rex.* And since planes have supplanted ships when it comes to people-moving, we could even imagine the prime minister flying off in all directions aboard the *Pterodactyl*! So much for fantasy, what about reality?

On May 13, 1911 the federal government took delivery of a vessel called the *Mastodon.* It was a special if strange-looking craft, designed for a particular job, which was to dredge the Narrows at the entrance to Burrard Inlet. The task kept the *Mastodon* working around the clock, six days a week, from 1912 until 1917. When it had finished the job, the channel—only 900 feet wide when work began—was 1,400 feet wide and markedly safer for marine traffic moving in and out of Vancouver's harbour. Before the First Narrows was widened, ships had to wait on the tide before they could safely enter or leave Burrard Inlet.

It was in 1909 that the federal government ordered the *Mastodon,* which was built in the yards of William Simons & Co., Ltd. at Renfrew in Scotland. The firm specialized in the design and building of dredges. Although the *Mastodon* was designed to do its job extraordinarily well, it was not the kind of ship that would have tempted anyone to run away to sea.

Laid down as hull number 508 in 1910, the steel-hulled vessel was 200.3 feet long with a breadth of 36.6 feet and a 10-foot draft. The *Mastodon* was described as a steam-powered barge-loading centre ladder type bucket dredge, powered by two compound engines. The engines were capable of producing 750 Indicated Horse Power, and moving the ship at eight knots. Incidentally, the rated speed was considered excellent for such an ungainly craft. The engines not only propelled the vessel from place to place, but powered the dredging equipment as well. Once the ship was ready to begin work, the propeller shafts were disconnected and the engines were coupled to the bucket dredge.

Its highly efficient dredging equipment gave the *Mastodon* its unique and rather bizarre appearance. Amidships was a 300-ton ladder, 139 feet long, that could be lowered to a maximum depth of 32 feet. Running over the ladder were 43 buckets travelling on an endless chain. Each bucket could dip and drag three-quarters of a yard of mud and rock, and had a five-ton capacity. The buckets emptied their contents into twin chutes, one on either side of the dredge that fed accompanying false-bottomed scows. When the scow on one side of the *Mastodon* was full, the mud and rock was sent to the other side where an empty scow would be waiting. At full speed the dredge could lift 1,200 tons of mud per hour, however, averaging 1,000 tons per hour it loaded a barge in 25 minutes. Tugs moved the loaded scows to one of two dumping grounds, depending on the way the tide was running. One dumping ground was off Point Atkinson and the other was in what was called the Moodyville Deep. To do its job the *Mastodon* dug away at the shallows, lowering its bucket ladder progressively so that mud and rock could continue to be scooped up until the maximum depth of 32 feet had been reached.

The *Mastodon* arrived in Victoria under the command of Captain William Redick on March 13, 1911. Redick remained in command while the ship completed performance tests. After Ottawa had accepted the new dredge it was registered by the Department of Marine and Fisheries on May 17, 1911. Initially the *Mastodon* was put to work at Port Alberni, and it was not until 1912 that it began the job for which it was designed and built, namely, widening the channel at the entrance to Vancouver's harbour.

Captain Albert William Dawe was the *Mastodon's* master. Born in Newfoundland in 1861, Dawe came to the West Coast in 1891 or 92—the year is uncertain. It seems that he left Newfoundland under something of a cloud. Though details are lacking, it seems that somehow he beached a 100-foot schooner that belonged to his brother, and at the same time became involved in a dispute with some French fisherman (regarding fishing rights) that for a while looked like it would become quite nasty. Whatever the details, Dawe concluded that moving to Vancouver would be a good idea. Once he found accommodation and a job he arranged for his wife Emma and their two children to join him.

Dawe got a succession of jobs on vessels in the coastal trade; he worked on one of the North Vancouver ferries for a time and operated his own tugboat, the *Constance,* for some years. Having passed the federal

The bucket dredge Mastodon *would never have been described as "a thing of beauty and a joy forever," but it was perfect for the job it was designed to do—to widen the First Narrows channel to make it safer for ships entering or leaving Burrard Inlet.*

ministry of Marine and Fisheries examinations, he got his master's ticket for "passenger steamers in the Coasting Trade" on February 14, 1898. In 1911, with twenty years experience on the West Coast, Captain Dawe became master of the *Mastodon*. His chief engineer was a man named McQuarrie. As the story goes, Dawe and McQuarrie were always at each other's throats keeping alive the traditional relationship between the bridge and the engine room. The dredge master who worked with him was William Kirkwood.

The *Mastodon* was accompanied by a tugboat that not only moved the scows or barges around but also repositioned the dredge itself at the job site. To do so was easier than connecting and disconnecting the propellor shafts each time a relatively minor move had to be made.

Captain Albert Dawe was a tallish man who was always careful about his appearance. As might be expected of a Newfoundlander and seaman, Dawe was something of a storyteller, although it wasn't always easy to know where fact ended and fiction began. Justifiably, he was immensely proud of his days as captain of the Mastodon. *He died in Vancouver at 81 in 1945.*

Government-owned tugs that worked with the *Mastodon* were the *Point Ellice* and the *Point Grey*. The *Point Ellice* was built at Wallace's shipyard in North Vancouver in 1911, and was specifically designed to serve as a dredge tender, as was the *Point Grey*, which was built a year later in the same yard. The *Point Grey*, however, was something of a novelty on the West Coast at the time because it was a steel tug. In 1912 alone, at least 25 wooden tugs over 50 feet in length were built in B.C. shipyards. Wood continued to be the construction material of choice for tugs until after the Second World War; it was plentiful, of good quality, and relatively inexpensive.

The job, which went on continuously from 1912 to 1917, was particularly difficult. Dredging the First Narrows wasn't simply a matter of sluicing out sand or gravel; the sea bed at the harbour entrance is comprised of blue clay and boulders. Many of the boulders to be removed were so big that they had to be broken up before they could be scooped into the *Mastodon's* buckets. To get the job done a derrick scow was anchored over the boulders and a steel rod, operating on the same principle as a pile driver, crashed down onto the rocks, smashing them into "bite size" chunks.

Widening and deepening the channel from near the mouth of the Capilano River to a point a mile or so east of where the Lions Gate bridge crosses to the North Shore kept the *Mastodon* working steadily on the north side of the Narrows for over four years. The 33-man crew worked around the clock six days a week. It was only because Albert William Dawe was a devout Christian that there was no work done on Sundays. People living on the North Shore were particularly thankful that Captain Dawe was such a religious man; the clattering, grinding and banging of the dredge's buckets and the rock crusher echoed up and down Burrard Inlet day and night.

Most of the crew were live-aboard. Dawe somehow managed to get the federal government to agree to supply food without charge for the crew. While quarters were of the traditional design, with officers forward and crew aft, the *Mastodon* did have both electric light and hot and cold running water. Interestingly, when the ship arrived on the West Coast it was equipped with a refrigeration plant. Soon after it arrived from Scotland it was removed, the belief being that there was no need for a refrigeration plant in B.C.'s coastal climate! The captain usually went home in the evening. One of the two motor launches that accompanied the *Mastodon* would run him over to the Gore Avenue wharf so he could catch the streetcar home to Kitsilano.

The *Mastodon* moved 100,000 cubic feet of rock and clay each month, meaning that by the time the job

This view from Prospect Point of the CPR's Princess Victoria *leaving the harbour clearly shows just how constricted the First Narrows was before the* Mastodon *began its work in 1912. A shelf of mud and boulders extended from 200 to 600 yards out into the channel from the North Shore high-water line.*

was finished in 1917 over 5 million cubic feet of material had been removed from the First Narrows which had become 1,400 instead of 900 feet wide.

After the dredging of the First Narrows was finished the *Mastodon* was moved on to other jobs. One of the most significant involved dredging the channel at the mouth of the North Arm of the Fraser River off Point Grey. The dredging coupled with the building of a rock jetty meant that the North Arm could be navigated by small freighters and by tugs moving barges and log booms. The improved waterway encouraged sawmills, fish packers, and a variety of small industries to locate along the Fraser's North Arm.

In 1925 the *Mastodon* was retired from full-time service and berthed near the Second Narrows Bridge with only its captain, chief engineer and a skeleton crew aboard. In 1934 the 71-year-old Dawe was retired, the crew paid off, and the vessel laid up. Not that the *Mastodon's* years of service were at an end. On May 13, 1942 the dredge was turned over to the Royal Canadian Navy, which had

Burrard Drydock convert it into a 60,000-barrel capacity oil tanker suitable for use in coastal waters.

With the end of the Second World War, the navy had no further use for the *Mastodon* and turned it over to the War Assets Corporation for disposal. The ship was sold to Imperial Oil on February 7, 1947. On July 4 in the same year Imperial sold it to Peruvian interests, and the *Mastodon* left Canadian waters forever.

Designed and built to widen the entrance to Vancouver's harbour, once that job was successfully completed, whatever else the *Mastodon* did—as either dredge or tanker—can only be viewed as an historical postscript. Certainly that's the way Captain Dawe would have seen things.

Vancouver
A DREAM COMES TRUE

Vancouver's first few years were good years in so far as the city's economy was concerned, but by the late 1890s the bloom was definitely off the rose. The building boom that had followed the fire of 1886 and the coming of the railroad in 1887 was over. There was little demand for real estate and merchants were seeing little growth in their businesses. It was becoming apparent that there was a need for secondary industry if long-term economic growth was to be sustained. And no one saw the situation more clearly than the city's hard-pressed realtors and merchants.

At the time most of the men on city council were either real estate agents or in the wholesale or retail trade. They were go-getters, and it wasn't long before they set out to attract both immigrants and business. The city advertised in Britain in its search for newcomers. One specific aspect of their program involved sending a year's subscription to local newspapers to 350 British working men's clubs.

While the city fathers also targeted industries that they thought might be tempted to relocate to Vancouver, or at least open a West Coast branch, they were wise enough to know that more than advertising was needed to attract them. The ratepayers supported council when it proposed offering both direct grants and indirect subsidies to manufacturers who would locate in Vancouver. The indirect subsidies were to include land grants, property tax exemptions, and attractively low water rates. Not that council was about to start shovelling money off the back of a wagon. Mayor David Oppenheimer summed up local sentiment when he suggested that the city "should proceed with caution but not with timidity."

Reflecting the mayor's perspective, city council was selective regarding firms that were to be considered eligible for special help. Those looking for a handout had to make a carefully detailed business plan available. They also had to offer assurances that they were unlikely to duplicate or compete with companies already established in the city. Even at that, proposals that received the go-ahead didn't always work out. One project that actually qualified for a civic grant called for the erection of a smelter. A London firm had agreed to build one at cost of $75,000 on condition that the city provide a bonus of $25,000. It was felt that a smelter would anchor B.C.'s mining industry to Vancouver, and so the city's ratepayers approved financial support for the B.C. Smelting Company, Limited.

The smelter attempted to begin production on February 14, 1889, but without success. It seems that the equipment installed wasn't able to process local ore with its high sulphur content. The smelter workers laboured on for ten days, hoping to solve the problem, but to no avail. The business had to shut down for good when the firm's London directors refused to invest any more money in the venture. Because no ore was successfully refined, the city did not have to make good on the $25,000 grant.

Another project that didn't work out involved the building of a graving dock for ship repairs. In 1891 the Glasgow firm of Bell and Miller proposed building the facility. Ratepayers approved a civic subsidy of $100,000; however, the project still didn't go ahead. The Scottish firm wanted both provincial and federal financial aid as well as a civic grant. Such generosity just wasn't in the cards.

Far more successful was a very different kind of enterprise, one that not only captured the imagination of the members of city council, but their financial backing as well. Astonishingly the man who talked the city fathers into providing a $30,000 bonus to cover the cost of buying and preparing a waterfront site, a fifteen-year exemption from taxes, and free water was a 24 year old! His name was Benjamin Tingley Rogers and he wanted to build a sugar refinery. Rogers was well-qualified to build and manage a sugar refinery, and had done his homework extremely well before approaching city council.

And just who was this brash young man? He was an American who was born on October 21, 1865 in Philadelphia where his father was president of the Columbia Steam Sugar Refinery. Rogers Senior later established his own refinery in New Orleans. Upon completing a private school education, son Benjamin signed up for a technical program in sugar chemistry at the Standard Refinery in Boston. Upon graduation he went to work for his father. Unfortunately his career in New Orleans was short-lived since his father died when the lad was only eighteen. After his father's death he went to work for Havemeyers and Elder, whose Brooklyn sugar refinery was the largest and most modern in North America. By 1887, when he was still only 21, he was

Even though he was only 24 years old, in 1898 Benjamin Tingley Rogers managed to convince both the directors of the Canadian Pacific Railway and Vancouver's city council that they should support his plan to build a sugar refinery in Vancouver.

appointed assistant to the refinery's demanding chief superintendent.

Opportunity presented itself in 1887 when he was sent to Montreal to oversee the installation of a Havemeyers and Elder filtering system at Redpath's refinery. While he was in Montreal everyone was talking about Western Canada as the land of opportunity, now that the Canadian Pacific Railway was completed to Vancouver. Rogers saw the chance of a lifetime opening up before him. At the time Redpath's was shipping sugar via the CPR all the way across Canada to the West Coast, where sales were protected by a tariff wall that made it impossible for San Francisco refineries to take over the market. For him the equation was obvious: reliable transportation, plus tariff protection, plus British Columbia and the Prairies as an exclusive market, plus

cheap raw sugar from Java and the Philippines equalled an opportunity for success and wealth.

Rogers was clever enough to realize that his knowledge and experience, coupled with his good looks and appealing personality would not be enough to give him credibility in the eyes of Vancouver's city council and voters. Therefore, in early January 1890 he asked Lowell Palmer, a New York City cooper who produced barrels for sugar producers in both New York and Montreal, for a letter of introduction to the CPR's president the American William C. Van Horne. Rogers got his meeting with Van Horne, who invited one of the railway's directors R.B. Angus of the Bank of Montreal to sit in on the meeting. Both men liked what young Rogers had to say and recommended to the CPR's directors that they support his plan for the establishment of a sugar refinery in Vancouver. Not only did the railway offer freight rates from Vancouver to Winnipeg at the same low rate as those enjoyed by refiners shipping sugar to the Prairie market from Montreal, but also offered "especially low rates" for sugar being shipped to Eastern Canada if there were empty freight cars returning east from Vancouver.

With the CPR's support, B.T. Rogers arrived in Vancouver on January 24, 1890, in time for the January 27 meeting of city council at which his proposal for a sugar refinery was to be considered. If it won approval he was prepared to have his refinery operating within nine months. The *Daily World* endorsed his proposal, as did Rogers' local CPR contacts chief of whom was J. M. Browning, the railway's land commissioner. As it happened, Browning was also an alderman and chairman of the city council's finance committee!

In next to no time Browning's committee had turned Rogers' plan into the "Sugar Refinery By-law." Browning had a strong ally in Mayor Oppenheimer when the proposed by-law went before city council on February 4. Before passing it, however, council amended Rogers' proposal in two ways. First, the bonus or grant to the new refinery was reduced from the requested $40,000 to $30,000, and second, it was stated that the sugar refinery would "not at any time employ Chinese labour in and about the said works." Alderman J.T.G. Carrall and the Labour Council's William Flemming led the crusade against the hiring of "Oriental" labour. On March 15, 1890 Vancouver's ratepayers approved the money by-law by 174 to 8, and on March 27 the British Columbia Sugar Refining Company was incorporated.

Rogers moved quickly to get his refinery up and running. As soon as he got back to New York City he ordered the latest and best equipment available for his new refinery. He also hired Walter Wayte, one of Havemeyers and Elder's skilled engineers, to help him get the project off the ground. Wayte not only helped design the five-storey refinery, but did much to get it into production. Rogers, too, had a lot of work ahead of him. He hired twenty men, some of whom had been employed on the construction gang, to work in the refinery. Not one of the crew had ever seen a sugar refinery, let alone worked in one.

Almost immediately Rogers started training the melt house gang, showing them how to do their jobs. He then went on to instruct those who would be responsible for succeeding steps in the operation. The initial melt was put through on January 16, 1891, and B.C.'s first major industry not related to fishing, forestry, or mining had taken its first tentative step along the road to success. At this point it is tempting to say, "and the rest is history." Even though Rogers did go on to become Vancouver's

wealthiest citizen, he didn't simply go from triumph to triumph. There were just too many factors beyond his control for life in the sugar business to be that easy.

Early on Rogers had to contend with unfavourable duties and tariffs, both American and Canadian. On April 1, 1890 the United States reduced its duty on imported raw sugar, thereby making it profitable for American refineries to sell their surplus sugar in B.C. This sugar, produced by Claus Spreckels in San Francisco, was sold to merchants in Victoria who detested the upstart mainland city of Vancouver and all its works and were only too happy to deal with anyone who could give Rogers a run for his money. Rogers quickly dealt with the problem. Since the United States had also reduced its tariff on refined sugar entering the country, B.C. Sugar's products soon appeared on grocery store shelves in Seattle and Tacoma at competitive prices. It didn't take Speckels long to realize that the only way out of a losing situation was to come to terms with the competition. It was soon agreed that each of the two manufacturers would only sell in his own country.

However, things were not going all that well for Rogers in Canada; on December 12, 1890 the federal government introduced a preferential tariff for raw sugar coming into Canada from the West Indies. The lower tariff substantially reduced the manufacturing costs of Montreal refineries, giving them a distinct price advantage on the Prairies. Since Rogers had to get his sugar from Hawaii, Java and the Philippines, he couldn't compete on the Prairies where he needed to sell sugar if his refinery was to become profitable. Rogers lobbied quickly and effectively, using all his eastern connections, to get the situation changed. He no doubt breathed a sigh of relief when the next federal budget dropped the duty on raw sugar, regardless of its country of origin, thereby creating an even playing field for all the country's sugar refineries.

Given that B.C. Sugar lost $13,105 in its first year of operation it may have looked as though the refinery was doing anything but growing and prospering. Rogers' answer to all this was to convince his directors that they should authorize a $10,000 refinery expansion, which would increase the refinery's production capacity from 100 to 300 barrels a day. The increased production would reduce the cost of refined sugar from $1.30 to 40¢ a pound. Even with increased production and reduced prices, however, there were problems.

In 1892 not one but two shiploads of raw sugar were lost when the chartered sailing ships disappeared en route from Java to Vancouver. The loss of 4,426 tons of raw sugar was mitigated only because the insurance payout allowed the refinery to show a marginal profit for the year 1893.

B.C. Sugar's next big headache was created by R.P. Rithet, Victoria's leading merchant who had planned to build his own sugar refinery until he was outwitted by the young upstart from New York. Rithet tried to crush Rogers by flooding the market with cheap sugar from Hong Kong. Fortunately for Rogers, the imported sugar was of poor quality, and the housewives of Victoria preferred both the more convenient smaller packages and the quality of Rogers' so-called fancy sugars to the coarse sugar sold only in large bags by Rithet. It was not long before Rithet was forced to end the sugar war. While there were still to be other problems along the way, by 1899 the most difficult years were over for B.C. Sugar. Thousands of settlers arriving on the Prairies and in the Interior from Britain and Europe meant that between 1897 and 1899 sales doubled to over $1 million annually.

While it might be more convenient not to do so, mention has to be made of B.T. Rogers' attitude toward organized labour, and his reaction to the idea that his employees might unionize. Rogers was an entrepreneur who was very much of his day; he would have happily and without apology have described himself as a capitalist. In 1917 a petition asking for higher wages and shorter hours was circulated to all B.C. Sugar employees by a man known today only as Irish Johnny. Nearly all of the company's 206 male and 36 female employees signed. The petition asked for a basic wage of 40¢ an hour with time and a half for overtime and Sunday work, and for a guarantee of a maximum ten-hour day, and a minimum five-day week. The petition also sought a 20 percent increase for mechanics, watchmen and women. Previously women were paid 20¢ an hour and received a daily hot lunch without charge.

The company responded on April 19, offering a 10 percent increase in pay for all men paid by the hour.

The women were not offered an increase, and no mention was made regarding hours of work. On Sunday, April 22 about 160 of the refinery workers walked off the job and marched up to the Vancouver Labour Temple at Dunsmuir and Homer where they decided to form a union. As far as Rogers and men like him were concerned, it was out of unions that revolutions came! As was common practice at the time, once the strike was on Rogers hired detectives not only to be responsible for refinery security but to infiltrate the would-be union and report on the strikers. Rogers was adamant, telling the *Vancouver Daily Province* that "there will be no conference between myself and any union.... I will receive a deputation of the men as individuals any time, but I will not recognize any union or union official." Typical of the day, he later said, "The men have the right to work or quit work as they see fit, and I insist on my right to employ or discharge who I see fit." Through all this the refinery continued to operate, staffed by those workers who chose not to go on strike and by newly recruited workers. Rogers let it be known that these new employees would be keeping their jobs when the strike ended, leaving only a limited number of jobs open to those who were on strike. As it happened, many of the strikers had already found employment elsewhere.

On July 20 a committee of strikers and longshoremen, whose union had actively supported the striking sugar workers, met with the local federal Fair Wages Officer J.D. McNiven to ask him to talk with Rogers without letting him know that they had spoken with him. At roughly the same time, McNiven was able to report to Ottawa that while Rogers remained unalterably opposed to dealing with a union, he was much more inclined to be conciliatory than he had been when he spoke with him on earlier occasions.

This postcard was sent to Vancouver voters on June 18, 1898. The voters approved the by-law, but the smelter failed to process local ore successfully and closed after only ten days. Luckily the city had "a good safe contract" and didn't have to pay out the agreed upon $25,000 subsidy. A similar card would have been sent out to ratepayers when it came time to vote on the sugar refinery by-law.

SATURDAY, June 18th, 1898.

VOTE TO-DAY FOR SMELTER BY-LAW

Vancouver needs a Smelter to establish it as the business centre of the Pacific Coast—to increase present business and to create more. The city has a good safe contract carefully amended and passed by the City Council. It is fully worthy of your attention and support to-day.

Located between the CPR tracks and the waterfront, the B.C. Sugar Refinery—facing onto Powell Street west of Clarke Drive—doesn't look vastly different today than it did in this pre-First World War picture taken by G.A. Barrowclough.

Again, Rogers agreed to reinstate as many of his striking workers as there were jobs available, but he was not about to dismiss those who had chosen to sign up for work at the refinery during the strike to make room for returning strikers. Since Rogers had already agreed to pay the men the 20 percent increase they had asked for in April and to regularize the working day to ten hours, McNiven advised the workers to accept the offer since, in his opinion, they had already lost the strike. On Sunday, July 22 the sugar workers voted to return to work.

Although Rogers would never had been described as an easy man to work for—he was

determined, always in a hurry, strong-willed and short-tempered—he nevertheless was probably a more enlightened employer than many of his contemporaries. The high percentage of employees who spent virtually their whole working lives at the refinery, coupled with the fact that not one full-time employee lost his or her job during the Depression perhaps better reflects the spirit of the place than does the strike of 1917.

B.T. Rogers worked hard and enthusiastically, but he was not an all work and no play kind of fellow. He very much enjoyed his family and the good life. Rogers had married Bella Angus in 1892, and the couple had seven children. He lived in the city's finest home, owned an impressive yacht, and loved "automobiling." The family's magnificent Davie Street home, *Gabriola*, was designed by Samuel McClure, the architect of choice for those building homes that were intended to make a

He had the distinction of being responsible for Vancouver's first traffic accident involving an automobile and a pedestrian. In 1904, driving his electric car, Rogers ran over William Roedde's leg. The boy, who was later to become owner of a prominent pioneer printing firm, had been playing in the sand at the curb on Barclay near Nicola when the accident happened. Rogers quickly drove the frightened but uninjured boy home. Roedde was so excited about his first ride in an automobile that by the time he got home, any thought of the accident had all but passed from his mind.

Beginning in March 1905 Rogers bought the first of a succession of Pierce Arrows, an expensive American luxury car. In 1911 he bought a 48-horsepower Pierce Arrow costing $8,000. The car came with two bodies: one enclosed for winter, and one open for summer. Twice a year men would be sent from the refinery to *Gabriola* to help the chauffeur make the necessary change-over.

It was just as well that Rogers enjoyed the fruits of his labour day by day, rather than waiting until his old age to do so, since he died suddenly of a cerebral haemorrhage on June 14, 1918 when he was still only 52 years old.

During his years at the helm he had managed the company well. He was able to write in February 1918, just four months before his death, that "since I started in business here … with a paid up capital of $250,000 the [B.C. Sugar Refinery] has earned $10,566,909 of which $5,289,375 has been paid out in dividends...there are few manufacturing enterprises in Canada which can equal that record …. Certainly there are none in British Columbia."

When the company celebrated its centennial in 1990 it was still controlled and managed by descendants of B.T. Rogers. And even though members of his family in each generation had exercised their stewardship responsibly and well, as the twentieth century drew to a close the days of B.C. Sugar as a family firm ended. Like so many other family-controlled businesses, it was to become part of a large international conglomerate. On June 1, 1995 B.C. Sugar ceased to exist, becoming instead a subsidiary known as Rogers Sugar Limited. Doubtless those who are concerned about things historical will be glad that the company isn't known as SugCoCan, or some other equally unattractive acronym, but bears the name of its imaginative and enterprising founder.

statement. And at a cost of $25,000, believed at the time to be twice the price of any other Vancouver home, *Gabriola* certainly made an impressive statement when it was completed in 1901.

The 160-foot *Aquilo,* which Rogers bought in 1912, was the largest private yacht in British Columbia waters. He became commodore of the Royal Vancouver Yacht Club in 1912, and remained in office until 1918. He played the part well, and his wife when speaking to others often referred in all seriousness to her husband as "the Commodore." When the Great War broke out in 1914, Rogers almost immediately made the *Aquilo* available to the government, which used it for a time as a coastal patrol vessel.

B.T. Rogers had a passion for "automobiling" that rivalled that of Mr. Toad in *The Wind and the Willows.* And his driving was just about as dangerous.

Vancouver's Pony Express employees are pictured outside the office with two of the company's horses and rigs. On what looks to be a hot summer day, neither the "ponies" nor the men appear ready to go anywhere in much of a hurry.

Vancouver

VANCOUVER'S OWN PONY EXPRESS

Vancouver's population went from 27,000 in 1901 to 100,000 in 1911. This four-fold increase in a decade fulfilled the hope expressed in the 1905 slogan of the local Hundred Thousand Club which proclaimed: "In nineteen hundred and ten Vancouver will have 100,000 men." The phenomenal growth meant, amongst other things, that were was plenty of business for the city's 42 transfer, express, and moving companies.

Doubtless before the First World War most of Vancouver's cartage firms consisted of no more than one or two men with a team and wagon hauling goods for the majority of city dwellers who owned neither horse nor rig. There were, as well, a few large cartage companies competing for business. As it happened, two firms each claimed to be the city's biggest. In 1912 Mainland Transfer was advertising itself as "easily the largest and best equipped transfer company in Western Canada [employing] seventy men [with] fifty-eight teams in constant use," while Vancouver Transfer was proclaiming itself to be "the largest and most up-to-date carriage and baggage transfer company west of Winnipeg … [with] forty-eight teams … and fifty men." Both cartage companies doubtless got somewhat carried away with their claims!

Somewhere in between the big boys and the little guys were firms that employed perhaps six to twelve men and offered a specialized service. One such business was owned by Robert Thorburn whose "furniture moving stable" was located at 646 Hornby Street, while another was the Pony Express Company at 500 West Cordova.

Thorburn advertised that he could provide "the most perfect equipment for handling furniture and pianos of any mover in the Canadian west." He took great pride not only in his padded moving vans but also in his horses, having won the P. Burns and Company cup for his six-horse team, the Stanley cup for his four-horse team, and the Stanley Furniture Company' cup for his three-horse team at the 1911 Horse Show. It is interesting that there was a cup awarded for the best three-horse team, given that the *troika* was never particularly popular in North America. Thorburn not only provided general storage space, but also "private rooms for those who desire." Although Queen Victoria had departed this world in 1901, a decade later many Vancouverites were still Victorians at heart, and would not have wanted their prized possessions mingling in general storage with the wrong kind of furniture!

Meeting a completely different need was the Pony Express Company, which stood on the southwest corner of Cordova and Richards. (The site is now occupied by the Spencer Building—a part of Simon Fraser University's downtown campus.) James Niven was the president, and Arthur Jervis the manager of the company that specialized in moving express and baggage. Given the firm's name, one wonders if its principals were American. The company's close proximity to the CPR train station doubtless worked to its advantage. Even at that, competition must have been keen, since over half the cartage firms listed in the 1912 city directory were located within four blocks of the station. Nevertheless, in the years between the turn of the century and the First World War there was plenty of business for everyone.

Newcomers were arriving in the city daily from overseas and the east, and most of them stayed temporarily with relatives or rented rooms in hotels or boarding houses while they found work and a permanent place to live. Although they would have been able to carry their valises on the streetcar to their temporary homes, the newcomers' steamer trunks were another matter. They had either to be delivered by wagon, or put into storage for at least a short space of time. These trunks were nearly as precious as life itself, since more often than not they contained all the worldly goods settlers were able to bring with them. Excepting hand luggage, third-class steamship passengers were only allowed ten cubic feet of baggage. Luggage in excess of the free allowance was charged at the rate of one shilling per cubic foot. Trunks were produced by manufacturers in the right size to meet the steamship companies' free allowance.

In 1912 Pony Express, which also did business as the Dominion Warehouse and Cartage Company, was offering express and baggage wagons "for hire, day or night" and "baggage transferred to all parts of the city." The firm also stored trunks at 25 cents a month. As well, the Pony Express Company advertised a "Hasty Messenger Service—Phone 743." One assumes that the "hasty messenger" travelled by bicycle.

Vancouver's future looked bright in 1912, but the boom times that literally brought a daily flood of newcomers to the city were soon to end. The world depression of 1913, and the war that began in 1914 reduced immigration to a mere trickle. Many of the able-bodied expressmen, baggage handlers, draymen and teamsters joined up and were soon overseas. When they returned home at the end of the war things were very different. Along with automobiles, motor trucks and vans were taking over the city's streets. The day when a man could make a living in Vancouver if he owned a horse and wagon was fast coming to an end.

Looking at the perfectly matched trio of horses, and the picture of galloping steads on the side of his moving van, it is apparent that Robert Thorburn took great pride in his animals. His horses were consistent winners in Vancouver's annual horse shows.

CENTRAL PARK

Central Park, as its name implies, is almost exactly halfway between Vancouver and New Westminster. Originally twice its present size, the park was set apart in 1860 as a military reserve by the Royal Engineers' Colonel Moody. In the same year a military road was put through, running along the northern edge of this Government Reserve to connect New Westminster with another military reserve on English Bay—an ice-free saltwater harbour. The military reserve on English Bay is now known as Stanley Park. The road was part of a defence system put in place to protect the colonial capital from American attack. People at the New Westminster end of the road called it the False Creek Trail, while those living in Granville (Vancouver didn't come into being until 1886) called it Westminster Road. Westminster Road was the name that stuck until the route was renamed Kingsway in 1911, in honour of the coronation of King George V.

In the 1880s both Vancouver and New Westminster began to see the Government Reserve as land that should be set apart for park and recreational use, and on January 14, 1891 the Lieutenant Governor proclaimed the military reserve to be a public recreation ground for the enjoyment of the citizens of Vancouver and New Westminster.

The development of both the park and the community on its north and west boundaries was hastened by the inauguration of Canada's first electric interurban service in October 6,1891. The Westminster and Vancouver Tramway Company's tracks crossed what is now Kingsway just east of Boundary Road as they came from Vancouver. They then cut diagonally southeastward through the new yet still unnamed park and on to New Westminster. The route was later to become the B.C. Electric's Central Park Line. A station was built and the name Central Park was chosen for the tram stop by Vancouver's Mayor Oppenheimer in honour of his wife who was a native New Yorker. The name given to the tram stop almost immediately became the name of the park.

With the coming of interurban service and the designation of the Government Reserve as parkland, Central Park became one of Burnaby's fastest growing communities. The park itself was soon being put to use by all sorts of people. The B.C. Battalion of Garrison Artillery set up a 200-foot rifle range in the park. It was completed in 1895, and was used for training by local militia units until it closed in 1904. The Central Park Farmers' Institute leased a 17-acre triangle of land bounded by present day Kingsway, Patterson, and the Skytrain right-of-way, which was originally the old interurban right-of-way. The Institute built a first-rate Agricultural Hall on the property. It was opened in time for the organization's Fall Fair in September 1901.

In 1899–1900 the B.C. Electric provided financial help so that a small octagonal bandstand could be erected in the park. Picnic grounds were laid out and playing fields were developed around it. In 1908 the provincial government passed an Act which provided for the formation of a parks board to "administer the Central Park Provincial Park." It was not until 1921 that Burnaby acquired a 99-year lease on the park that allowed the municipality to develop the acreage as it saw fit.

It was in 1911 that the province allowed Burnaby to erect a 90-foot-high steel water tank and a pumphouse in the park as part of a $350,000 waterworks improvement program. The pumphouse was torn down in 1936, and the huge unsightly steel water tower was sold and dismantled in 1948.

In 1910 the community that developed to the north and west of Central Park had a population of about 2,000. This figure included those living in Collingwood East and Collingwood West in what was then the municipality of South Vancouver.

Henderson's B.C. Gazette and Directory provides a profile of the community as it was in 1910. While there were still many who made a living off the land—including twenty farmers, eight ranchers, six gardeners, one poultry man, one miller, and one land steward—most of the district's men worked in blue collar jobs. Listed were twenty carpenters, seventeen labourers, nine painters, five teamsters, five stonecutters and quarrymen, three mill hands, a plumber, a blacksmith, a tinsmith, a patternmaker and an electrician.

In 1910 there were also five realtors and ten men in trade in Central Park. Their number included grocers, general merchants, a florist, a baker, and a jeweller. White collar workers included the postmaster, the school teacher, three clerks, a male stenographer, two brokers,

The Central Park Rifle Range ran east and west, with the eight targets at the end of the 200-yard range. The rifle range was used every Saturday afternoon from April through October. The facility closed for good on November 12, 1904, replaced by the Richmond Rifle Range, which opened on Thanksgiving Day in the same year. Major Matthews, Vancouver's long-time archivist, was the officer in charge at both the closing of the old rifle range and at the opening of the new one.

a dentist, and rounding out the list with class were two "gentlemen." Interestingly, the community was without a doctor. While all these people lived in Central Park it cannot be said for certain that they were all employed in Central Park; there is a possibility that some of them, other than those in agriculture, were employed in nearby Collingwood or New Westminster or Vancouver.

The community also had three resident clergy. One, the Methodist, held services in the Agricultural Hall, while the Presbyterian and the Anglican both had church buildings where their congregations could meet for services and fellowship. As it happened, the Anglican Church of St. John the Divine was the first church to be established in Burnaby.

After meeting in homes for a time, the congregation built its first building in 1899 on land bought from Ed Mahon. The property, on what is now Kingsway, cost the congregation $100. Although unfinished, the new church was used by the congregation until it was destroyed by fire in 1904. In 1905 the parish of St. John the Divine built a new church. It was designed by Joseph Bowman, a Vancouver architect who was a member of the congregation. The simple building was well-proportioned and featured an attractive tower and spire. While the building has been remodelled and enlarged over the years, this bell tower remains unaltered.

Like so many older buildings that have been "improved" over the years, St. John's is now clad in a

1950s coat of pinkish-brown stucco. As the twenty-first century begins the future of St. John's, Central Park is uncertain. Its members have joined with a neighbouring Anglican parish to form one larger congregation, and the old building has become redundant. As Burnaby's oldest surviving church building, however, there will be many people suggesting ways to make appropriate use of this historic Central Park landmark.

Central Park's Anglican Church of St. John the Divine looks very much the country church in this photo, circa 1910. To the left of the church is the rectory and to the right is Central Park Real Estate's office and Philip Oben's general store. Regarding Westminster Road, the Vancouver Annual *of the period points out that "Burnaby has been the pioneer district ... to adopt the use of crude oil in perfecting the surfaces of its magnificent motor highways."*

New Westminster

MAY DAY

Annie Tidy, the newly crowned May Queen, and her Royal Suite, are at the centre of this 1907 picture taken at Queens Park. To the left of Queen Annie and her party is J.J. Cambridge who served as Master of Ceremonies on alternating years with J.J. Johnston from the 1889s to the 1930s. On either side of the platform, wearing pill box hats, are the Boys' Brigade lads.

Although the origins of May Day are lost in the distant past, there is no doubt that it was essentially a pagan celebration of the coming of summer. Even though the festival was of special significance to post-pubescent youth and maidens, and knowing full well what that implied, the medieval church—albeit with misgivings—allowed the celebration to continue. Central to the festival was "bringing in the may," which meant that the young people spent much of the night and early morning in the woods and meadows looking for blossoms to bring home triumphantly at dawn. While "may" could be any kind of tree in bloom, in England it generally meant hawthorn and in Scotland rowan, which is more commonly known in North America as mountain ash. At the same time, in some places the maypole would also be brought home with great rejoicing and revelry. It was not uncommon, however, for towns and villages to keep their maypoles from year to year since much time and attention had often been given to their decoration.

During the Middle Ages the maypole was the focal point of the May Day celebrations, in the shadow of which morris dancing, sports and simple plays took place. And needless to say there was maypole dancing. Even though the maypole and not the May Queen's crowning—was central to the whole celebration, the day was still presided over by the May Queen or May Lady. Always an adult, the May Queen or May Lady was in some places a man in woman's clothing!

The English and Scottish Puritans soon put a stop to all the fun—innocent or otherwise. As one Puritan Philip Stubbs put it, for the revellers the "chiefest jewell … is the May-pole (this stinking Idol rather) … covered all over with flouers and herbs bound about with strings … and they fall then to dance aboutt it like as the heathen people did at the dedication of Idols." And still speaking of the youth and maidens, Stubbs went on to say that "of the fortie, three score, or a hundred maides going to the woods overnight, there have scaresly the third part of

New Westminster's May Queens have always travelled in style. In 1909 Queen Helen Hale and her attendants paraded through the streets in a lavishly decorated carriage that may have been either a sociable or a barouche.

The rube band pictured in front of the courthouse took part in New Westminster's 1908 May Day program. Over the years bands of all kinds have quite naturally had an important place in the parades that are an integral part of the May Day celebrations.

them returned home again undefiled." Finally in 1614, parliament banned May Day celebrations altogether as a "heathenish vanity [full of] superstition and wickedness." At the restoration of King Charles II to the throne on May 29, 1660, a great number of maypoles were quickly erected as evidence of loyalty to the crown.

Toward the end of the eighteenth century interest in May Day had begun to decline, and by the beginning of the reign of Queen Victoria in 1837 British youth and maidens had found other and more interesting ways to amuse themselves. All was not lost, however, for by the last quarter of the nineteenth century a nostalgic longing for the "Old Englishe" May Day moved the sentimental hearts of middle class Victorians to revive the festival. It was, as would be expected of the Victorians, purged of its "grosser elements."

Maypoles reappeared, and around them danced not love-stuck youths and longing maidens but children who danced "innocent Measures" taught by the members of the local "Guilds of Merrie England." The proceedings now took place under the watchful eyes of squires, parsons, and school teachers. May Day in their guiding hands became "a pretty affair for children." With the village beauty no longer as the Queen of the May but instead a tinsel-crowned schoolgirl, thousands of May Day celebrations marked the first of May throughout Britain.

It was this laundered Victorian version of May Day that was brought across the waters to British Columbia by British Immigrants in the later part of the nineteenth century. May Day celebrations were once held in a number of communities in the Lower Mainland, and in what where then called Church of England (now Anglican) parishes; however, the only one to survive is that of New Westminster, which incidentally was the first held on the Mainland. The year was 1870. Since it was a year in which May Day fell on a Sunday the May Day celebrations had to be scheduled for Monday, May 2. Puritanism died a very slow death, and "worldly entertainments" on the Sabbath were still very much frowned upon in Victorian New Westminster. As it happened Mother Nature took a hand in things, and rain on May 2 meant that the city's very first May Day had to be postponed until Saturday, the May 7.

New Westminster's first May Queen Nellie McColl was crowned on the Cricket Ground, later the site of the provincial asylum, and still later of Woodlands School. Over the years the venue for the city's May Day festivities has varied. The lawn in front of old Government House (later the site of the B.C. Penitentiary), Moody Park, Mercer Stadium, and Queens Park have all been used as sites for May Day events.

Each year's May Day activities have included a procession or parade through the streets, bands and music, maypole dancing, and the crowning of the year's May Queen. The fact that May Day is a school holiday makes it a day well worth celebrating in the eyes of the city's children. In the official program for the 125th anniversary year, May Day is described as "an important part of the heritage and cultural traditions of New Westminster. It highlights [a] rich past and provides a legacy to future generations." And in the same vein the School Board chairman wrote that "heritage is more than just buildings, it is events like May Day that children and the community have enjoyed for 125 years. Its continuing popularity relates to the fact that New Westminster's May Day has been transformed over the years from something of a Merrie England that never was, to something that successfully brings together traditional and contemporary elements in a unique mix that gives visible expression to the strong sense of community that is to be found in the Royal City."

This 1915 photo of maypole dancing was taken at Queens Park, the most frequently used site for May Day. It appears as though various schools have entered maypole "teams." Rather surprisingly, the dancers on the right-hand side of the picture would seem to be Boy Scouts.

HOMEWARD BOUND

Westerners have always been intrigued by what they perceive to be the mysterious East. Nowhere was the fascination with things eastern more apparent in the years before the Great War than in Vancouver. Perhaps the greatest mysteries associated with Chinatown were those associated with the Chinese cult of the dead.

Before anything can be said about Chinese burials in Vancouver, something has to be known about the Chinese who came to British Columbia between 1858—the year when they first arrived in the province—and July 1, 1923, when the passage of the Chinese Immigration Act ended Chinese immigration for nearly a quarter of a century. They were Cantonese-speaking and came from eight rural counties in the Pearl River delta in the southern province of Guangzhou (Kwangtung).

While some parts of the exclusionist Act were repealed by Order in Council in 1947, it continued to restrict Chinese immigration to wives of Canadian citizens and their children under eighteen years of age. It was not until 1956 that the Act in its entirety was removed from the statute books. By then, of course, mainland China was under Communist control and virtually all emigration had been halted by the new Chinese government.

Those Chinese who arrived from the region then known to Westerners as Canton Province were men who came for the most part to work in the gold fields or in the building of the Canadian Pacific Railway. While some were merchants and entrepreneurs, most were landless farmhands or sharecroppers from rural areas, or peddlers, and labourers from the city of Canton itself. Regardless of their differing backgrounds, the majority of these immigrants shared Taoist beliefs and values. This is not to say that they weren't also Buddhist and Confucian as occasion demanded.

For the Chinese religion has always been syncretic, that is, able to reconcile the diverse (even opposite) beliefs and practices of Buddhism, Confucianism, and Taoism. During the Ming dynasty (1369-1644) there were actually a number of official attempts to harmonize China's three great religions, saying that in reality they are one. Although the government didn't succeed in its attempts, the Chinese people in their own minds have "harmonized" their

beliefs for centuries. They are not like Christians, Jews or Muslims who see the claims of different religions as mutually exclusive. In popular practice the three great religions of China are inextricably intertwined, but each does have its own tenets.

Buddhism calls the individual to awaken from darkness and error in order to live in freedom from selfishness, greed and ignorance. There is the Noble Eight-fold Path, which when followed perfectly leads the believer to *nirvana*: to escape from the wheel of successive reincarnations into absorption with the godhead where the individual ceases to exist as an identifiable being who is capable of knowing and being known.

The second great religion of China reflects the thinking of the 5th B.C. philosopher Confucius. Confucianism was the most important single force in Chinese daily life until the advent of Communism. While many consider Confucianism to be a religion, it teaches nothing about the worship of a God or gods, or about an afterlife. It is essentially a guide to morality and good government. The good people are those who are truly reverent and sincerely respect their fathers and rulers. Individual are to think for themselves, guided by rules of conduct. Confucianism suggests that the enduring state will be built on the merits of its rulers' advisers. Perhaps not surprisingly, by the 1700s candidates for the civil service had to pass examinations based on the teachings of Confucius. Confucianism emphasises above all else the ethical meaning of human relationships, believing that it is in the perfecting of humanity in the world that the secular will become sacred.

And then there is Taoism in which everything is seen as relative. There are no absolute purpose or values in Taoist thought; purpose and values only exist in relation to something else. Judging what is right or wrong depends on one's perception, situation, and needs. It could be said that Taoism invented situational ethics! Taoism also calls for non-action or non-striving, that is, respect for the natural course of events. This call, in turn, precludes the expending of effort to fight for or against whatever will be. The whole belief system is predicated on belief in a balance of complementing energies (yin-yang). For guidance in discerning appropriate or propitious future actions, the *I Ching* is the most important written guide to important clues.

Weather permitting, the seven days of public mourning required by Taoist tradition would be outdoors. In this 1910 photo, family mourners dressed in hemp-cloth are on the left. The man wears a headband, and the two women are wearing cowl-like headdresses. Food offerings, wine and joss sticks are in the right foreground. Chinese seem to be outnumbered by brazenly curious White onlookers.

In the years before the First World War Chinese burial rites in Vancouver, as in South China, reflected Taoist rather than Buddhist or Confucian beliefs, if for no other reason than Taoism has the most to say about life after death and about gods and ancestors. Taoists worship a full pantheon of deities, some of which are ancestors, and others the spirits of famous people. In popular practice each trade or profession has a patron deity. To communicate with the dead there is belief in astrology, fortune telling, and witchcraft.

Ancestor worship became a fact of life in the Chou dynasty (1122-325 BC). It was then that it was first officially decreed that filial piety demanded honour and respect for parents and elders while they were alive, and that they should continue to be reverenced after death. S.A. Nigosian has summed up the relationship between the living and the dead by saying that, "Through

their close association with the Supreme Ruler in Heaven [ancestors] have power to intercede on behalf of living descendants …. Their relationship with living descendants is one of mutual dependence: they offer protection in exchange for filial sacrifices."

The eldest male heir is obliged to perform established memorial rites and sacrifices. According to ancient tradition those who abandon or betray the ancestral rites are subject to two fates: they are doomed to suffer the vengeance of ancestral spirits, and in death are to wander as unlucky hungry ghosts with no one to perform memorial rites and sacrifices for them.

It has been said that death ceremonies in most religions are the ones least likely to change with the passage of time. Regardless of current practice in Vancouver, and taking into account the fact that the members of Vancouver's pre-1914 Chinese community were living in a foreign land, funeral rites would have been as similar as they could be to those followed in their native land by their ancestors.

So what was a Chinese funeral in Vancouver like in 1905 or 1910? Writing of ancestor worship, the theologian Chua Wee Hian says, "the soul has to be assisted as it journeys to heaven [and, therefore] rituals are meticulously carried out … the family chants prayers, offers sacrifices of food and burns [imitation] paper mone … in some cases even paper cars, planes and servants [are burned] so there will be no lack of provisions [along the way to heaven]. Evil spirits who oppose the deceased are propitiated by appropriate sacrifices and by loud wailing."

When death occurred in a Chinese home in the early years of the 20th century, the family would follow ancient custom as closely as practicality would allow. Because seven is a most auspicious number in Taoist belief, the body remained at home for seven days of private family mourning. While the corpse was usually placed in a closed coffin, it was sometimes simply laid out and covered. If available, a photograph of the deceased was placed on or near the coffin.

Seven days of public mourning, when friends came to pay their respects, followed the seven days of private mourning. Weather permitting, the closed coffin was outdoors where other family members would join the eldest son in displays of mourning. Since the colour for mourning is white, family members wore clothes made of unbleached linen or hemp cloth. Wine, rice, incense, cooked chicken or pork, and candles painted with texts were placed near the casket. The food was a symbolic nourishing of the deceased spirit as it journeyed heavenward. Some of the food was consumed by mourners, suggesting a oneness with the departed.

Ideally, there would have been a third seven-day period of mourning when the body was taken to a Taoist temple where specific prayers would have been offered and rituals observed. Since there were no temples in Vancouver at the time, temporary burial would have taken place immediately after public mourning had ended.

There is much conjecture regarding burials in early Vancouver, whether they be those of Chinese or non-Chinese ancestry. It seems that burials initially took place in what was to become Stanley Park, above the shoreline between the site of the Nine O'clock gun and Brockton Point. It is estimated that there were around twenty burials in the park, of which a few were Chinese. Given that segregation was the order of the day, it has been suggested that Chinese burials took place at a different site, one that was closer to the Aboriginal burial ground near what is now Lumberman's Arch. What about Deadman's Island, it may be asked? While there are a

This 1893 Chinese funeral procession is heading east on Westminister Avenue (now Main Street). It is crossing Princess Street (now East Pender) on its way to Mountain View Cemetery. Given the banners, musicians, and the platoon dressed in white, it was probably the funeral of a Chinese Freemason (the Chi Kong Tong). There are many White spectators, but it is only the uniformed bobby who seems to be showing any appropriate respect as the cortege passes by.

number of anecdotal tales told by descendants of "those who were there," there is no documented proof that non-Aboriginal burials ever took place on the island which is virtually solid rock.

Wherever the Chinese were buried was only of limited importance since in time their remains were dug up, and their bones cleaned of any remaining flesh, so they could be sent back to China for permanent burial. In 1893 the Park Ranger complained about the Chinese lighting fires in the park. Why they lit fires is uncertain; they could have been preparing food offerings for the departed or they could have been cleaning bones in preparation for re-burial in China. In September 1886 the provincial government granted twenty acres on North Arm Road (now Fraser Street) to the city as a cemetery site, and in 1890 the Chinese community—acting through a lawyer—asked that it be given a piece of land in the new city-owned cemetery.

The graveyard, which was named Mountain View Cemetery by the city's Health Committee on June 18, 1903, was racially segregated with Chinese, Japanese, and Jews each having their own section. They had to arrange for their own caretakers and were billed for grass cutting. In 1902 the Chinese erected a substantial and rather forbidding cut stone ceremonial altar in their one-acre plot. It remained in use until the Chinese Benevolent Association replaced it with a much more colourful and attractively sheltered altar in 1973.

Regardless of where Chinese burials took place in the days before the First World War, they were always accompanied by elaborate ceremony. Many years after the event Frank Scott, whose family moved to Vancouver in 1887, recalled a Chinese funeral procession making its way down Georgia Street to Stanley Park in 1888. Even though he was only about ten years old at the time he remembered it clearly, saying "the coffin was on a spring wagon, drawn by horses and followed by another spring wagon with a whole roast pig … and many roast ducks, and Chinese delicacies, and [there were] numerous Chinese in Chinese costumes and pigtails. Following the improvized hearse was a Chinese standing on the back end of the rear wagon; he was distributing small pieces of thin paper with … the name of the dead person on it to those who followed."

The ceremony was even more elaborate when a prominent member of the Chinese Freemasons died. Although the organization originally known as the *Chi Kung Tong* is a traditional secret fraternal order, it has no connection whatsoever with the Masonic Order. Locally its members supported Dr. Sun Yat-sen, who was working to overthrow the Manchu monarchy with a view to establishing a republic based on nationalism, democracy and social well-being.

Reporting on the funeral of a Chinese Mason Chew Yuh on May 21, 1907, *The Province* wrote, "It is not often that the streets of Chinatown are disturbed by the weird notes of Chinese funeral dirges, and still less frequently are such occasions the obsequies of a celestial Mason …. The funeral rites … afforded interest if not information for a multitude of spectators. The clashing of cymbals and beating of tom-toms, the shrill notes of the Chinese clarinet, and the rattle of the snare drum bones attracted a large concourse of people …. [In front of] the house of the late Mr. Chew, was the usual display of offerings to the gods and the votive tributes which take the place in European funerals of floral offerings—the roast carcasses of two fattened porkers and an indescribable variety of confections which in their richness far exceed what it is often the privilege of a western spectator to behold …. At last … the casket with its rich trapping was carried into the street. Here it was deposited upon a catafalque and the ceremonies resumed …. The ceremonies completed, the casket was carried to the hearse a block away where the procession formed to follow the body to its temporary resting place, for it will not remain in Canada in sacred soil, but will be stripped of its flesh and carried back to the land of flowers and sunshine …. The marshalled guards of honor (sic), led by the horseman who scatters inscribed paper clippings along the way, the continued beating of the drums, the long procession of hired mourners and afterward empty wagons to give eclat and importance to the affair. So passes Mr. Chew, and Chinatown has one less of the bosses, whose authority was final among so many of his fellows, and whose far away relatives have already been informed by cable of his departure from this earthly life."

The article refers to the body being taken to its temporary resting place. When the Chinese exhumed bones for shipment to China, Mountain View on behalf of the city charged a fee even though no work was done by city employees. In 1910 the Chinese Benevolent Association asked that exhumation be free. While at the time the city turned down the request, in 1919 the fee was temporarily reduced to $2.50. Later on remains could be exhumed without charge, provided the grave reverted to the city for resale. By the mid-1930s, however, Mountain View had forbidden disinterment, and the Chinese community had to make other arrangements for interment of those wishing their bones to be buried with those of their ancestors in China. By 1951 the bones of 860 Chinese, some of which had been waiting return to China since war broke out in 1939, were being held in Vancouver. The Kuomintang, or the Chinese Nationalist League as it was called in Canada, together with other Chinese-Canadian organizations

This postcard pictures the 1902 altar in the Chinese section of Mountain View Cemetery. Grave markers can be seen in the foreground. The message on the card, which is postmarked December 10,1910, reads in part, "This is the place I was telling you about ... don't it seam (sic) funny they lay the body on the cross peise (sic) & dance & sing .... 'Nellie.'" At least Nellie didn't say, "having a wonderful time, wish you were here."

decided the remains would be permanently buried in Vancouver. The Kuomintang was seen as the stalwart defender of ancient Chinese values and customs, while the Communists were widely regarded as the enemies of Chinese tradition.

Whether the grave was temporary or permanent, it was important that it be well maintained. In popular Chinese religious belief, the soul of the departed resides in three places: heaven, the grave, and the ancestral tablet or shrine. The soul within the grave is there to receive sacrifices. Not only are food offerings and the lighting of joss sticks (incense) a part of the burial rite but also the burning of coloured paper or even gold leaf to represent money. These rites would not only take place at the time of burial but also on special days in each succeeding year.

Chinese folk religion—Taoism—with its belief in fortune telling, astrology, witchcraft, and the ability to communicate with the spirits of the dead, leaves Westerners in wonderment. Bewildering though it was to non-Asians living in Vancouver at the beginning of the twentieth century, the fact that popular Taoist belief has had great meaning for countless millions over the centuries suggests it deserves to be both understood and respected.

157

The grounding of the Princess May *on Sentinel Island gave an enterprising photographer the chance to produce a spectacular picture of a Pacific Coast marine mishap.*

On the Coast

"FOR THOSE IN PERIL ON THE SEA"

Peril at sea is not limited to vessels crossing the world's great oceans. A "protected" Alaskan waterway, Lynn Canal, provided more than enough peril for those travelling aboard four CPR coastal vessels. At the north end of this 90-mile long fiord is Skagway and near its southern end is Juneau, Alaska's capital.

The first CPR vessel to find its watery grave in Alaskan waters was the *Islander*. In 1901 it struck an iceberg and sank with a loss of 42 lives. The fourth and last CPR vessel to founder in Alaskan waters was the *Princess Kathleen*, which sank off Lena Point in 1952, fortunately with no loss of life. Although the stories of the second and third CPR ships to run into troubled waters on the Alaskan coast have certain similarities, their ending could not be more different.

The second vessel to find itself in difficulty in Lynn Canal was the *Princess May*. Built in 1888 for the government of Formosa for service on the China coast, the CPR bought the vessel in 1901 for $175,000. The newly acquired ship allowed its owners to offer a weekly sailing to Alaska. In March 1910 the ship became the first of the company's vessels to be equipped with wireless. And just as well, too, for on August 5 in the same year it was used to report a spectacular accident.

Having left Skagway near midnight on August 4, a mere two hours later the *May* was high and dry on a reef at the north end of Sentinel Island. A sudden fog had settled over Lynn Canal, and while the ship was proceeding cautiously, it was off course and carried onto rocks which were submerged at high tide. The wireless operator then had his moment telegraphing, "*S.S. Princess May* sinking Sentinel Island; send help." Fortunately the ship was so firmly caught on the reef that there was no real possibility that it would founder, in spite of the fact that fully 107 feet of hull was unsupported with the bow 30 feet above the water at low tide. The 80 passengers and 68 crewmen were landed safely on Sentinel Island, from whence rescue vessels took them to Juneau.

Saving the vessel was not easy. The salvage operation ended up costing $115,000, and it was a month before the ship could be freed from its rocky perch. After repairs were made in Victoria's Esquimalt dry dock the *May* continued to sail the coast until 1919.

In 1913 another CPR coastal steamer the *Princess Sophia*, built in 1911–12 expressly for the Alaskan run, also ran aground on Sentinel Island. Damage was minimal. The *Sophia* was easily refloated, and continued to sail regularly to Alaska before disaster overtook the steamer in 1918. That story unfolds as follows:

Wednesday, October 23: The *Princess Sophia* left Skagway at 11:00 p.m. for the return trip to Vancouver. A gale from the northwest brought swirling snow that reduced visibility to zero as the ship sailed down the two and one half mile wide Lynn Canal.

Thursday, October 24: Suddenly at 3:10 a.m. the *Sophia* ran aground on Vanderbilt Reef. Lifeboats were made ready, and lifejackets were issued to the 343 passengers and crew. Given that the ship was held fast and a blinding storm was raging, the captain decided all were safer remaining on board than they would be rowing lifeboats on a cold rough sea, in hope of reaching land they could not see.

As dawn approached the storm abated somewhat and it was hoped the vessel would float free on the 6:00 a.m. high tide. The ship did not float free, and as the day wore on the storm grew worse. Pounding waves worked the *Sophia*'s keel into a groove in the reef, and lifted its stern, exposing it to the raging gale, forcing the vessel farther onto the reef. By afternoon the winds had increased to the point where the vessels that had arrived in answer to the *Sophia*'s distress calls could not get close enough to rescue those aboard the stricken vessel.

Friday, October 25: By morning the gale force winds had assumed hurricane proportions, and in the afternoon matters grew still worse. Not only had darkness fallen, but snow was swirling furiously in 50 knot per hour winds and the ships standing by were forced to take shelter nearer shore. At 4:50 p.m. the wireless operator telegraphed, "Taking water and foundering. For God's sake come and save us." Within the hour the final message was sent, "Just time to say goodbye. We are foundering."

Saturday, October 26: By the time the first rescue vessel reached Vanderbilt Reef all that was visible above water was one of the *Princess Sophia*'s two masts. There were no survivors.

What happened during the final hours of the *Sophia* remains a matter of conjecture. The official enquiry concluded that in all probability the worsening storm had driven the ship across the reef in such a way that the bow alone remain wedged between the rocks. It is believed that the wind and waves, then swung the vessel in a half circle, breaking the bow free, and allowing the damaged ship to sink in minutes with the loss of all on board. The enquiry also stated that neither the captain nor the company were blameworthy, and that "the ship was lost through peril of the sea."

Though it may seem strange, "peril at sea" can be as real in a narrow coastal inlet as it is in mid-ocean.

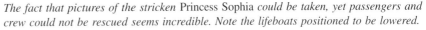

The fact that pictures of the stricken Princess Sophia *could be taken, yet passengers and crew could not be rescued seems incredible. Note the lifeboats positioned to be lowered.*

Vancouver

METHODIST ROMANESQUE

Vancouver's first church was Methodist and stood on Water Street. Built in 1876 when the town was still officially named Granville, and unofficially called Gastown, it was destroyed in the Great Fire of 1886. Immediately rebuilt, the second structure, like its predecessor, was a simple frame building with little style. Early in 1888 the congregation decided to move uptown. The Water Street building was sold to J.B. Lovell for $7,500 and property on the northwest corner of Homer and Dunsmuir was purchased. At the same time, three lots on the northwest corner of Princess (later East Pender) and Dunlevy were bought as the site for a future East End church.

The new Homer Street Church was built in the High Victorian Gothic Revival style, in which historical detail was taken from several periods, and which seemed to reflect a belief that if a little bit of decoration is good, then more is bound to be better! It was also an architectural fashion that was already dated when the church opened in May 1889.

Vancouver's population was growing at such a rate that even before the Homer Street church opened there was a need for a second Methodist church.

A new congregation was organized and held its first services in the police court in the Powell Street building that had initially served as Vancouver's first city hall. Carrall Street marked off the territory that was to be served by each of the two churches. The new congregation, which not only served the area now known as Strathcona but also Vancouver's first suburb Mount Pleasant, was self-supporting within a year of its founding. On April 9, 1889 Thomas Hooper, an architect with offices in both Victoria and Vancouver, was asked "to prepare plans for a place of worship in the East End of the City." The building was to be 30- by 65-feet, not to cost more that $1,750, and to stand in the middle of the Princess Street property. The new church was of frame construction, without any particular distinction. On July 30, 1889 Homer Street and Princess Street Methodist churches became independent entities with each managing its own affairs. By 1901 the Princess Street congregation had grown to the point where a larger church was needed. Hooper was again called upon to prepare designs for the relatively affluent congregation.

Hooper had picked up some new ideas since he last worked for the people at Princess Street Methodist Church. His earlier buildings such as the Winch building (the Robson Street addition to the courthouse), and courthouses in Vernon and Revelstoke had been in the Beaux Arts idiom—a 19th century French amalgam of Greek and Roman styles with much additional ornamental detail—but, by 1901 he was architecturally in a very different space.

In 1890 Hooper had been commissioned to draw up plans for Victoria's new Metropolitan Methodist Church. He was told to design a church in a style that would underscore the theological and liturgical distance between the Methodists and both Anglicans and Roman Catholics. At the same time he was expected to create a design that would reflect the bond that existed over the years between Canadian and American Methodists. The congregation sent him to the eastern United States so he could see what was currently being designed and built elsewhere. There he discovered Richardson Romanesque, a style created by Henry Hobson Richardson, an architect who was bringing together the fine craftsmanship of what was called the Arts and Crafts movement and the grandeur of Romanesque.

Romanesque is defined as the prevailing style in Western Europe from the tenth to the thirteenth centuries. The name was invented by a French archeologist to describe the architecture that was developing at the time when Romance languages were evolving from Latin. While Romanesque varied according to local needs and influences, its constant features were simplicity in planning, sequences of interesting spaces, rounded arches and vaulted or domed rather than flat ceilings, large rough-hewn masonry blocks, groups of deeply set windows, asymmetrically positioned short circular towers with conical roofs, tall castellated towers, and huge rose windows. It was not by accident that the style became popular at the time when church music was taking on a new liturgical importance: Gregorian chant was heard to best effect in a vaulted church. Given the importance of music—both vocal and instrumental—in 19th century Methodism, Romanesque Revival had a practical as well as an aesthetic appeal for Methodists.

Vancouver's Princess Street Methodist Church was Thomas Hooper's successful shingle and clapboard adaptation of Romanesque Revival, a highly popular architectural style at the beginning of the 20th century.

Hooper's Metropolitan Church was a huge success; so much so that a year later he was called upon to remodel and enlarge Victoria's Centennial Methodist Church on the Gorge Road. While Metropolitan is of stone, Centennial is of brick. Back in Vancouver, Hooper's Romanesque churches were going to have to be of wood since local congregational budgets couldn't be stretched to meet the cost of either stone or brick.

The enlarged Princess Street Church needed to seat 475 people comfortably for a service. To accommodate the required 58- by 73-foot addition, Hooper had to move the existing building to the back of the property. The *Methodist Recorder* of May 1902 told its readers that the new Princess Street Church was commodious with a "choir gallery in the centre of the west end, with a choir vestry and minister's vestry at the sides of it …. The pulpit is in the corner adjoining the old building, and the seats are arranged in amphitheatre form round it. The incline of the floor is such as to give an uninterrupted view to all … [and] the old building has been converted into a modern Sunday school room with a gallery all around and classrooms above and below …. Large folding doors unite the two

sections of the building … so that when required at least 300 more can be accommodated in as good a view of the speaker as those in the main auditorium."

Hooper's design made optimum use of a difficult piece of property, and even though he was working in wood, he was able to use Romanesque features effectively. Large rose windows, groupings of windows, an asymmetrical layout, oversized bell tower, round arches, and so forth, all found a place in the design. The new work cost $6,700, and the total church plant was valued at $15,000. As it happened, the remodelled and enlarged Princess Street Methodist Church wasn't Vancouver's first church built in Richardson's Romanesque Revival style.

In the late 1890s there had been talk of building a Methodist church that would serve the West End. Homer Street Methodist Church wisely decided that the answer was not to build an additional church but to relocate closer to the West End. On January 12, 1899 the official board passed a resolution unanimously favouring one strong Methodist church that would serve those living in the West End as well as those in the downtown area. In August twenty men each subscribed

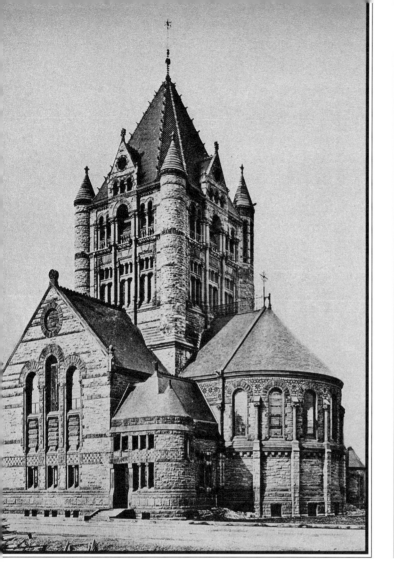
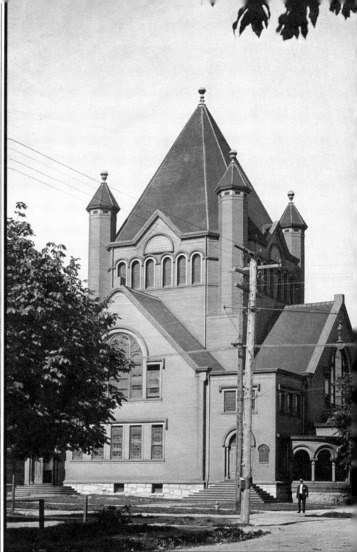

Trinity Church in Boston, Massachusetts (left) was designed in 1872 by H.H. Richardson in the Romanesque Revival style. The building was an immediate sensation, and "Richardson Romanesque" became the style to be imitated. Wesley Methodist Church (right), which stood on the southwest corner of Georgia and Burrard from 1902 until 1934, bore a copycat resemblance to Richardson's Trinity Church.

$250 for a new church, and in September the Homer Street Church was sold to the Vancouver Trades and Labour Council for $7,000. Property diagonally opposite the Anglican's Christ Church at the corner of Georgia and Burrard was bought as a site for the new church. The congregation set about developing plans for a church "costing $25,000 or more." It had already made arrangements with the Labour Council to continue using the old church for services until the new one was ready for occupancy.

On January 1, 1901, in the midst of a heavy snowstorm, Mrs. A.E. Malkin laid the cornerstone for what was to become Wesley Methodist Church. One wonders how many members of the congregation realized that their new church was in reality a simplified copy of an Episcopalian (Anglican) church in Boston! William Blackmore, the building's designer, had in fact done little more than create a scaled-down "carpenter Romanesque" copy of Richardson's Trinity Church in Boston. In 1872, because he had been faced with an irregularly outlined square, Richardson developed a plan featuring a compact footprint, a pyramidal mass, and a central tower that would be equally conspicuous from any angle. With its galleries on three sides and its relatively shallow semi-circular chancel, Trinity's design needed little adaptation to make it suitable for use by a Methodist congregation, a fact that quite obviously had not been lost on Mr. Blackmore. It would be interesting to know if Blackmore ever bothered acknowledging the source of his design. Wesley Church was dedicated and opened on December 22, 1901.

The third in Vancouver's trio of Methodist Romanesque churches stood on the northwest corner of 10th Avenue and Ontario Street in Mount Pleasant. The church started life as a mission of Princess Street Church on April 14, 1889. In the same year a building site on the corner of what is now Broadway and Main was purchased for the new Mount Pleasant Methodist Church, which was up and ready for dedication in May 1890. Even though the building was enlarged (a decade later) to seat 500 people it wasn't long before the congregation was looking for a larger and better site for a new and bigger church. The 10th and Ontario property was bought, and in 1906 the church began to make plans for a new building. Thomas Hooper, who had designed Mount Pleasant's "mother church" Princess Street Methodist, was hired to prepare the plans for the new church. By this time Hooper's firm was known as Hooper and Watkins; he had entered into partnership with C.E. Watkins, his former apprentice. While the building's rounded windows, towers, and rose windows were parts of the Romanesque architectural vocabulary, the building's exterior still managed to suggest that it owed some debt to the earlier High Victorian style with all its fussiness. To be fair to Hooper, it has to be remembered that he was expected to produce a monumental building in shingles and clapboards that should have been built of stone or brick and marble.

An architect's drawing for Vancouver's Wesley Methodist Church that appeared in the January 1901 issue of the Methodist Recorder *suggests that there may have been some thought given to the idea of building a brick church with cut stone decoration.*

Hooper's interior was truer to Romanesque Revival than was his exterior, and it gave the Methodists both the kind of space they wanted, and a stylish church. As *The Daily Province* reported on June 29, 1907, the day before the church opened, there "is a very spacious auditorium, the floor of which slopes down to the preaching platform on the west side. On this side also is an arched recess for the organ. It was evidently one of the objects of the designer of this auditorium to provide [everyone with] an unobstructed view of the minister, and in this he has amply succeeded. There is a large gallery, the front of which starts from either side of the organ recess … seats rise in tiers in the usual way. On the floor [the seats] form concentric circles … as is also the case in the gallery."

Although the Methodists of Mount Pleasant wouldn't have allowed a cross, candlestick, or saint in either plaster or stained glass within a mile of their church, they were not averse to spending money on "suitable" decoration. As *The Province* write-up went on to say: "It would seem that the Mount Pleasant Methodists, having determined to have a new church, desired to make it an exceedingly good one." The gallery railings weren't of simple panelling, but of "bronzed open work," and the seating was not of local fir or pine, but of "very substantial joinery in oak." The windows were filled with tinted glass, and the interior decoration was in " tones of yellow ochre and old gold with hints of light blue and brown designs in the arched ceilings...which [exhibited a combination that] hit the exact desirable medium between the too flamboyant and bizarre, and the mediocre and petty." The paper also pointed out the top of the concave organ recess was finished in azure with bronze stars. All this sounded like the congregation had travelled a long way from the whitewashed Methodist meeting house of an earlier generation.

Methodist Romanesque had a short life in Vancouver of roughly 30 years. The enlarged and remodelled Princess Street Church, which opened in 1907, fell on hard times within a decade. Rapidly changing demographics meant that by 1914 the church, which had changed its name to Central Methodist after Princess Street became East Pender, found itself in a neighbourhood in which 75 percent of the children attending nearby schools were of non-English-speaking parentage. The congregation numbered less than 150 people, and was unable to survive financially. The church tried to meet the needs of the changing population and was heavily involved in what was then called social service work. In 1917 the Methodist Conference of Vancouver allowed the church to again change its name; it became the Turner Institute. Much needed financial help came first from the local Methodist City Mission Board, and then from the church's national headquarters in Toronto. By the time of Church Union in 1925 when

Thomas Hooper's "Methodist Romanesque" Mount Pleasant (later Chown) Church stood on the northwest corner of 10th and Ontario from 1907 until it was destroyed by fire in 1936. The church held 1,200 people and even in the middle of the Depression was valued at $90,000.

the Methodists, most Presbyterians and some Congregationalists joined forces to become the United Church of Canada, the Turner Institute's days were numbered. Work in the downtown East Side was centralized in the former First Presbyterian Church at Hastings and Gore, which at Church Union had become First United. The Pender Street property was sold, and Princess Street Methodist Church became nothing more than a memory.

The last United church services in the old Wesley Methodist Church at Georgia and Burrard were held on May 21, 1933. Wesley had joined forces with

St. Andrew's Presbyterian Church to build the new St. Andrew's Wesley United Church on Burrard Street. In June 1933 the old Methodist building was taken over by continuing Congregationalists—those who did not become members of the United Church—and became known as Vancouver City Temple. The Temple only lasted until the end of April 1934; its congregation couldn't bear the cost of city taxes that were $400 a month. The building's new owners tore it down and announced that they would be building a night club, the Palamar, on the site. When they first got wind of that piece of news there must have been more than a few very unhappy old-time Methodists!

Only one of Vancouver's trio of "Methodist Romanesque" churches went out in a blaze of glory. Mount Pleasant Methodist, which at Church Union in 1925 had chosen to be renamed Chown United Church, was destroyed in a spectacular $90,000 three-alarm fire in the early hours of May 8, 1936. Firefighters had no hope of saving the building; all they could do was prevent the fire from spreading to neighbouring houses and apartments. Since Chown was only a block west of St. Giles United Church (the former Mount Pleasant Presbyterian Church) the congregation decided to relocate to South Cambie where the new Chown Memorial United Church opened in March 1937.

Altogether "Methodist Romanesque" was only popular in Vancouver for a relatively few years. The three principal churches built in the style were erected during the first decade and destroyed in the third decade of the twentieth century. Almost without exception, those United Churches that were built in the 1920s and 30s were not built in the architecture of their time, whether it was Modern Classical (Vancouver City Hall) or Art Deco (the Marine Building). Instead, the builders of new United Churches chose to build in what came to be called Modern Gothic—a very "safe" style. Their Methodist parents or grandparents had been much braver when they chose to build their churches in the Romanesque Revival style of Henry Hobson Richardson.

With its bronzed balcony railing, solid oak pews, elaborate and colourful stencilling, not to mention its "large electroller [chandelier] hanging from the apex of the roof," Mount Pleasant's congregation worshipped in what was certainly the city's most expensively furnished Methodist church.

Vancouver

SHOWING THE FLAG

In peacetime there aren't too many things that can be done with a warship. Of the limited options, one of the more popular in times past seems to have been to send them off on world cruises so they might show the flag, and stir the blood of colonials in the far off corners of the Empire. In 1913 Vancouver was one of the ports of call for the battlecruiser *New Zealand* on its eleven-month world cruise to the Dominions.

In 1908 it had been rumoured that Germany was secretly embarking on a dreadnought building program. It was alleged that by the spring of 1912 Germany would have 21 dreadnoughts ready and able to do battle: the same number as Great Britain. But, as any English schoolboy of the time would have known, that would never do. It was after all Britain's God-given right and solemn duty to rule the waves. Launched on the Clyde in July 1911 and completed in February 1912, the *New Zealand* was one of eight capital ships built in response to the threat posed by the German Imperial Navy's building program. The *New Zealand* was so-named because the government of that country had borne the cost of construction, and presented the battlecruiser to the Royal Navy as a gift. Interestingly, one of the *New Zealand's* sister ships the *Australia*, which was also launched in 1911, was paid for by the Australian government. This ship, however, was not presented to the mother country, but became instead the flag ship of the new Royal Australian Navy.

The *New Zealand,* like the other battlecruisers of the *Indefatigable* class, was a formidable fighting ship with 12-, 4-, and 3-inch guns, beam and stern torpedo tubes, and armour as thick as 10 inches in some places. Of 22,110 tons deep load, it was 590 feet long with an 80-foot beam. It had four propellers, each powered by eight coal-fired boilers. The vessel could attain a speed of over 27 knots, and cruising at a leisurely ten knots could travel 6,330 nautical miles before refuelling. To be sure there would be no problem coaling on its world cruise the *New Zealand* was accompanied by its own collier, the *Glenartney*. The ship arrived in Vancouver on Saturday, July 27, 1913 at 3:30 in the afternoon. Following a brief official welcome by Mayor Baxter, preparations for coaling-up were underway by five o'clock. For the most part, Monday and Tuesday were taken up with coaling and the extra cleaning that such a

dirty business made necessary. Once chores had been dealt with, however, it was party time!

One man who got an early start on R and R was the ship's captain, Lionel Halsey. *The Sun* dutifully reported in its Monday edition that "Capt. Halsey took a good rest last night, having engaged by wireless a suite of rooms at the Hotel Vancouver." Rank does have its privileges.

It has to be said that the city outdid itself entertaining the 800 officers and men of the *New Zealand.* Doubtless some of the credit has to go to E.R. Ricketts who was often called upon to help plan and stage civic events. For many years he had been manager of the Vancouver Opera House, and his involvement with the theatre and the world of make-believe doubtless more than qualified him for his unofficial civic role. At the time Ricketts' greatest challenge and triumph was still a month off in the future when he was to mastermind the visit of the Governor General, the Duke of Connaught.

On the Tuesday, July 30 the officers were guests at a Canadian Club luncheon, which was followed by a motor tour around town that ended at 606 Powell Street, allowing the officers to be present at the opening of the British and Foreign Sailors' Society's new sailors' home by their captain. In the evening both officers and men took in a lacrosse match at Athletic Park. On the Wednesday the ship was open to the public from 9:30 to 11:00 a.m., and from 2:00 to 5:00 p.m. Those crew members who were not on duty were taken for an afternoon drive around the city in private automobiles. Mayor Baxter had earlier recruited volunteers who would make themselves and their motor cars available for the day. It was also arranged that vehicles and drivers would be available on the following day to take those sailors who were on duty on Wednesday for their sightseeing trip.

Wednesday was also the day when the officers were off to Minoru Park in Richmond for luncheon and the races. A feature of the afternoon was the running of the New Zealand Cup. Only horses owned by members of the Vancouver Hunt Club were eligible for the race. It was reported that "several noted riders [were] to be seen under silk. Among the more prominent [was] Lord Burghersh." He was the son of the Earl of Westmount and a midshipman on the *New Zealand.* Burghersh was one of a number of sons of the nobility aboard ship. His fellow midshipman, included the Earl of Carlisle and sub-

Passing through the First Narrows, H.M.S. New Zealand *comes into the harbour for a week-long visit in the summer of 1913.*

lieutenant, His Serene Highness Prince George of Battenberg. The 21-year-old Battenberg was rather well connected. His father was Prince Louis of Battenberg, Britain's First Sea Lord. His younger brother, also named Prince Louis, was to become much better known as Earl Mountbatten of Burma. Their sister, Princess Alice, who upon her marriage became Princess Andrew of Denmark and Greece, was to become Prince Philip's mother in 1921.

On the Thursday morning there was a special reception aboard ship for New Zealanders, and in the afternoon a by-invitation-only reception for the local elite, all of whom could have the satisfaction of seeing their names in print in the next day's papers. Friday was taken up with more of the same sort of programming. In the morning "the ship [was] thrown open to Boy Scouts and Indians," while the officers were taken to Canyon View Hotel on the Capilano River for a luncheon tendered by the City of North Vancouver. At 3:00 p.m.

the crew took part in an aquatic sports program at Coal Harbour. In the evening the officers were guests of honour at Vancouver's civic banquet which was held at the Terminal City Club.

During most evenings during its visit, from approximately nine until eleven, the ship was illuminated and had its search lights turned on. As reported in *The Sun* on the Thursday morning, "with a suddenness that stopped pedestrians in their tracks and caused dumb brutes to shy, the great light flashed suddenly out into the sky, then slowly swung along from one end of the city to the other with a dazzling glare." The paper was of the opinion that the operation of the searchlights was the most memorable feature associated with the ship's visit. Each of the four searchlights was of 25,000 candle power, and had a range of five miles.

As guests of the Royal City, the visitors were taken to New Westminster, Colony Farm, Fraser Mills and Steveston on Saturday. After lunch in the Beatty Street Drill Hall, the crew paraded with local military units to Brockton Point for an afternoon of sports. In addition to the full round of laid-on events at which attendance was compulsory, a number of the city's clubs and societies hosted dances and social evenings to which either officers or crew were invited. Doubtless to their relief, the crew members were left to find their own entertainment on Saturday night. It can be assumed they did so quite successfully!

On Sunday, the officers were once again off to a luncheon. This time it was tendered by the Navy League of Canada at Wigwam Inn at the head of Indian Arm. At 6:00 a.m., on Sunday, August 4 the *New Zealand* left Vancouver for a week in Victoria and another round of duty drinking for its officers, and a continuing mixture of work and play for the crew. The next call after Victoria was Mazatlan in Mexico, and then on to ports along the west coast of South America.

The *New Zealand* completed its world cruise in December. It then joined the 1st Battle Cruiser Squadron for a trip to the Baltic. When war broke out in August 1914 the ship joined the Grand Fleet. At the Battle of Dogger Bank it fired 147 12-inch shells with no known result, and at the Battle of Jutland fired more shells—420—than any other dreadnought. The 12-inch shells fired resulted in only four hits. The *New Zealand* took one hit from an 11-inch enemy shell, but sustained little damage and no serious casualties.

The war over, in 1919 the *New Zealand* set off on another world cruise, this time taking Admiral Lord Jellicoe on his tour of the Dominions. And then came the end. Under the terms of the Washington Conference of 1922 treaties were negotiated for limiting the naval strength of world powers. One of the British warships to be scrapped was the *New Zealand*. On December 19, 1922 a ship that only ten years before had cost 10 million dollars (Canadian) to build was sold to be broken up.

One wonders if any of the *New Zealand's* officers and men defending the flag at Jutland had a momentary longing for the days when all they had to do was show the flag in far off and peaceful places like Vancouver.

The heading for a Vancouver Sun *article read, "Night-time Demonstration of War Vessel's Electric Eyes Greatly Enjoyed." With a radius of 5 miles, the* New Zealand's *searchlights were much talked about while the battlecruiser was in port.*

In 1907 the Orange Hall was at the farthest edge of the city's urban core; the properties to the east were still largely residential. Immediately behind the former lodge hall is Fire Hall No. 2, which was also designed in 1905 by the Orange Hall's architect, W.T. Whiteway.

Vancouver

THE ORANGEMEN ON PARADE

The Orange Order had its beginning in Ireland some 200 years ago as one response to the religious and political problems of the day. In 1672 the future James II, who was Duke of York and Albany at the time, publically acknowledged his conversion to Roman Catholicism. In response Parliament passed the Test Acts, disqualifying Roman Catholics from holding public office. In 1679 parliament unsuccessfully attempted to bar James from the succession. By his first wife Anne Hyde he had two Protestant daughters, Mary and Anne, so it seemed that the Protestant succession was assured. He succeeded his brother, Charles II, as king in 1685. When a son was born to James and his Roman Catholic second wife Mary of Modena in 1688, however, it was the Roman Catholic succession that

appeared to be a certainty. His enemies, and he had made many—both Anglican and non-conformist—invited James's son-in-law the Protestant Dutch Prince William of Orange to take the throne. With considerable courage William landed (with a quickly assembled force) in Devon in 1688. James almost immediately fled to France, and the bloodless "Glorious Revolution," as it was called, was successful. In February 1689, James's daughter Mary and her husband, William of Orange, jointly ascended the British throne as King William III and Queen Mary II.

In 1690 James landed in largely Roman Catholic Ireland with an insufficient number of troops, intending to regain his throne. He was decisively defeated at the Battle of the Boyne on July 12, 1690. James escaped back to France where he lived out the rest of his life in exile. William became not only the hero of the hour, but the hero for all time of those who choose to see the Church of Rome as the enemy of religious and personal freedom. It is William's victory in Ireland that the Orangemen commemorate annually on "the Glorious Twelfth" of July.

After nearly a century of continuing intersectarian rivalry and all too frequent outbursts of violence in Ireland, the Orange Order was formed in 1795 in county Armagh to support the continuation of British rule in Ireland, and to maintain a Protestant monarchy.

Overseas it was in Canada that the Orange Order found its greatest success beyond Ulster. Perhaps it was more successful in British North America than elsewhere because of the challenge—real or imagined—presented by French-speaking Roman Catholic Quebec to the English language and to Protestantism, and by the republican United States to the monarchical principle. It is no mere coincidence that in Canada the Orange Order has been strongest in Ontario and New Brunswick, the two provinces that are next door to both Quebec and the United States. In Canada the Orange Order's twin allegiances are to the Protestant monarchy and to the continuation of Canada's present constitutional arrangement with Great Britain.

It has been suggested that an Orange Society existed within the Halifax Militia as early as 1799; however, there is no substantiating proof to back up the claim. The first bona fide Orange Lodge in what is now Canada was formed in St. John, New Brunswick in 1818. It was not until 1830 however, that the Grand Lodge in British North America came into being. Its founder was Ogle R. Gowan, late of county Wexford in Ireland. He convened a meeting of like-minded men on January 1, 1830 in Brockville, Ontario, to establish the mechanism for the centralized administration of existing lodges and the creation of new ones. In April 1832 the grand master of the empire, the Duke of Cumberland, acknowledged British North America as a separate jurisdiction.

British Columbia's first Orange Lodge—Loyal Orange Lodge No. 1150—opened in New Westminster on May 21, 1863. It was an Irishman, William Holmes of Kilkenny, who organized the Royal City's first Orange Lodge and became its first Worshipful Master. Within the year it had 25 members, mostly men who had moved west from Ontario, and a small number who had come directly from Ireland. Vancouver's first Orange Lodge—No. 1560—was instituted on May 14, 1886. By the beginning of the twentieth century there were 34 active lodges in the province.

A very special day for Vancouver's Orangemen was July 12, 1904, the day upon which 4,000 took part

Even though the County Parade Marshall wasn't decked out in the traditional costume of William III, as custom required he was astride King Billy's white horse. Each lodge was encouraged to develop its own distinctive uniform, and prizes were awarded with a possible 25 points being given for uniformity of dress, 15 points for uniform regalia and lodge designation, and 10 points for marching. Lodges entering the competition had to have at least twelve members on parade.

in the ceremonies for the laying of the cornerstone for the new Orange Hall to be built on the northwest corner of Hastings and Gore Avenue. The newspapers reported that the expected cost of the new building was $30,000 and that most of the money was already on hand. Responsibility for erecting and managing the building was vested in the County Orange Hall Building Association.

Visitors came from the Fraser Valley, Vancouver Island, and the Interior for the special day. Prior to the laying of the cornerstone, the Provincial Grand Lodge held a meeting in Sutherland's Hall on Cordova Street. Following the meeting, the officers put on their full regalia for the parade to the new site. Led by the band of the Duke of Conaught's Own Rifles, all the local and visiting Orangemen paraded to Hastings and Gore. A number of mementos were placed in the cornerstone, including an elaborately embossed and illuminated scroll listing lodges officers, members of the building committee, and others; local newspapers; a number of current coins; statistics about Vancouver; and other items.

The inevitable speeches followed with "a few words" from the mayors of Vancouver and New Westminster, the American Consul, the Grand Chaplain, and others. The "oration of the day" was delivered by the Order's Grand Organizer who had come from Toronto to deliver the address, which *The Province* reported "was lengthy but masterful." Looking back over time, the most interesting remarks were those of the Royal City's Mayor Keary. To quote *The Province*, "He said that although he was not a Protestant yet he admired the stand which the Orangemen took for religious freedom. He was glad to be able to join with the Orangemen in celebrating the anniversary of William, Prince of Orange's victory which he contended had given both Protestants and Roman Catholics the right to worship as they preferred. Orangemen had done much both for Great Britain and America. There were none more loyal and he admired them for it." Not surprisingly, Mayor Keary's speech "was received with ringing cheers." He may not have been a Protestant, but he certainly was a politician!

The new building was to be all that a lodge could want. It would be of three stories over a full basement with a twelve-foot ceiling. The ground floor would accommodate six stores, three fronting on Hastings and three on Gore. On the second floor there was to be a spacious assembly room, a banquet hall, cloakrooms, and so forth. The large high-ceilinged lodge rooms were to be on the third floor. A band room was also to be built on the top floor. It would be "directly over the hallway, and so constructed that the Orange Band can practice without the sound of music being heard in the lodge rooms." The kitchens were to be in the basement with an elevator in place for transporting food to the upper floors.

The exterior would be of pressed brick with stone trimming. Its decoration was to be limited to an attractive cornice, round-headed windows on the top storey, and a most attractive and complementing Romanesque entrance of decorated carved stone. Horizontal sandstone bands were to delineate each floor. The Orangemen hired a quality architect, W.T. Whiteway. He is best remembered as the architect who

The Provincial Grand Lodge of the Orange Order met at New Westminster's Queens Park on a number of occasions. Arranged behind Revelstoke's Orange Band are women who may have been members of the Ladies' Orange Benevolent Association. Why there are four young girls at the centre of the picture is difficult to say.

was later to design the Sun Tower. A man by the name of James Gillott was hired to put up the building.

A certain amount of mystery surrounds the building of the Orange Hall. Although the cornerstone was laid in 1904, the building was not ready for occupancy until 1907. Memories fade, time passes by, printed records are lost or destroyed, and we are left to guess at possible reasons why it should have taken so long to erect a three-storey building. Perhaps the $30,000 promised to meet the building costs hadn't materialized; or possibly there was some hold up relating to building permits. Then again, all along it may have been the plan to build in stages as funds became available. Gillott who was listed in the city directories of the time as a plasterer, may only have built the stone foundation, which according to the building permit issued in his name, cost $2,900. While he was also known as a carpenter and mason, it may be that he proved to be insufficiently skilled and experienced to handle the job. Regardless, at the beginning of 1907 there was still no Orange Hall to be seen on the corner of Hastings and Gore. *The Province* reported on March 8, 1907 that a $45,000 contract had been awarded to David G. Gray "who will rush the construction [of the Orange Hall] with all possible dispatch [and have it] ready for occupancy in four months' time." Gray was a well-known and reputable contractor and builder.

The Orangemen, whose numbers had declined steadily since the mid-1920s, hung on to their hall until early 1944, but they had only been able to do so by renting out the large top floor. In 1935 they had been fortunate enough to find a tenant in the person of Jack Whelan to help pay the bills. Whelan operated a gym and staged popular wrestling matches each week on Wednesday and Saturday nights.

The end came in May 1944 when the building was sold by the Vancouver Orange Hall Company Limited to the National Housing Administration, which hired the architect W.F. Gardiner to redesign the interior in such a way that it could be divided into 27 suites. The building was virtually gutted, and three floors were created above the ground floor where there had formerly only been two. Exterior changes were minimal; to create windows for the uppermost floors, the tall Romanesque windows were replaced by two rows of square-headed windows. In spite of the changes made in 1944, the building looks much as it did in 1907. And even in its rather run-down state it still has more style to it than many of its newer and more flashy neighbours.

Bowen Island
CAPTAIN CATES' CREATION

Bowen Island, like so many places on the West Coast, was named by George H. Richards, captain of H.M. surveying vessel *Plumper*. The year was 1860 and the island was named to honour Rear Admiral James Bowen, captain of H.M.S. *Queen Charlotte*. Named or not, it was only in the 1880s that serious White settlement began. The most prominent of the early Bowen Island settlers was Joseph Mannion, a Vancouver hotel owner and alderman.

In 1884 Mannion had bought two acreages, one on the west side of Gambier Island, and the other on the west side of Bowen Island. A year later he bought a much more highly desirable property on a beautiful bay on the east side of Bowen Island. Mannion and his family used this bay-side land as a summer campsite until 1888 when they decided to move permanently to Bowen Island. He built a year-round home and called it Terminal Farm, overlooking the cove that was successively known as Mannion's Bay, Hotel Bay, and Deep Bay. Over the ridge to the south of Mannion's home was a natural harbour which came to be known as Snug Cove. It has been the site of a deep water dock of one sort or another ever since Mannion built his first wharf. Other settlers moved to Bowen Island, and by the turn of the century the island had a small scattered community of year-round residents.

In 1900 Mannion sold his Bowen Island property to John A. Cates' Terminal Steamship Company. Jack, as he was called, was one of the five sons and six daughters of Andrew Jackson Cates. Cates and his wife Katherine Kelly were natives of Maine who had moved to Nova Scotia where their children were born. Eventually the whole family ended up on the West Coast, but it was Jack who first arrived in Vancouver. He and his four brothers were all master mariners, and each became well-known locally for his own accomplishments.

This 1910 cartoon successfully underscores Captain John A. Cates preeminent position in the local excursion business of the day.

The excursion steamers Britannia *and* Baramba *are shown leaving Vancouver for Bowen Island. To alter Cunnard's slogan ever so slightly, getting there was surely half the fun.*

When he arrived on the coast Jack went into tug boating. It wasn't long, however, before the lure of Klondike gold called him to the Yukon. In 1899 he came out of the north with enough money to be able to buy a small wooden steamer in partnership with Vicker Wallace Haywood who had been in the gold fields with him. Their ship, the *Defiance,* had been built in Tacoma in 1897. With it they served the settlers and summer campers along the shores of Howe Sound and on its islands.

Cates and Haywood set about turning the Mannion property into what would have been called a summer pleasure garden back then. The Mannion home became the rather pretentiously named, Hotel Monaco. They laid out campgrounds, and developed picnic sites to attract holiday crowds. For whatever reason, Cates and Haywood parted company in 1901. Cates, who was now sole owner of the business, sold a half interest to Percy Evans, George Coleman and Ernest Evans. As Evans Coleman & Evans, they were shipping and commission

merchants, who described themselves as "importers and dealers in builders' cannery and railway supplies." More importantly, they had a corporate thumb in a number of waterfront-related pies. The new partners incorporated as the Terminal Steamship Company, Limited.

Business was good, and in 1902 Jack Cates arranged to have his brother George build a new and larger vessel for the company. George had set himself up as a shipbuilder in False Creek. The ship was to be a single screw, 221-ton wooden-hulled vessel, powered by a Glasgow-made triple-expansion engine. The 104.8-foot long ship was designed to accommodate 300 day passengers. It featured both ladies' and gentlemen's saloon accommodation with seats of maroon plush, a full dining service, and a spacious promenade deck. In other words, it had all the attractions that would make it the ideal excursion vessel. Costing $45,000 to build, it was easily the most modern and best equipped excursion vessel of its day sailing out of Vancouver. Named *Britannia*, it

This wonderful Philip Timms photograph of a group of men on their way to Bowen Island, circa 1910, is entitled, "The Half Holiday." Whether the half holiday was a Wednesday or a Saturday half day off will never be known. Note the member of the ship's band with his clarinet.

The Sons of England's 1909 Bowen Island picnic included the inevitable races. The woman who is obviously coming in first is just about to cross the finishing line.

It's lunch time for the staff of the Vancouver News-Advertiser at their first Annual Picnic. The bottles look interesting; were they pop or? Obviously casual picnic wear was still some time off in the future.

The ladies' tug-of-war looks like it called for an all-out effort. The "anchor" has certainly thrown her weight into the contest!

was launched and named by Jack's sister, Lillian, on July 7, 1902.

Almost from the day the *Britannia* first set sail, Bowen Island became *the* place for annual outings. Churches and Sunday schools, businesses and unions, social clubs and fraternal orders, were all soon there for picnics, races and games, and the inevitable tug-of-war without which no group outing would have been considered complete.

Cates not only planted 300 fruit trees, laid out 5,000 feet of water pipe, and opened a store, restaurant and bakery, but also introduced a system of camping permits for those wanting to tent on the 320-acre estate. As well, he kept a herd of cattle to provide fresh milk for those using his facilities.

In 1906 Evans Coleman & Evans gave up its interest in the firm, but the three principals continued on as shareholders and directors. In 1908 the business was capitalized at $200,000, and reorganized as the Terminal Steam Navigation Company, Limited. Business was such that Cates bought the *Belcarra*—formerly the *Unican*—in 1906 to help cope with the ever increasing numbers literally wanting to get on board.

He had the *Belcarra* refitted to double its original size in 1908, but it was still not large enough to handle the summer weekend excursion crowds. To solve his problem, Cates bought John Irving's *R.P. Rithet* in 1908 from the CPR to replace the *Belcarra*. A sternwheeler that had been built in 1882, the 817-ton *Rithet* was 177 feet long, and built for service on the Fraser River. The ship had come to the Canadian Pacific Navigation Company when Irving was bought out, and thence to the CPR in 1901 when the railway took over Canadian Pacific Navigation. During its CPR days, the *Rithet* had regularly crossed the Strait of George to Victoria and called at the landings along the lower Fraser River three times a week during good weather. When Cates acquired the sternwheeler he renamed it *Baramba*.

Even with the *Britannia* and the *Baramba* Cates was still having difficulty accommodating everyone wanting to picnic or camp at his Bowen Island resort. In 1912 and 1914 he bought two more ships from the CPR—the *City of Nanaimo,* which became the *Bowena,* and the *Joan,* which he renamed the *Ballena.* At the time it was not at all unusual to see at least three of Cates' excursion steamers leaving the Evans Coleman & Evans wharf within the space of an hour for Bowen Island on holidays such as May 24th or July 1st.

A big change came about just before the Great War, when Coleman and the Evans brothers withdrew

In this 1916 photograph the Britannia *is approaching the landing stage in Bowen Island's Snug Cove. The horse and cart were probably waiting on the wharf ready to pick up supplies for the hotel and general store.*

An architect's sketch of the Terminal Summer Resort, Bowen Island, is subtitled, "British Columbia's Paradise for the holiday seeker." Fortunately the reality of beautiful Bowen Island far surpassed the artistic fiction of this promotional postcard.

from the company, selling their interests to Jack Cates who then became virtually the sole owner of the Terminal Steam Navigation Company and all its assets. Cates, together with his sister Lillian and her husband Robert Turner, entered upon a renewed program of expansion and improvement. He bought an additional 300 acres around Lake Killarney and a further 220 acres on Snug Cove, and the trio built what was to become the development's centrepiece, the Terminal Hotel. They also developed the Terminal Farm which supplied produce not only for the hotel, but for the resort's general store and the company's ships as well. Barns, stables, silos, a dairy, slaughterhouse, and a greenhouse were all there. The contractor hired to oversee development was T.M. Behrens, Jack Cates' future father-in-law. Interestingly, much of the construction, maintenance work, and gardening was done by Japanese staff. Cottages for weekly renters were built in 1917, and more were added over the next two years.

Cates and the Turners went on to develop a 364-acre park with a lagoon and boat rentals, a Japanese tea garden, and a dance pavilion. They even went so far as to run a telephone cable across to the mainland, creating a phone line to Vancouver. And if all that wasn't enough, they also inaugurated moonlight cruises!

As the Great War ended another pioneer Vancouver firm called the Union Steamship Company (formed in 1889) came into the picture. It had already bought out the All Red Line in 1917 for $117,500. That company owned two luxuriously built steam yachts built in Glasgow by John Elder & Co. for John A. Rolls (of Rolls-Royce) and the Marquis of Angelsea. The All Red Line served a dozen or so communities between Vancouver and Powell River and owned seven acres of waterfront property at Selma Park. It wasn't long before the new owners had built a dozen waterfront cottages, picnic sites, and a dance pavilion with a large verandah at Selma Park. And business was booming.

Having tasted success in both the resort and excursion business, Union Steamships was looking to expand that side of its operation. Finally, in December 1920 Jack Cates agreed to sell his business—lock, stock and barrel—to the Union Steamship Company for a quarter of a million, an amount equal to just slightly less than two million in today's dollars.

Cates seemed happy to move on, taking up new challenges along the way. Among other things, he invested in properties in the Okanagan, along the Tulameen River, and at Crescent Beach. While few people will know that it was Captain John A. Cates who created one of Vancouver most popular pre-Second World War holiday spots, it was his imagination and flair that created the setting on Bowen Island that gave hundreds of thousands of people cherished memories of happy days gone by.

On Wednesday, September 4, 1918 Dr. J.C. Farish came home to find a seaplane on his roof, and a rather stunned pilot on his upstairs landing. While this was not Vancouver's first plane crash, to that point in time it certainly was the city's most spectacular.

Vancouver

IS THERE A DOCTOR IN THE HOUSE?

On September 4, 1918 anyone in Vancouver would have told you that the luckiest man in town was Lieutenant Victor A. Bishop. While flying over the West End his aircraft stalled and fell 1,200 feet, landing on Dr. J.C. Farish's roof. The Farish home stood on the northwest corner of Alberni and Bute Streets.

As the seaplane crashed onto the roof, Bishop seemed to have bounced out of his seat and hit one of the wings, which were covered in unbleached linen. The

relatively soft fabric somehow broke his fall, and when he was helped out of the wreckage he appeared to have no more than minor facial lacerations and bruises to his back. The somewhat stunned pilot was assisted down through the hole in the roof that the seaplane's engine had made when it broke free from its mountings. From the upstairs landing Bishop was able to walk virtually unassisted down the stairs, onto the street, and into the ambulance that had been called. While Dr. Farish wasn't at home when the accident occurred, he did get there minutes after the crash in time to provide Bishop with initial first aid before accompanying him to the Vancouver General Hospital's Military Annex.

The pilot fared better than the $7,500 single engine flying boat which was a total loss. It had been built by the Hoffar brothers, Henry and James, who owned the Hoffar Motor Boat Company located on Coal Harbour between Gilford and Chilco Streets. The aircraft was a two-seater biplane powered by a 100-horsepower pusher engine. A pusher engine was one mounted above the cockpit with the propeller facing "backward." One of the design advantages was that the pilot had an unobstructed view of what lay ahead, not that it did Victor Bishop much good! Being the second plane built by the Hoffars, it was known as the "H2."

With an option to buy, the plane had been chartered by the provincial government for the forestry department of the Ministry of Lands. The minister in charge, the Hon. T.D. Pattullo, was enthusiastic about the idea of using planes to implement a provincial aerial forest fire patrol.

And just who was Victor Bishop? He was born in Britain and in 1913 emigrated to Vancouver where he got a job in the wharf office of Evans, Coleman & Evans. In 1915 he joined the Seaforth Highlanders, and after nine months in the trenches he transferred to and was commissioned in the Royal Naval Air Service, which later together with the Royal Flying Corps formed the Royal Air Force. He flew frequent trips to Paris, ferrying new planes to where they could be used in combat. In time he became a qualified armament flight instructor. Bishop had come to Vancouver in mid-August on three months furlough, and was staying with an aunt whose Robson Street home was only two blocks from where he crashed.

It might also be asked what an R.A.F. pilot on furlough was doing flying a B.C. government plane? While the *Daily Province* did mention that Bishop, "had a regular military permit … to make the ascent," nothing was said in any of the daily papers as to why it was that Bishop was flying the Hoffars "H2." It was probably taken for granted that he had been asked by the ministry's forestry department to give a second opinion regarding the suitability of the aircraft for forestry fire patrol. It is only in Bishop's diary that the full answer to the question is found. It seems that on the morning of the accident he had been offered a $225 a month salary if he accepted a job with the forestry department. Having received the offer of a post-war job, he took the plane up in the afternoon to try it out, presumably to see how the aircraft performed before accepting the invitation to become a provincial government employee.

The plane's builders, as would be expected, were quick to defend their name and the aircraft they had built. James Hoffar said that he had flown the boat three times, and had no trouble with it. He also said that he had carefully examined the wreckage and could not account for the accident. He did, however, say that if Lieutenant Bishop had kept up speed, pointing the plane's nose downward he could have landed successfully. Hoffar also stated that he had spoken to a number of aviation cadets (student pilots?) who agreed that Bishop could have landed the plane safely had he kept the nose of the machine pointing downward. Earlier Bishop had said that when the engine stopped he then attempted to volplane, that is, descend on a relatively steep angle, in the direction of English Bay. When he realized that he wouldn't make it, he attempted to turn back toward Coal Harbour. It was then that the plane went out of control and fell in a spinning nose dive. None of what he had to say in any way altered the opinions of the experts on the ground!

Captain W.H. MacKenzie, R.A.F. who had been hired by the Department of Lands to test the plane before the lease was signed, joined the chorus. He said that when he tested the machine he found it to be an excellent aircraft that would fly itself. He also was quoted as saying that "the machine was quite satisfactory for the work for which it was built but that it was by no means a machine with which an aviator might do stunts, such as nose dives or loop-the-loops," implying that Bishop was in some way showing-off when the engine stalled. The *Vancouver Sun* wasn't too impressed by the excuse-making, stating with a note of finality that "there were many theories advanced [as to the cause of the accident] but Aviator Bishop's own story makes them valueless."

With a speed not usually associated with government, Pattullo quickly announced that the Ministry of Lands would not only pay for the plane which was a write-off but also meet the costs involved in repairing Dr. Farish's house. As well, it was announced almost immediately after the accident that a replacement plane would be built, to be leased by the government with a view to purchase. Beyond the announcement nothing further was said. The idea of using airplanes for forestry patrol was quietly abandoned for a number of years.

And what of Lieutenant Bishop? Discharged from the hospital on September 16, 1918 he was bothered for the rest of his life by what turned out to be a serious spinal injury. In fact, in 1950 he underwent surgery to relieve the pain created by a crushed vertebrae. Even with his back problems, he was probably a lot luckier than most pilots that fell from the skies. After all, he lived to tell the tale.

The poorly proportioned Cheslakee *is pictured at a float landing in Lewis Channel, which is approximately 15 miles north of Lund in Desolation Sound.*

On the Coast

THE "CHESLAKEE"

Sometimes its tempting to think of ships as being like people, that is, living in an *Upstairs/Downstairs* world. Just as there are beautiful patrician upstairs people and rather plain downstairs people, so there are ships with obvious quality and style, and ships that look like they were made for drudgery. With few exceptions, most of the Union Steamship Company's vessels had a definite below stairs look about them. True, there were a few with pretensions; they were the half dozen day boats that ranged in size from the 1,396-ton *Lady Alexandra* down to the 199-ton *Lady Rose* that also served as excursion vessels. But compared to the Grand Trunk Pacific's princes and the CPR's princesses and empresses, even these "ladies" weren't all that beautiful.

Handsome or not, the Union Steamship's coastal vessels, were certainly the most popular with people living in the fishing, mining and logging communities on the West Coast. Not only had the Union Steamships, established in 1889, been first to provide a safe and reliable scheduled service to places big and small up and down the coast, but it did so with a courtesy and good humour that made the company seem like an old and reliable friend. For all their qualities, neither the CPR nor the Grand Trunk Pacific (later the CNR) ships were able to engender anything like the affection felt by Coast people for the Union Steamship's vessels and the men and women who sailed in them.

Of course Union Steamship service wasn't always perfect, and accidents did happen. In its 70-year history the line had a number of accidents. With 53 ships sailing the coast for seven decades there were bound to be mishaps. The most serious involved the 526-ton *Cheslakee,* a ship that looked like the sort drawn by school children—a hull topped by a pyramid of boxes topped with an ill-proportioned "smoke stack."

In 1910 it had been the plan of the company's managing director Gordon Legg to have two large ships built in Britain for the line. His plans changed apparently when the size and quality of the Grand Trunk Pacific's new ships, the *Prince Rupert* and the *Prince George,* became known. They were luxurious, indeed, and Legg rightly guessed that they would siphon off both passengers and freight as they plied the route between Skagway, Prince Rupert, and Vancouver. However, there was one small point of consolation: the *Princes* were too large to be accommodated at many of the wharfs and landings that were regular ports of call for the Union Steamships. At any rate, it seemed more prudent to build a small ship that could be used on the run between Vancouver and Kingcome Inlet.

The *Cheslakee* would provide relief on the route for the *Cassiar* and the *Comox.* The fact that M.J. Scanlon and other Americans had bought timber rights in the vicinity of Powell River and on Vancouver Island to be sure of a supply of logs for the pulp and paper mill they were about to build in Powell River made the need for more tonnage just that much more imperative. Designed by A.T.C. Robertson, a Scottish-trained Vancouver naval architect, the steel single-screw *Cheslakee* was laid down in Ireland at the Dublin Dockyard in 1910. Only the hull, main deck and crew's quarters were completed in Dublin; the cabins and superstructure were to be built in Vancouver. From Dublin the ship was towed to MacColl & Co. in Belfast were it was fitted with triple expansion engines. Leaving Belfast on June 29, 1910, what there was of the *Cheslakee* arrived 89 days later in Vancouver. Wallace's Shipyard in North Vancouver was awarded the contract for the completion of the superstructure and general fitting out. Even though some last-minute design changes were made, the *Cheslakee* was ready for service by mid-December.

All went well until the night of January 7, 1913 when the *Cheslakee* sailed from Vancouver at 8:45 p.m. with 97 passengers and 45 tons of cargo aboard. The ship arrived at Van Anda on Texada Island at 3:25 a.m.,

The salvage vessel, Salvar, *is pictured preparing to right the Union Steamship Company's sunken* Cheslakee *at Van Anda (now Vananda) on Texada Island.*

The B.C. Salvage Company was hired to raise, pump out, and move the Cheslakee *to Vancouver. Being the depression days that preceded the First World War, Union Steamship's general manager was able to hire the firm with the understanding that it would only be paid if it completed the job successfully.*

allowing twenty minutes for eight passengers to disembark and for freight to be unloaded. At 3:45 p.m., by which time the seas had become very rough, the ship set sail for Powell River. Ten minutes later, a mile and a half across Malaspina Strait, the ship was struck starboard by a 65 mile per hour squall. The vessel then shipped two heavy seas, and took on a dangerous 25-degree list to port. To make matters worse, the list dislodged some of the cargo. Chief Officer Robert Wilson quickly turned the ship against the storm and headed back to Van Anda. In turning back, the vessel

righted itself somewhat, however, it was again listing heavily to port when it reached the dock at Van Anda.

Captain John Cockle had ordered all passengers to be awakened, and once a starboard line had been secured to the dock and a gangplank run out, passengers were quickly put ashore. This docking and unloading took place in almost pitch black darkness since rising waters had reached the ship's generators and put its power plant out of commission. Fortunately most of the passengers and crew were safely on the wharf when the line snapped, allowing the *Cheslakee*

Once on an even keel, the Cheslakee *had to be raised and pumped out. Cold as the January day appears to be, there seems to have been no shortage of sidewalk super-intendents.*

to heel over. Within four minutes the vessel was lying on its side, submerged in the icy waters. Six passengers and one crewman lost their lives when the ship went down in what would come to be recorded as the only accident involving fatalities in the 70-year history of the Union Steamships.

E.H. Beazley, the company's general manager, arranged to have the B.C. Salvage Company raise, pump out, and return the *Cheslakee* to Vancouver for repairs. The recovery of the ship was accomplished by the salvage vessel *Salvor*.

On January 20, 1913 a marine court of enquiry was convened. It found that "the seamanship exhibited by the Master [Cockle] and the Pilot [Wilson] … was commendable, and was the means of avoiding what might have been a much more serious and lamentable catastrophe." At the same time, the court of enquiry criticised those who authorized changes in the design of the ship's superstructure without a further marine survey having been undertaken, making it "heavier than allowed by the designer." Stated more simply, the court was saying that the departures from the architect's plan had made the ship top heavy.

Once the vessel was safely back in Vancouver Beazly set about having it redesigned. This re-planning included lengthening it by 20 feet. Although slicing a vessel in two in order to add a section midships has become a relatively common procedure, the *Cheslakee* was the first vessel on the Pacific Coast be extended in this way. The "operation" was successful, giving the vessel much greater stability. To accommodate mariners' superstitions there was one more change; in June 1913 the *Cheslakee* returned to service as the *Cheakamus*. With the exception of the "Lady boats," all the ships in the early Union Steamship fleet were given Aboriginal or Spanish names beginning with the letter "C."

In spite of its inauspicious beginnings, the salvaged *Cheslakee* managed to have a long and productive career as the *Cheakamus*. In early 1942, after 32 years sailing the B.C. Coast for the Union Steamship Company as a passenger ship, the vessel was converted into a tow boat to be used in the transporting of war materials north for the American military. Later in the same year the vessel was sold for $75,000 to the United States government whose Department of Transport put it to work as a salvage tug. History does have its ironies.

This 1920s photograph was taken in West Howe Sound some years after the extended and refurbished Cheslakee *had been renamed* Cheakamus, *which means "a fish trap" in Coast Salish.*

Vancouver

THE CENOTAPH

In so far as planning for a First World War memorial is concerned there is certainly no question that the men's Canadian Club of Vancouver was first off the mark. The war was barely five months old when in December, 1914 the club petitioned the provincial government to set aside the vacant block that had been the site of the 1898 provincial courthouse as the location for a war memorial. The nine-tenths of

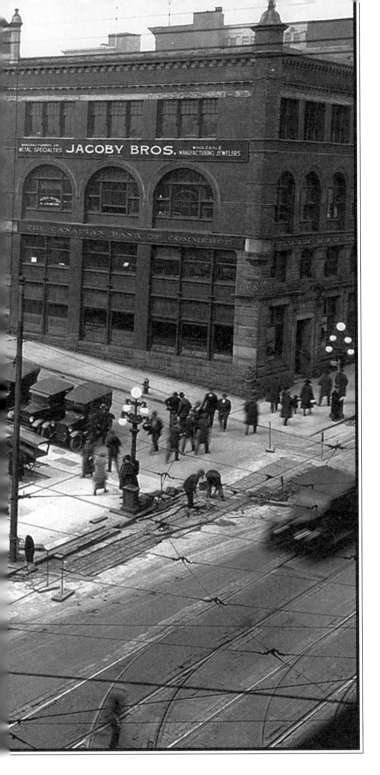

The ancient Egyptians probably used sturdier timber for their scaffolding, and more advanced hoisting equipment to build the Sphinx, than that used for the construction of Vancouver's cenotaph! Although the structure appears to be of solid granite, as the picture clearly shows, the cenotaph is in fact a hollow shell.

an acre requested was and is bounded by Hastings, Cambie, Pender and Hamilton Streets. As it happened the club's request was compatible with the city's own plans for the property.

These plans, unveiled in April 1915, were for the development of a proposed civic centre that was to include a new city hall. The grand design encompassed a number of surrounding blocks and included the parcel of land now known as Victory Square. At the time the block was envisioned as providing a ceremonial approach to the civic complex. In January 1917 city council formally asked the provincial government for a lease on the land, and on March 12, 1916 a 99-year lease was granted at an annual rent of one dollar. As with other later schemes for a civic centre, nothing came of the 1915 plan, which had been selected from those submitted by 31 applicants.

In 1918 the Canadian Club renewed its initiative of 1914 and formed a committee to work toward the erection of a war memorial. At the same time the city brought into being its own Civic War Memorial Committee. Hard to believe though it might be, there were now two committees working separately and simultaneously "to erect a war memorial as soon as possible." And so it continued for four years until the two committees brilliantly came up with the idea that they should work together. Only in Vancouver, you say! No one will be surprised to know that each committee was chaired by a brigadier-general.

Although the joint Vancouver War Memorial Committee was organized in 1922, it didn't meet until 1923. Half its membership was appointed by the Canadian Club and half by the Civic War Memorial Committee. The new joint committee's tasks were to raise the money needed to erect a cenotaph, and to get the memorial built. It was of course to be built at Victory Square and not to cost more than $15,000. Money was solicited from the general public, and given the worthiness and popularity of the cause, the necessary funds were raised quickly and without difficulty. Once funding was secured, a call went out to the city's architects asking them to submit designs. Preference was to be given to those architects who had served overseas.

The winning design for the cenotaph was that of G. Thornton Sharpe. Perhaps the best that can be said of it is, that while there is nothing about the cenotaph that will inspire, there is also nothing about it that will offend. If the structure has to be labelled it could probably be described as an example of what is called Modern Classicism, a style that has variously been described as a child of its time, an architecture of post-First World War sobriety, and as an abbreviated classicism. Modern Classicism's building materials of choice were white or neutral stone or artificial cast stone, and its details were simplified to the point where surfaces became little more than grids of horizontal and vertical

The original intention was to have the cenotaph dedicated on November 11, 1923, but delays were such that the unveiling could not take place until April 27, 1924. Beyond the cenotaph, on the south side of Pender Street, the old Central School can be seen.

lines. Not surprisingly Modern Classicism, which wasted little money on ornamentation, became the preferred style for public buildings during the 1920s and 30s. In November 1923 city council approved an expenditure of $1,000 to grade the site so construction of the cenotaph could begin.

The cenotaph is made of cut blocks of grey Nelson Island granite supplied by the Vancouver Granite Co., Ltd. It is a 30-foot high three-sided obelisk, which aligns well with the more or less triangular shape of Victory Square. The contractors responsible for its erection were Stewart & Wylie. They completed the job for $10,666. Unfortunately Stewart was so seriously injured while working on the job that he did not live to

see it completed. Each of the three sides bears a quote from the Old Testament and a simple decorative device. Facing Hastings Street is a downward-pointing sword, facing Hamilton Street is a laurel wreath entwined with maples leaves, and facing Pender is a wreath of poppies also intermingled with maple leaves. On Sunday, April 27, 1924 in the presence of some 25,000 people, the cenotaph was unveiled by Mayor W.R. Owen. The first wreath, that of the City of Vancouver, was put in place by his wife. The monument was dedicated by the Rev'd C.C. Owen, Anglican rector of Christ Church, assisted by the Rev'd G.O. Fallis of the Methodist Church. Both men were much-decorated veterans. One does not even have to wonder how hard the committee responsible for arranging the service tried to find a Roman Catholic priest or Baptist minister, let alone a Jewish rabbi or Buddhist priest to take part in the dedication. The fact that it was the Buchan version of "O Canada" with couplets like, *"At Britain's side whate'er betide Unflinchingly we'll stand,"* and, *"With heart we sing, 'God save the King',"* that was sung at the service puts it all in perspective.

In January 1924 the city asked the Parks Board to assume responsibility for the landscaping and upkeep of Victory Square. Fortunately the property was already ringed with a border of thirty mature maples. They had been bought as saplings from the Dominion Experimental Farm at Agassiz by A.E. Beck, K.C., the court registrar and government agent soon after the old courthouse had been built. Aside from the maple trees, the property looked like any other vacant lot.

The city and the Parks Board were lucky that a neighbour came to the rescue. As it happened, in early 1925 Frederick Southam, president of his family's newspaper chain, was in Vancouver meeting with F.J. Burd, the publisher of the *Vancouver Daily Province*. So the story goes, Southam looked across from Burd's office window in the Province Building at the untidy grounds surrounding the cenotaph and said something to the effect that someone should do something about the situation. The outcome of all this was that Southam and *The Province* donated $11,500 toward the cost of landscaping Victory Square.

Hindsight being an exact science, it is easy to be critical of the cumbersome process that brought the cenotaph into being, to see its design as pedestrian, and to marvel at the sentiments of its builders who really did believe the British Empire to be the greatest structure for political good the world had ever known. At the same time, however, their desire to remember, to honour, and to express their gratitude to all those who gave their lives for King and County in the Great War can only be admired and appreciated.

SELECTED BIBLIOGRAPHY

Books and Periodicals

Agassiz, A.R.N. *A Short History of the English Branch of the Agassiz Family*. Shanghai: The Oriental Press, 1907.

Alexander, Pat. *The World's Religions*. Oxford: Lion Publishing, revised edition 1994.

Appleton, Thomas E. "Captain John T. Walbran, 1848-1913," *BC. Studies*. No. 5 (Summer 1970): 25-35.

Armitage, Doreen. *Around the Sound*. Madeira Park: Harbour Publishing, 1997.

Atkin, John. *Strathcona: Vancouver's First Neighbourhood*. Vancouver/Toronto: Whitecap Books, 1994.

Barr, James. *Ferry Across the Harbor*. Vancouver: Mitchell Press, 1969.

Breen, David, & Kenneth Coates. *Vancouver's Fair*. Vancouver: University of British Columbia Press, 1982.

Burnes, J. Rodger. *Echoes of the Ferries*. North Vancouver: self-published, n.d.

Basque, Garnet. *Fraser Canyon & Bridge River Valley*. Langley: Sunfire Publication Ltd., 1985.

Bernard, Elaine. *The Long Distance Feeling*. Vancouver: New Star Books, 1982.

Billington, David P. *The Tower and the Bridge*. Princeton: Princeton University Press, 1983.

Boam, Henry J. with Ashley G. Brown. *British Columbia*. London: Sells, 1912.

Bridge, Kathryn. *By Snowshoe, Backboard and Steamer*. Victoria: Sono Nis Press, 1998.

Broom, Giles T. *Ships That Sail No More*. Lexington: University of Kentucky Press, 1966.

Burrows, Roger G. *Railway Mileposts*. Vol. 1. North Vancouver: Railway Milepost, 1981.

Cenotaph, The, Vancouver: Vancouver City Archives, 1956.

Clapp, Frank A. "West Vancouver Municipal Ferries." *Steamboat Bill*. Vol. XLVI, No. 3 (Fall 1989): 172-181.

Corley-Smith, Peter. *Barnstorming to Bush Flying*. Victoria: Sono Nis Press, 1989.

Delgado, James, "Mastodon: Vancouver Harbour's First Dredge." *Harbour & Shipping* (June 1998): 18-20.

Durant, John. *The Heavyweight Champions*. New York: Hastings House, new revised edition 1976.

Ewert, Henry. *The Story of the B.C. Electric Railway Company*. North Vancouver: Whitecap Books, 1986.

Foster, Mrs. W. Garland. *The Mohawk Princess*. Vancouver: Lions' Gate Publishing, 1931.

Frontier to Freeway. Victoria: Queen's Printer, 3rd edition 1986.

Futcher, Winnifred, ed. *The Great North Road to the Cariboo*. Victoria: Roy Wrigley Printing & Publishing, 1938.

Gardiner, Robert, ed. dir. *All the World's Fighting Ships, 1906-1921*. London: Conway Maritime Press, 1985.

Gosnell, R.E. *The Year Book of British Columbia and Manual of Provincial Information*.
    Victoria: Government of the Province of British Columbia, Coronation ed., 1911.

Goodfellow, Florence. *Memories of Pioneer Life In British Columbia–A Short History of the Agassiz Family*.
    Harrison: Harrison Lake Historical Society, reprinted 1982.

Green, Ruth. *Personality Ships of British Columbia*. West Vancouver: Marine Tapestry Publications Ltd., 1969.

Hacking, Norman, and W. Kaye Lamb. *The Princess Story*. Vancouver: Mitchell Press, 1974.

Harris, Lorraine. *Fraser Canyon: From Cariboo Road to Super Highway*. Surrey: Hancock House, 1984.

Haws, Duncan. *Merchant Fleets in Profile*. Cambridge: Patrick Stephens, 1979.

Merchant Fleets in Profile:4. Cambridge: Patrick Stephens, 1980.

Henry, Tom. *The Good Company*. Madeira Park: Harbour Publishing, 1994.

Hill, Beth. *Sappers–The Royal Engineers in British Columbia*. Ganges: Horsdal & Schubart, 1987.

Historic Yale. Vancouver: Vancouver Section, British Columbia Historical Association, 1954.

Howard, Irene. *Bowen Island*. Bowen Island: Bowen Island Historians, 1973.

Howey, F.W., and E.O.S. Scholefield. *British Columbia from the Earliest Times to the Present:*
    *Biographical:*Vols. 3 & 4. Toronto: S.J. Clarke Publishing, 1914.

Humphreys, P., and S.G. Wong. *The History of Wigwam Inn*. Vancouver: Perfect Printers, 1982.

Imredy, Peggy. *A Guide to Sculpture in Vancouver*. Vancouver: self-published, 1980.

Ito, Roy. *We Went to War*. Stittsville: Canada Wings, Inc., 1984.

Jagpal, Sarjeet Singh. *Becoming Canadians*. Madeira Park: Harbour Publishing, 1994.

James, Rick. "Melanope: A Witch of the Waves," *Foghorn*. Vol. 7 Issue 4 (November 1996): 10-13.

Johnston, Hugh. *The Voyage of the Komagata Maru*. Delhi: Oxford University Press, 1979.

Kalman, Harold. *A History of Canadian Architecture,* Vols. 1 & 2. Toronto: Oxford University Press, 1994.

Kearney, J. *Champions.* Vancouver: Douglas & McIntyre, 1985.

Kightly, Charles. *The Customs and Ceremonies of Britain.* London: Thames and Hudson, 1986.

Kluckner, Michael. *Vancouver the Way it Was.* North Vancouver: Whitecap Books, 1984.

   Vanishing Vancouver. North Vancouver: Whitecap Books, 1990.

McCombs, Arnold, and W.W. Chittenden. *The Harrison–Chehalis Challenge.* Harrison Hot Springs: Treeline, 1988.

MacEwan, Grant. *Pat Burns:Cattle King.* Saskatoon: Western Producer Prairie Books, 1979.

McLaren, Keith. *Light on the Water.* Vancouver/Toronto: Douglas & McIntyre, 1998.

McRaye, Walter. *Pauline Johnson and Her Friends.* Toronto: Ryerson, 1947.

Maiden, Cecil. *Lighted Journey.* Vancouver: British Columbia Electric Company Limited, 1948.

Maltin, L., S. Green & L. Sader, eds. *Leonard Maltin's Movie Encyclopedia.* New York: Dutton, 1994.

Marlatt, Daphne, and Carole Itter. *Opening Doors: Vancouver's East End.* Sound Heritage Series, Nos. 1 & 2, Vol. VIII.
   Victoria: Provincial Archives of British Columbia,

Matches, Alex. *It Began With A Ronald.* Vancouver: self-published, 1974.

Matthews, J.S. *Early Vancouver: Narratives of Pioneers of Vancouver, B.C., Collected During 1931-1932.*
   Vancouver: Vancouver City Archives, 1932. *The Founding of the Salvation Army, Vancouver.*
   Vancouver: City Archives, 1962.

Melvin, George H. *The Post Offices of British Columbia: 1858-1970.* Vernon: self-published, 1972.

Mills, Edward, and Warren Sommer. *Vancouver Architecture 1886-1914*, Vols. 1 & 2. Ottawa: Environment Canada, n.d.

Moogk, Peter N. *Vancouver Defended.* Surrey: Antonson Publishing Ltd., 1978.

Nigosian, S.A. *World Faiths.* New York: St. Martin's Press, 2nd edition, 1994.

Peacock, J. *The Vancouver Natural History Society, 1918-1993.* Vancouver: Natural History Society, 1993.

Reeve, Phyllis. *Every Good Gift.* Vancouver: St. James' Anglican Church, 1980.

Rifkind, Carole. *A Field Guide to American Architecture.* New York: New American Library, 1980.

Rushton, Gerald. *Echoes of the Whistle.* Vancouver: Douglas & McIntyre, 1980.

Sparks, Dawn, and Martha Border. *Echoes Across the Inlet.*
   North Vancouver: Deep Cove and Area Heritage Association, 1989.

Sleigh, Daphne. *The People of the Harrison.* Deroche: self-published, 1990.

Steele, Richard M. *The Stanley Park Explorer.* North Vancouver: Whitecap Books, 1985.

Tanaka, Tosh. *Hands Across the Pacific.* Vancouver: Consulate-General of Japan, 1990.

Tucker, Gilbert N. *"The Career of H.M.C.S. Rainbow."* BC Historical Quarterly. Vol. VII, No. 1 (January, 1943): 1-30.

Turner, Robert D. *The Pacific Princesses.* Victoria: Sono Nis Press, 1977.

   Vancouver Annual. Vancouver: Progress Club, 1912.

Van Rensselaer, Marina G. *Henry Hobson Richardson and His Works.* New York: Dover Publications Inc., 1969.

Waite, Donald E. *The Fraser Canyon Story.* Surrey: Hancock House Publishers, 1988.

Walbran, John. *British Columbia Coast Names: 1592 - 1906.* Vancouver: J.J. Douglas for Vancouver Public Library, 1971.

Walker, Elizabeth. *Street Names of Vancouver.* Vancouver: Vancouver Historical Society, 1999.

Woods, J.J. *The Agassiz-Harrison Valley.* Sidney: Kent Centennial Committee, 2nd edition 1958.

Woodstock, George. *British Columbia: A History of the Province.* Vancouver: Douglas & McIntyre, 1990.

Working Lives Collective. *Working Lives.* Vancouver: New Star Books, 1985.

Yee, Paul. *Saltwater City.* Vancouver/Toronto: Douglas & McIntyre, 1988.

Newspapers

New Westminster Columbian (title varies)

Vancouver Daily Province (title varies)

Vancouver Daily World (title varies)

Vancouver News-Advertiser (title varies)

Vancouver Sun (title varies)

All unattributed quotations in the text are from the *Vancouver Daily Province*.

INDEX